DR. CHI'S FINGERNAIL and TONGUE ANALYSIS

Third Edition

Chi's Enterprise, Inc.
Anaheim, CA 92807

Dr. Chi's Fingernail and Tongue Analysis
Third Edition
January 2010
ISBN 0-9657847-2-X

Printed in the United States of America

First printing: July 1997
Second printing: January 2002

DISCLAIMER

All material in this book is provided for your information only and may not be construed as medical advice or instruction. No action or inaction should be taken based solely on the contents of this information; instead, readers should consult appropriate health professionals on any matter relating to their health and well-being.

The information and opinions expressed here are believed to be accurate, based on the best judgment available to the author, and readers who fail to consult with appropriate health authorities assume the risk of any injuries. In addition, the information and opinions expressed here do not necessarily reflect the views of every contributor to the book.

ACKNOWLEDGMENTS

I would like to express my appreciation to Jonathan Wright, MD, David Williams, MD, and Adrian Barber, DC, for their contributions to this book.

Thank you to my wife, Cheryl Chi, MS in Biochemistry, for your constant support and always worthwhile advice.

To my assistant, Kristina Libay Gatal, BS in Computer Science, your help in researching and collecting data as well as organizing and editing this edition of the book is invaluable.

I express my deepest gratitude to my father, Kui-Chen Chi, MD, for his knowledge and guidance throughout the years.

To my daughters, Shirley Chi, MD, and Jennifer Chi, JD, thank you for your medical knowledge and editorial recommendations, respectively.

I express my heartfelt thanks to all my colleagues and patients who have shared their testimonies.

TABLE OF CONTENTS

FOREWORD

Returning to the Roots of Medicine

Medicine and health care are returning to their roots, especially here in the United States. While natural medicine has co-existed with Western Style medicine in many areas around the world, it has been forced underground in the United States (and much of the world which considers itself civilized) for most of the 20th century.

However, the constraints of western, high-tech health care have initiated patient interests in alternative medicine. Since drugs and surgery have little influence, our long-term, chronic illness, patients often seem to look to herbal formula's satisfaction. Indeed alternative medicine is often cost-effective and more affordable for those in need of long-term health management.

Thus, western markets are rapidly exploring eastern "healing" techniques. The media commonly alludes to vitamins, minerals, herbs, botanical remedies, acupuncture, homeopathy, Qi gong, etc. Even "orthodox" physicians are beginning to take note of the growing trend toward Asian methodologies.

But before healing comes diagnosis and Western medicine has too often categorized "diagnosis" as a high-tech, laboratory-intensive, x-ray and CAT scan affair. Many older physicians still deplore the marked decline in the teaching of "hands-on", observation-based physical diagnosis skills in modern medical schools.

Along with the 'roaring renaissance' in natural treatments comes a quieter but equally important trend: the resurgence of interest in hands-on physical diagnosis, using close observation of the patients and extensive knowledge of body systems in health and disease.

Applied kinesiology, foot reflexology, iridology, and intuitive methods of diagnosis are gradually emerging from the far fringes of diagnostic techniques.

I have been quite ignorant of tongue and fingernail diagnosis (except that they existed), and was surprised when Dr. Chi asked me to write this foreword to this book about them. Having read it through, I can see I once again have something to learn. This training will no doubt help me greatly in treating patients at the Tahoma Clinic. Perhaps that was Dr. Chi's intention. I am moved to have a page or two to write for you in the book of an accomplished master of the art of physical diagnosis.

Jonathan V. Wright, MD
Tahoma Clinic
Renton, Washington
USA

FOREWORD

It was a pleasure to meet you and to witness your methods during the Atlanta conference. I am a veteran traditional medical practitioner with some experience in herbal and alternative biological therapies. Your accurate assessment of my medical condition was indeed astonishing. Recently, there have been several specialized tests of my health using the latest high tech electron beam CT scan device. Your application of the fingernail and tongue diagnosis was faster and more impressive than any condition-analysis method I am aware of.

Later the same day, I watched as you diagnosed another patient of mine with unnerving precision. This man is a middle-aged disabled airline pilot who has impairment from a stroke. He has hypertension and lipidemia, which are well controlled. Your exam sheet indicated you detected these major problems within minutes. Without a BP cuff, stethoscope, or any other medical device you made a most rapid diagnosis. This patient has fooled other doctors as he has a type of slow expressive aphasia and yet does not appear sick or in distress.

Your book is highly informative. Since our brief encounter, I have already used my newly acquired knowledge to assess over hundreds of case studies. The summary of my findings in enclosed. There is indeed a deadly triad of signs not to be ignored. Your work is nonetheless monumental. You are calling attention to the most sick and urgent situations, where standard medical texts devote hundreds of pages to thousands of rare diseases. A medical student would be years ahead to learn and use your system while in a standard clinic. In this way, a doctor could be trained to be more sensitive to physical diagnostic methods. As it is, young doctors are beset by enormous texts and only get to see few patients. A standard text of internal medicine is now so lengthy as to be difficult to carry from room to room. Your book enables a doctor to save time and money in rapidly getting to the core of the problems. It should be made available to those in training.

Best Wishes,

David A. Williams, MD
Federal Aviation Medical Examiner
Immigration Medical Examiner
November 28, 1999

Why Study the Chi Diagnosis System?
By David A. Williams, MD

- Improve diagnostic skills through fast and effective means
- Save large quantities of time by avoiding long clinic lines
- Detect serious disease earlier and improve provider profile
- Further patient trust by offering routine examinations Dr. Chi's methods
- Conserve time and money by applying the diagnostic system

FOREWORD

My wife and I had the pleasure of meeting Dr. Chi and his wife Cheryl six years ago while attending a Parker Chiropractic Seminar in Las Vegas. I later attended a seminar where Dr. Chi presented a program on his method of Fingernail and Tongue Diagnosis. Since implementing Dr. Chi's methods in my practice, I have seen many exciting patient responses to his products.

Dr. Chi's Fingernail and Tongue Diagnosis book detailing the way to diagnose and treat conditions found in a patient has proved to be an invaluable reference for early screening and diagnosis without a batter of expensive tests. I have used Dr. Chi's Fingernail & Tongue Diagnosis book to examine many patients and found them to have conditions they were totally unaware of. Further investigation revealed some of the patients did have unexplained symptoms that could be accounted for by the findings I made using Dr. Chi's methods. Unfortunately I have had patients who did not believe the findings from a fingernail or tongue diagnosis was important. They ignored the findings and later suffered severe consequences with their health by opting not to treat the conditions found because they did not have symptoms at the time the diagnosis was made.

An eighty-nine-year old patient of mine suffered from an open sore on her right foot for a period of three years. All prior medical attempts to resolve the sore had failed. The patient was not diabetic. I treated her with Dr. Chi's Whole Skin ointment and the Mineral Infrared Frequency Device (MIT). In three weeks the patient's open sore was completely healed.

I treated a 72-year-old patient who was suffering from severe left leg pain that interfered with his sleep and caused him to limp. His personal physician and a Mayo Clinic physician evaluated his condition. Both doctors concluded the patient's left leg symptoms were due to a significant loss of circulation in that leg. He was told his only solution to the condition, if the circulation continued to deteriorate, was amputation. I started the patient on Vein Lite and Wine Extract for an initial period of six months. The patient noted he felt improvement every month for three months and then the response plateau. He was able to walk without a limp and slept without pain at night. When his physician evaluated the leg some six months later, he estimated a 50-60 percent improvement in his leg circulation.

I could relate many other cases of heart problems, high lipids, hypothyroidism, and etc. that I have worked with successfully using Dr. Chi's methods and products. There is no sufficient space in the foreword to go into the details of each one. I have used Dr. Chi's herbals on many patients safely and the products have proved to be very effective.

Adrian G. Barber, DC

PREFACE

Fingernail and tongue diagnosis has evolved over thousands of years, resulting in a methodology so precise and natural that it is hailed among practitioners as an enlightened art form. Over the years, doctors have learned to derive qualities from fingernail and tongue diagnosis specific to their field of medicine. My own father was a doctor for forty five years, and I myself have had over thirty years of experience in the field. Together we have been able to combine both eastern and western methodologies to create a unique program of physical diagnosis. Both patients and doctors alike have been urging me to secure this valuable information in print. I hope this book will serve as both an innovative guide to medical diagnosis and a means to carefully bridge together two important schools of thought, culminating in an advanced look at the future of medicine and preventative diagnosis based on physical markers. And unlike most other handbooks on Chinese medicine, dismissing what is fundamental to the teachings of Western science, my approach allows one to combine culturally competent methodologies to achieve the most accurate and effective results.

My method of physical diagnosis started out as an analysis of the fingernails and the tongue. Throughout the years, I have had the opportunity to analyze many patients and have managed to compile the clinical data of over 10,000 cases from around the world.

Readers should note that diseases do not always have easily detectable causes and symptoms. In some cases a disease may manifest as quite different symptoms in different people. Similarly, different diseases can cause the same symptoms in people. In the old days, primary care physicians spend a lot of time with patients to check their medical history, their physical symptoms and so on. It was a more thorough checkup in many ways. However, primary care checkups now are not what they used to be. With more patients than doctors and with the arrival of managed care, patients end up spending more time with the nurse than with their doctor. And even then, nurses are unable to spend enough time with each patient.

Preventive care is important so each of us needs to be more observant of our body's changes. This is where fingernail, tongue and body analysis will be most helpful. By learning how to recognize physical markers and what they mean, health issues can be addressed very early and complications can be avoided.

Arriving at an accurate analysis is often a difficult task. Looking at one or two physical markers may not be enough to determine a health issue. It is therefore important to use other symptoms or physical markers as confirmation of a diagnosis.

I have written the first edition of this book, *Dr. Chi's Fingernail and Tongue Diagnosis*, in response to the large demand of people who wish to learn more about this cultural and family treasure. From the mention of my techniques in an October 1996 Scientific American article to countless phone calls to our office in Anaheim, the public is becoming increasingly interested in my diagnostic methods.

This diagnostic technique is an evolving process. Therefore, as I see more patients, I am able to collect more case studies that are worth sharing. Five years after the first edition, I updated the book and came up with *Dr. Chi's Fingernail and Tongue Analysis*. The second edition had additional diagnostic tools as well as illustrations.

Since the last edition, I have compiled more data and pictures supporting the analysis. Over these past seven years, I have changed the technique to include not just the fingernail and tongue but other body markers as well for a more thorough examination. In this third edition I have provided numerous pictures that clearly illustrate these physical markers and which I hope will aid you as you learn this method.

Sometimes it is not enough to evaluate the physical markers and determine which health conditions are associated with them. We must also learn how to address these health issues. Throughout the book, I make dietary recommendations and herbal supplement suggestions so that you will have a more complete care plan. I briefly outlined each herbal formula I mentioned in one of the appendices. A more detailed discussion of herbal usage for various illnesses is explained in my recent book, *Dr. Chi's Herbal Formulas 2nd Edition*.

Finally, this book seeks to provide patients and practitioners with a better understanding of my life's work. I hope you will find the information I impart invaluable either in your health practice or for preventive care.

Tsu-Tsair Chi, NMD, PhD
Anaheim, California
January 2010

INTRODUCTION

Doctors have long been socially responsible for the implementation of new and more affordable methods of healthcare. However, as information becomes increasingly accessible through the Internet, the concept of healthcare is less nebulous to the public. People have learned the importance of early diagnosis. Indeed, one of the major methods of early diagnosis is regular self-examination. Medical statistics show that, of the cases of breast adenocarcinomas, about 95% of patients detected the problem themselves by self-examination and the finding of lumps in their breasts. Doctors diagnose only about 5% of cases. The number of women who detected the cancers themselves outnumbers doctor diagnoses by a factor of 18, showing the relevance and importance of self-examination.

Many other diseases besides breast cancer can be self-diagnosed, and if every family knew the basics of self-diagnosis, then the important task of early detection leading to early treatment could finally be carried out. Therefore, we feel that a widespread familiarization with the methods of self-diagnosis is necessary. Individuals must learn how to take preventative steps toward the improvement of a condition that could lead to disease. This has become the role of doctors in today's world of growing populations and health concerns, to not only diagnose and treat, but to teach others the methods of preventative and early self-diagnosis.

By far, the most widely accepted method of diagnosis in Asian medical culture is the tongue. This along with pulse diagnosis is especially popular among the Chinese. Pulse diagnosis, while helpful, is a very subjective method and difficult to learn. You would need a very well-trained and experienced practitioner to conduct the diagnosis. And even then, it might not be very accurate if there are factors affecting the patient's pulse.

So why have I chosen to use the fingernails and tongue to do quick and accurate readings of organ function? The fingernails have the capacity to show very openly detectable characteristics that correspond to organ function and bodily health. The physical clarity of nail markers presents conditions of the body in a clear and distinct way. An entire adult fingernail usually takes from six to eight months to grow, so their markers are generally slow to appear and disappear as the bodily condition changes. The tongue, however, regenerates its entire topmost epithelial layer every three days. This fast rate of re-growth allows for immediate detection of problems, faster than any other form of physical diagnosis.

In addition to the fingernails and the tongue, markers may also appear on the ear, the face, the torso and other parts of the body. For example, a cardiovascular problem may show up on the fingernails (lack of lunulae), the tongue (dark veins under the tongue), the ear (earlobe crease), or the forehead (cherry angiomas). In some cases, it may appear on all these areas. Another example is hormonal imbalance, which may appear as white spots on the nails or cherry angiomas on the abdomen.

An evaluation that combines all these markers can give a comprehensive and more accurate look at a patient's overall health. Thus, it is my belief that the tongue, fingernail and body analysis method should be introduced to everyone, and I hope that this technique can stir discussion among professionals and trigger input from these groups.

This method of analysis is amazingly accurate. Studies by doctors indicate that using this method to discern a patient's problem has over 80% accuracy rate, even before any blood tests, hair analyses, or urinalyses results come back from the lab. This type of analysis can direct the doctor's attention to one of the five major areas of the body and the exact problem can be further pinpointed after that by the physician. Thus, doctors have a good idea of their patient's problem without having to research blindly using exploratory techniques, and can perhaps start treatment early enough to stave off future complications. For patients, this would prove quite advantageous with respect to saving money on unnecessary laboratory fees.

In the first section we shall discuss how to analyze the fingernails as the first step in the combined self-diagnostic method I have developed. Section II is dedicated to diagnosing the tongue as the next crucial component of self-diagnosis. In Section III, we will look at markers in other parts of the body, such as the abdomen, the eyes, and so on, which will work to confirm the results of the fingernail and tongue diagnosis. Finally, Section IV will provide you with a comprehensive look at all the different analyses combined, categorized according to the different systems of the body. You may want to read this section more carefully as it combines the different analyses and provides you with a more complete picture of what signs to look for in certain health conditions.

Throughout the book, references will be made to figures and pictures located in the appendices. Please notice the distinction between references to 'Figure' and 'Picture' as these will be found in different appendices. You will also find actual case studies that will provide you with an essential learning tool in how to combine fingernail, tongue and body analysis when you evaluate a patient.

SECTION I

FINGERNAIL
ANALYSIS

Chapter 1

OVERVIEW OF FINGERNAIL DIAGNOSIS

A good practitioner should be able to distinguish between healthy or weak organs by carefully examining the nails' appearance. Because the hands are flexible, they reflect a person's physical and spiritual condition. In addition, nails never finish their cycle of growth and, thus, are an accurate record of a person's systemic and physical situation.

Nails are the transfer points for all nutrients in the body. Blood runs through these specific points, which are the meridian points of the body. Many physical deficiencies can be seen in the appearance of the nails. If in good health, the nails will be shiny in luster, pink colored and transparent, with an even, smooth arch. If one maintains a proper diet, they are quite healthy.

Although there are many different systems in the body to speak of, my family has always referred to several specific ones that correlate to each fingernail. Thus, the five fingernails of each hand refer to a certain part of the body:

The Thumbnail

The thumbnail reflects the condition of the brain and of the excretory system. For instance, if the thumb is the only nail that presents a problem, then this person may have a localized malady.

The Index Fingernail

This nail reflects the condition of the liver, gallbladder, and the nervous system. If the index finger is brittle and of a grayish yellow or a dark green color, and is the only finger that presents a problem, then this person is easily prone to liver, gallbladder, or nervous system maladies.

The Middle Fingernail

If the middle fingernail is the only nail that presents a problem, then this is generally not a good sign. If the middle fingernail is abnormal, then this patient has a heart and circulatory problem.

The Ring Fingernail

The ring fingernail has, throughout ancient times, been related to reproductive organ function, along with hormonal balance to a certain degree.

The Pinky Fingernail

The condition and appearance of this fingernail reflects the condition of the digestive system and gastrointestinal tract, including the intestines, and colon.

Generally, nails should have a hard, epithelial cornea layer. Hardness of the nails can also say a lot about the patient's physical situation. A patient who has overly soft nails has very sensitive nerves and suffers from poor nutrition. Thin, soft nails also indicate calcium deficiency. Nails that appear brittle and plagued with large cracks signify that the patient suffers from malnutrition and adrenal gland problems. Brittle nails also signify problems in the patient's excretory, endocrine and reproductive systems. Healthy people often have nails that can be characterized as elastic and strong. Healthy nails are also translucent in color, showing a pink hue with a smooth, even face and a slight shine. Healthy nails should be somewhat elastic and should be of the correct thickness. The correct amount of thickness is 0.5-0.75 mm.

One thing that should be noted first off when performing a fingernail analysis is the consistency of the nails overall, and their general appearance. Many basic, important facts can be drawn from this kind of general diagnosis. Shriveled, atrophied, or thin nails, for instance, signify that the patient is malnourished and may often experience cramps in the extremities. Scaling in the nails often signify tinea, athlete's foot, or ringworm caused by trichophyton, which is a difficult fungal infection to treat. Heat rash and prickly heat can also cause tinea, which is also very difficult to cure. Nails that separate from the nail bed usually indicate fungal infection.

If a patient's nails become rough and yellow and if the nail growth diminishes in speed, then this person may be suffering from diabetes, heart disease, or poor capillary circulation. If the matrix of the nails is experiencing atrophic changes such as discoloration or sudden swelling, this may be due to lupus (hardened skin). Nails that conform to the above symptoms, as well as matrix atrophy, signify that the patient has diabetes.

If nails are brittle, or if they can be flexed and bent too easily, then bones may be similarly weak. Brittle nails indicate that the kidney is in bad condition and that blood supply to the nails is inadequate to bring enough nutrition. Anemia, chemotherapy, or poor blood circulation may have side effects that result in dull, weak and brittle nails.

Lastly, before we begin our detailed journey into fingernail analysis, let me suggest following along the next few chapters with my diagnostic kit, a turntable wheel designed for easy clarification of fingernail condition. It may prove helpful in the general schema to study this kit while reading this book.

Chapter 2

NAIL SHAPE or GROWTH CHANGE

The size of the nail, which should be proportional to the hands and the rest of the body, can certainly reveal how the body is functioning. For instance, a patient with short nails should proportionately have short fingers. The nails of a patient should not deviate notably from one another. They should be arched in a slightly curving structure, transparent, to reveal the pink flesh beneath, and normal in size.

Length and Width of Nails

If a patient has short, square-shaped nails, then he or she has a hyper-excitable condition. If the nails are short to a certain level and very small, then the patient may have heart disease. If the nails are too long, then the patient may have respiratory problems.

Narrow Nails

If the patient has nails that are very narrow and light in color with a base that is dull yellow or dark blue, then this person has skeletal problems. Narrow nails that are elongated with vertical ridges (whose significance will be discussed later) running along them, especially if they are dark-colored, tend to indicate respiratory disorders of a chronic nature. If the nails are extremely narrow and elongated proportionally to the body, and a dark yellow or gray color, then it is even more indicative of the bone and skeletal problems mentioned above (Figure 1C).

Short and Wide Nails

Short, wide, reddish nails (Picture 1a) signal cardiovascular problems including high blood pressure, atherosclerosis, and the possibility of stroke or brain hemorrhage.

Triangular or Shell-Shaped Nails

Triangular or shell-shaped nails (Figure 1D, Picture 1b) signify blood or bone marrow disease. So whenever you see this type of nails, always check your hemoglobin, platelets, white blood cells and red blood cells.

A patient who has triangular or shell-shaped nails could also be experiencing symptoms of a stroke. This type of patient also runs a higher risk of developing paralysis.

If the nails are also slow-growing, this may signify that the patient has cirrhosis, neurodermatitis, or a nail disease.

Spoon-shaped Nails (Koilonychia)

Koilonychia refers to nails that are concave, shaped like spoons. This signals hemoglobin deficiency and is often seen in patients with anemia or blood disease (Figure 2B, Picture 1c). A person with symptoms such as these may also be suffering from rheumatoid fever, hookworms or syphilis.

In anemia, koilonychia is also associated with these symptoms: dizziness, headaches, ear ringing, blurred vision, flashes/floaters, tired, no energy, lack of sleep, lack of concentration. Taking Vitamin C will help absorb iron and help produce hemoglobin.

Nail Clubbing

Normally, the nail should be slightly horizontally arched. Clubbing of the nails is a very distinctive physical sign of systemic diseases and one that even western physicians commonly use to assess the severity and morbidity of their patient's long-term struggle with an illness. In this condition, the base or matrix of the nail loses its curvature from the fleshy tissue of the finger with a resultant curved appearance. Often the fingertips themselves are enlarged, and therefore *clubbed* (Figure 1E, Pictures 1d, 1e).

An extremely curved, clubbing nail can be caused by lung disease, such as lung tumors or emphysema, where alveoli are not completely exchanging air. This is usually accompanied by opaque nails. In these cases, hemoglobin has a low binding potential, causing insufficient oxygen exchange and too much carbon dioxide.

Besides lung diseases, nail clubbing is also an early sign of heart disease, some cancers, liver cirrhosis and autoimmune disease (e.g., Crohn's disease). If the opaque nails turn thick, hard, and begin to lose its luster, then this person may be experiencing external trauma such as a fungal infection or several congenital diseases. Thick, yellow nails that grow at an extremely slow pace signify respiratory, lymphatic, or thyroid problems.

Nail clubbing has actually been used historically as an indicator of certain diseases. One comprehensive study (Table 1) reveals that unilateral or bilateral nail clubbing is associated with lung disease, cardiovascular conditions, infectious diseases, gastrointestinal disorders and other systemic conditions (*Journal of the American Academy of Dermatology*. 2005; 52(6)).

Table 1. Incidence of nail clubbing in lung disease, heart disease and cancer

Condition	Total number of cases	Cases with clubbing	%
Cystic fibrosis	73	73	100
Hepatopulmonary Syndrome	14	9	64.3
Hypersensitivity pneumonitis	82	44	53.7
Infective endocarditis	60	30	50.0
Interstitial Pulmonary Fibrosis	588	289	49.2
Asbestosis	167	72	43.1
Mesothelioma	77	23	29.9
Bronchogeneic carcinoma	111	32	28.9
Tuberculosis	426	72	16.9
Hemiplegia	87	12	13.8

Based on these statistics, bilateral nail clubbing is a very strong indicator of lung diseases (Table 1). For instance, clubbing was present in all 73 cases of cystic fibrosis. In fact, nail clubbing is one of the definitive signs to look out for in diagnosing cystic fibrosis.

Unilateral clubbing is mostly found in those with heart problems like hemiplegia.

When a person has nail clubbing, teeth marks on the tongue, opaque nails and lunulae only on the thumbs, there is a high chance for lung cancer.

Beau's Lines

Beau's lines are horizontal indentations across the nails (Picture 1f). These indentations are seen in most or all of the patient's nails and usually located in the same spot. These lines may be caused by trauma or by an illness severe enough to interrupt nail growth. For instance, a period of malnutrition or a heart attack can cause this interruption. Since these lines usually occur on the same spot, you can actually estimate the time of the illness through the location of the lines. It takes approximately six months for an adult nail to completely grow out. So a line that appears in the middle of the nail can tell you that the illness occurred approximately three months ago. The depth of the lines determines the severity of the illness: the deeper the lines, the more severe the illness.

In some cases, an interruption in nail growth may manifest not as an indentation but as a major change in the quality of the nail. As seen in Picture 1g, chemotherapy interrupted nail growth in this patient. Approximately half of the nail towards the tip is yellowish in color and is somewhat raised from the nail bed. The rest of the nail has grown normally after chemotherapy treatment.

Chapter 3

COLOR CHANGE

Nail color is often indicative of a person's health. A healthy, energetic individual should have slightly flexible, pink-colored nails that are shiny and strong. On the other hand, a person who suffers from malnutrition or anemia has very pale nails and shows no signs of the fast, healthy blood circulation that should be present. For instance, a patient who has just undergone surgery usually has no color in the nails. A person whose nails have changed from yellow to green to black has a chronic disease in her internal organs. A patient who is severely ill, for example, will have nails that are completely covered in a dark, near-black tint.

White Nails

White nails signify that the patient suffers from anemia. If the nails also appear waxy, opaque and dull, then the patient may have ulcers, hemorrhaging, or hookworms. Liver problems can also cause white nails.

Drink more water to improve circulation, digestion, absorption, and excretion of waste. Reduce metabolic waste/toxins that could damage the liver. Follow a balanced diet. Do not overeat or skip meals. If hungry, you will tend to overeat. This causes an imbalance in digestive enzymes and fluid secretion. As a result, liver function is impaired.

If the nails are not exactly white but are more of a cloudy, opaque color, then this should be indicative of a lung or heart problem. Further indication of this would be nail clubbing.

The following types of nails are variations of white nails, with distinctive characteristics.

Half-and-Half Nails

In half-and-half nails, the upper half of the nail appears dark while the bottom half appears white (Picture 1h). This is commonly seen in chronic renal failure patients (may be autoimmune-related as well), and sometimes in liver patients.

Terry's Nails

Terry's nails are a type of half-and-half nails where almost the entire nail appears white or opaque and there is a dark band on the tip (Picture 2a). The lunula is barely, if at all, visible. This type of nails is associated with liver cirrhosis or kidney problems. It may also signal cancer, congestive heart failure, diabetes, or autoimmune disease. If, under the dark band, the rest of the nails are opaque or white as in Picture 2a, then it definitely signals a kidney condition. This picture is of a glomerulonephritis patient. If the rest of the nail is still pink and not opaque, then it signals a liver condition (Picture 5a).

Mee's Lines

Mee's lines are white bands across each nail (Picture 2b). It is not to be confused with random white lines on the nails. Mee's lines actually parallel the lunula and go across the entire surface of the nail. The lines also move with nail growth. This is classically attributed to heavy metal poisoning (e.g., arsenic, etc.) but may also be caused by Hodgkin's disease, chemotherapy, carbon monoxide poisoning, and other systemic conditions.

Muehrcke's Lines

Similar to Mee's lines, Muehrcke's lines are also transverse white lines that parallel the lunula (Picture 2c). This also indicates kidney disease, particularly hypoalbuminia. What distinguishes Muehrcke's lines from Mee's lines is that the former occurs on the nail bed, so it does not move with nail growth. Muehrcke's lines move with nail growth and usually disappear once the albumin level normalizes.

Yellow Nails

Yellow nails often signify liver or digestive problems (Picture 2d), mainly due to jaundice caused by hepatitis or a chronic bleeding disease. This may also be caused by other problems, such as:
1. Hyperthyroidism, kidney problems, nail fungus, or an excess of beta carotene
2. Water retention in the lymphatic system, especially possible if the nail has a slow growth rate.
3. Hair loss (if the nails are almost of a copper color).
4. Melanoma, liver problems, or poor digestive functions if the tip of the nail is yellow instead of white. These people, who are typically smokers, may have an excessive amount of tetracycline in their system.

If the nail becomes yellow or grayish, is thick and hard and grows slowly, then it is associated with chronic respiratory, thyroid or lymphatic problems. It may also be associated with diabetes-induced coronary heart disease (risk is three times higher than normal).

Red Nails

Redness of the nails can sometimes be attributed to the function of the circulatory system. However, other problems may result in the redness of all or part of the nails.

If the colors of the nails are reversed, that is, switched so that the lunula is red (Picture 2e) and the rest of the nail is actually white, then this patient has a circulation or heart problem and may be prone to coughing, with other symptoms that include vomiting blood. This may also indicate an autoimmune disease such as rheumatoid arthritis or lupus. If the color of the nails appears to be completely red, then the patient may have heart or lung disease. If there are red spots underneath the nails, then the patient may have capillary vessel bleeding, high blood pressure, skin problems or heart disease.

Reddish bruises around the circumference of the nails may be due to lupus infection or dermatitis. If a red band covers the tip of the nail, then this signifies that the patient's gastrointestinal tract should be treated for inflammation. This condition may also signify that the patient is suffering from a heart valve problem. If the nail is dark red, then the patient's organs may be experiencing inflammation.

Normally when you press down on the fingernails, it turns white. However, if it still appears red or pink despite the pressure on the nail, this means that the blood still carries over and an artery valve may not be closing well. There may be disease of the blood vessels (atherosclerosis) or hyperlipidemia. Vein Lite, Wine Extract and Asparagus Extract are recommended.

A patient may be suffering from carbon monoxide poisoning if the flesh beneath her nails as well as her lips and cheeks are a bright cherry red color.

Purple Nails

Purple nails usually signify that the patient lacks oxygen and suffers from circulatory problems. This condition generally stems from either hereditary disorders or habitual problems such as lack of exercise and hence low oxygen saturation levels on a cellular level.

Those with purple nails covered with dots may be prone to cramps in various parts of the body, particularly in the extremities. Asparagus Extract and Vein Lite should be taken.

Green Nails

Nails of this color often suggest irritation caused by cleansing agents or detergents. A patient with these symptoms could also be suffering from bacillus infections. Greenish or purplish colored nails could also signal a serious case of emphysema.

Blue Nails

Nails of this color (Picture 3a) are usually due to a lack of hemoglobin binding to oxygen, resulting in the bluish tint of venous blood, slow and deoxygenated. The lunulae may appear blue as well. A patient with nails of this color often suffers from copper or silver poisoning or gas poisoning, which can bind to hemoglobin competitively and make the oxygen carriers dysfunctional. In some cases, only the area around the lunulae appears dark or blue (Picture 4h), which is typically caused by heavy metal or carbon monoxide poisoning. Patients should use Metal Flush, Vein Lite, OxyPower and Asparagus Extract.

A patient with blue nails may also be suffering from rheumatoid arthritis or autoimmune diseases such as lupus. It would be beneficial to use other techniques to verify these conditions.

If nails are a dark blue or reddish color, showing coagulated blood, then this may be due to a prior stroke, elevated blood lipids, atherosclerosis, Raynaud's disease, blood viscosity, liver cirrhosis or hepatitis. People with blue nails have a higher chance of coronary heart disease and brain embolism.

Black Nails

Black nails are often caused by trauma or are signs of silver deposits. Bacterial infection will also cause black nails. If the tip of the nail is black, then this suggests that the patient could be suffering from chronic kidney failure. A patient with this nail color may also be suffering from a lack of Vitamin B12 and/or a deficiency of adrenocorticosteroids. If the nails are opaque, glassy, and blackish-red in color, then this person has a chronic kidney problem.

Most importantly, if the thumbnails and toenails have black edges or black bands that vertically cover the nails, then the patient must be checked immediately by a physician, as many melanoma patients display this type of condition. If no trauma was involved and the nail is black, then a nevi or melanin may be causing the growth, usually related to melanoma that is difficult to treat. About 84% of melanoma cases are related to black nails.

Chapter 4

LUNULAE AND MITOCHONDRIAL FUNCTION

One of the first and most important factors when evaluating fingernails is to look at the lunulae on the nails, the small white half-moons at the bottom of the nail. These lunulae represent the cellular oxygen levels in the patient, and can tell whether there is proper intracellular oxygen saturation.

When children reach two years old, they should have lunulae on the thumbs. By the time they are around four years old, they should have lunulae on the thumbs and index fingers. By nine years old, they should have lunulae on the thumbs, index fingernails and middle fingernails. By 14 years old, all lunulae should be present except on the pinkies.

Each adult person should be able to see eight lunulae on their fingernails, four on each hand except on the pinkies (Picture 2f). These lunulae should also be of a certain length; they should not be too large or too small. Absence of one of more lunulae, or smaller lunulae than normal, signals a deficiency in cellular oxygen levels and poor circulation. This type of deficiency leads to symptoms such as cold hands, cold feet, and sometimes a general numbness in certain parts of the body. Poor circulation could be caused by circulatory blockage, which may be due to the presence of toxic heavy metals or the accumulation of triglycerides and other lipids in the system. The patient may also feel weak and fatigued, with instances of memory loss. There are greater risk of candida infection and cancer in those who lack lunulae.

The existence of lunulae means that that particular area of tissue is saturated with oxygen. Each lunula is led by meridian lines to the areas of the body they represent. If the fingernail has no lunulae (Picture 2h), it signifies a lack of oxygen saturation in cells, which must not be confused with shallowness of breath or any other voluntary process. Thus, any administration of such substances as ozone and hydrogen peroxide will not help the oxygen situation. If your tissues are not completely saturated with oxygen, it is due to some sort of circulatory or lymphatic system blockage and needs to be cleared as soon as possible to prevent furthers damage.

Lunulae also represent a person's Chi (or Qi) energy, a term the Chinese use to mean a form of bodily energy, referring specifically to persons spirit and inner strength. Lunulae should appear on all fingers but the pinkies. The size of the lunulae on the thumb should be much larger in area than that on any other finger. The lunulae should, beginning with the thumb and ending with the ring finger, decrease in size and should take up no more than 1/4 the size of the nail. Size of the lunulae is due to lung function varieties. This has to do with oxygen uptake and the cell's own oxidation potentials and aging potential. Hormone functions are also lower with smaller lunulae.

If there are large lunulae on every fingernail (including the pinky nail, where lunulae should not appear), then the chance for heart disease is high (Picture 2g). People with pinky lunulae are hyper excitable and generally have a ruddy complexion. Stroke is also possible if the lunulae are oversized and quite large. A person has a greater chance of having a stroke if the lunulae on one hand are markedly smaller than on the other. This, though common in people who use one hand much more than the other (i.e. writers, pitchers, etc.), can also indicate the possibility that one side of the body has a circulation blockage that does not affect the other side. If the problem worsens, risk of a stroke is greatly increased, and is more likely to occur on the side of the blockage.

Fewer than eight lunulae on the fingernails represent poor circulation. Other coexisting symptoms are cold hands and feet, numbness, and memory loss. A person who has no lunulae at all (Picture 2h) often suffers from anemia, depression, and low blood pressure and is highly at risk for cancer (more details in later sections).

If the lunulae skip fingers (e.g., a lunula on the thumb, none on the index finger and a lunula on the middle finger), then there is a blockage on the side of the body that this occurs.

Lack of lunulae can be improved by taking Vein Lite. With each missing lunula, three months of Vein Lite must be taken. If used together with Asparagus Extract and OxyPower, results will be faster.

Finally, a thyroid problem can be seen if a person's lunulae have a shoot-like growth sprouting from its border (Figure 3B). Pro-Metabolic is excellent for this problem.

Although rare, some people may have red lunulae (Picture 2e). This may signal lupus or rheumatoid arthritis. It may also be related to a heart or respiratory problem.

You may also see azure or blue lunulae (Picture 3a). This is associated with silver poisoning, Wilson's disease, or quinachrine therapy. Other causes may be circulation blockage, heart disease, Reynaud's, finger/toe spasms after severe coldness, Rheumatoid arthritis, and lupus. Closely related to azure lunulae is the presence of Mee's lines (Picture 2b), which may also signal heavy metal toxicity.

Chapter 5

RIDGES, BUMPS, SPOTS AND OTHER MARKINGS ON THE NAILS

Ridges, bumps and white spots on the fingernail point to several potential problems in areas such as the adrenal glands, the liver, kidney, the endocrine hormones, etc., and can locate problems such as arthritis, parasites, and respiratory diseases. Contrary to popular belief, these spots and ridges are not caused by simple zinc or calcium deficiency. This is why many patients who are prescribed zinc or calcium supplements for their condition see no improvement even after prolonged usage of the minerals. Zinc has been shown to be good for fertility, but white marks on the nail are a type of disorder that requires more comprehensive evaluation of the excretory system as well.

A person with vague or shallow vertical or horizontal ridges need not worry. Such marking are perfectly normal and commonly seen in patients over the age of forty. These ridges can often be attributed to kidney problems (Figure 1B). However, if the vertical or horizontal ridges are blatantly noticeable, then this patient may be suffering from an illness and the ridges are symptoms of the disease.

Vertical Ridges and Lines

Parallel solid vertical ridges are a sign of several conditions (Figure 1A, Picture 2d, 3b). Vertical ridges are normally seen in adults over 50 years old as a sign of aging. If seen in young children, they may be predisposed genetically to kidney problems, such as IgA nephritis (check for bubbles in the urine or enough hydration). If seen in teenagers, check for drug or marijuana use. If seen in young adults, check for respiratory problems. Among the middle aged, vertical ridges may signify an adrenal problem or peripheral artery disease (Picture 3b). Ridges may also be due to a mineral or vitamin deficiency. What this means is that the body's essential trace elements are not being absorbed properly. This could be due to a lack of vital minerals or the body is just not using the minerals as it should.

The minerals we ingest, either through food or supplements, are in their nonreactive, and thus unusable, form. For our bodies to be able to use these minerals, they must be in a charged or ionized form, undergoing an energy-expending process. This bioenergy is missing from our natural consumption of sunrays due to carbon dioxide and moisture absorption. However, this phenomenon can be prevented by using the Mineral Infrared Therapy device (Refer to *Dr. Chi's Herbal Formulas 2nd edition* for more details on this device). An example of this can be seen in hemoglobin, the oxygen-carrying substance in our blood. Hemoglobin has a protein component called porphyries, which is bound to positively charged iron before it can be active. However, the iron that we ingest is in its uncharged form, and thus it takes an amount of energy to remove some electrons (thus leaving a positive charge on the molecule) before it can become part of the porphyries ring.

While vertical ridges are frequently seen in the elderly, this does not imply that they are a natural part of the aging process. Proper health care can prevent these ridges from forming. If the vertical ridges appear only on the thumbs then they refer to excretory system conditions. Ridges that are on only the other four fingers are due to respiratory problems. An entire nail covered with vertical ridges may also be caused by trauma sustained by the patient, either recently or within the last year. If the ridges are very conspicuous, then the patient may be suffering from peripheral artery blockage, or a yeast or fungus infection.

Vertical ridges and black lines across the nails that appear in a young person may be nothing to worry over as the person develops. Nails with dark vertical banding can indicate normal variations of melanin deposition on skin (Picture 3c, 3d). However, this may still signal melanoma risk. African Americans, especially, are at higher risk for melanoma than other ethnic groups. Sometimes, a dark strip may be a birthmark. But if it continues to grow, this may still be a sign of melanoma risk. Vertical lines on the nails may signify Vitamin A or B deficiency as well as chronic inflammation.

If the nails have vertical ridges that can be very easily split down the middle, this could be due to adrenal gland problems (Figure 3F). For those under the age of forty, vertical ridges definitely indicate problems as imbalance in the five-element system. These types are usually chronically fatigued, nervous, and suffer neurasthenia. Young people also possibly suffer bronchitis, asthma, or laryngitis.

Location of the ridges can also help determine certain conditions. Ridges on the thumb signal spleen and heart problems and may be related depression. Those on the index finger signal depression, while middle finger ridges show nervousness and hyperactivity. Vertical ridges on the ring finger signal the possibility that the patient is suffering from emotional trauma, while those on the pinky nail show long-term stress and the overexertion of energy leading to liver and kidney damage.

Central Nail Canal or Ridge

A central nail canal or ridge is a vertical cavity running down the center of the nail, usually on the thumb (Picture 3e). Central nail canals are associated with malnutrition and trauma. There is a type of central nail canal that splits at the tip of the nail, creating a fir tree appearance. This "fir tree" abnormality is related to peripheral artery disease or a heart problem (Picture 3f).

Beading Nails

Vertical ridges that are bumpy, appearing like beads on a string (Picture 3g), are associated with arthritis or osteoporosis (Figure 2C). If seen in women in their 30s, this may be a sign of early osteoporosis. In men, beading nails are more indicative of arthritis. For osteoporosis, Youth Chi and Chi-F are recommended. For arthritis, Myosteo and Joint Force are recommended.

Onycholysis

Nails detached from the flesh (onycholysis) may be due to a fungal infection, if not from trauma or chemical irritants (Picture 3h). It may also be due to chemical sensitivity (e.g., cleaning solvents), malnutrition, protein deficiency, or anemia. More accurately, it is caused by imperfect cell differentiation and poor capillary circulation, allowing fungus to invade and cause widespread infection. Kidney Chi and Asparagus Extract are recommended in this case.

Horizontal Ridges and Indentations

A patient who has deep horizontal dips is likely to have suffered from one of two possibilities if it is not due to a major illness or external damage on the hand (Figures 2D and 2E). If these horizontal dips are very shallow but continuous over the nail, they signify that the patient either lacks certain essential nutrients, which are necessary to good health and healthy nails, or has poor circulation and heart disease, in which the nail will have usually one very deep dip. However, stress is also a factor that can cause many shallow horizontal lines. One can estimate approximately when the problem happened by measuring the distance of the dip from the matrix, or bottom of the nail. For adults, it usually takes six months to grow the entire nail. In Figure 2E, you can see that, based on the location of the dips, the problem took place about 2 to 3 months ago.

How do horizontal ridges appear? Horizontal ridges on the nails are typically due to poor blood circulation or poor growth and development, or in my opinion, a consequence of stress and sudden changes in diet. If a patient suffers from a condition or ailment that allows the nails to grow slower, then the body returns to normal and the nail growth rate speeds up again, this causes horizontal lines in the nail to appear, as the nail starts and stops growth.

Horizontal indentations, also known as Beau's lines (Picture 1f), may be caused by anemia, irregular kidney function, kidney failure, lupus, or be the effects of chemotherapy. Radiation therapy and excessive drug use will affect kidney function and result in anomalies. These indentations may also be signs of connective tissue cell differentiation and nutrient absorption deviations. If one is dieting, these markings will be caused by malnourishment. Horizontal lines across the nails could also signify that the person may be suffering from measles or mumps.

If the nails are covered with numerous horizontal ridges and with bumps like a washboard, then the patient may be suffering from a matrix/cuticle inflammation, or matrix damage. This may also signify that the patient suffers from some kind of pressure from a tumor. Especially if one has an ear crease (Picture 6a) or the pinkies have lunulae (Picture 2g) indicates there is a high chance for a heart attack. Vein Lite and Asparagus Extract are excellent for cardiovascular health.

Horizontal white lines or strips are most commonly caused by chronic kidney problem, such as proteinuria (Pictures 4a and 4b). This condition is particularly noticeable if the patient has more than one horizontal white line with a fuzzy appearance. However, horizontal white lines can be the result of many other things, such as arsenic/lead poisoning and/or Hutchinson's disease. Muehrcke's lines (Picture 2c), white lines that are parallel to the lunulae, also indicate kidney problems.

Pitting

Pitting of the nails represents as small, point-sized depressions or indentations on the surface of the nail, sometimes with scaling (Pictures 4c and 4d). It may or may not be uniform throughout the nail and is associated with autoimmune disorders such as psoriasis, eczema or fungal infection. In fact, approximately 10% to 50% of psoriasis patients manifest this symptom (Ref: Mayeaux EJ Jr. Nail disorders. *Primary Care*. 2000; 27: 333-51). Pitting is also seen in other autoimmune conditions such as chronic dermatitis and alopecia areata. For fungal infections, Kidney Chi, Happy Skin

Tonic and Asparagus Extract are recommended. For autoimmune conditions, either Autocin or Psoricaid is recommended.

White spots

White spots that appear on the nails of men, women, and children may have to do with hormonal imbalance (Pictures 4a and 4e). Zinc and calcium deficiencies are also possible, but this is not necessarily all that is the case. In children and adolescents, this may be due to developmental changes or hormonal changes that occur in the normal growth stages. This changing can also cause air bubbles to form underneath the nails, which should not cause alarm.

Other reasons for white spots include excessive chemical or drug use, which causes the kidneys to be overworked while cleansing the system. Detoxification is necessary in these cases. Another indication of poor kidney function is the presence of fuzzy white strips running horizontally across the nail (Pictures 4a and 4b), signaling the chance of protein and excess nitrogen in the urine. In these cases, Asparagus Extract, Cordyceps Extract, Bathdetox and Kidney Chi have been shown to be very helpful.

Certain infectious entities can often manifest themselves in the nails of a patient. Of the infectious etiologies, fungal infections of the nail are probably the most noticeable and one of the most common as well. Tinea, a specific nail fungal infection, is often seen in the nails as yellowish-white, thickened, brittle or scaly nails with numerous markings and pinpoint indentations. It can also involve the skin around the nail. Earlier signs will show few indented points on the nails (Figure 1E). Happy Skin Tonic, Kidney Chi and Asparagus Extract are recommended.

If one has fuzzy-looking white splotches, like little elliptical patterns, this signals the possibility of a condition such as incontinence, any genital or uterine infection, or sexually transmitted diseases (e.g., Chlamydia or syphilis) associated with symptoms such as white discharge. This may also signal vaginitis, in which case Kidney Chi and Happy Skin Tonic (for washing and douching) are recommended. For incontinence, Night-Dry and Kidney Chi can be taken.

Gray dots

Nails that are covered with gray dots signify that this patient suffers from dry nail fungus, a condition known as tinea which is also related to hair loss, alopecia, and other autoimmune diseases. One way to tell whether fungal infection has spread throughout the body is to press the associated meridian points and test for sensitivity: either on the insides of the thighs halfway between the hip and the knee or in the notch where the collarbone meets the shoulder blade. If one feels a sharp pain, this means that she has a low immunity and a systemic candida infection. At this point, it would be very beneficial to take Asparagus Extract, Kidney Chi and CFC.

Red spots

If the middle fingernail has red spots on it, this could be due to a heart problem (Figure 3B). This problem is seen in many patients, and is one that doctors should be especially aware of. If this condition is seen, then other symptoms of the same disorder should be checked to confirm the suspicion.

Black/Red Line

If the nail has a dark line, which moves when nail grows, it is internal bleeding or ulcers (Figure 2F, Pictures 2g, 4f and 4g). If a spot shows on the nail, and not move with nail growth, it could be digestive cancer.

The black or red line usually signifies microvessel bleeding, chronic hypertension, psoriasis, endocarditis, or bleeding in the prostate or within the digestive system.

If caused by trauma, avoid water to prevent infection.

If caused by blood disease, avoid spicy food that can cause gastrointestinal bleeding. Avoid fish bones that can cause gum bleeding. Avoid hard foods to prevent fecal bleeding.

J.N., 30 y/o/m from CA, had several black lines on his fingernails. I told him he may have some internal bleeding. Two days later, he relates that he had dark urine, an indication of bleeding. He later found that the bleeding was caused by kidney stones.

Dark, longitudinal Band

A dark, longitudinal band or streak (Pictures 3c, 3d), not to be confused with a line, on the nail can either be a benign nevus or can signal melanoma. Sometimes black or brown spots may also signal the early stage of melanoma and these spots may grow in size.

Hammer nail

A hammer-shaped nail is related to cardiovascular disease. Some cardiovascular diseases are related to nutrition: atherosclerosis, CHD, hypertension, myocardial infarction. Factors are high lipid level, high sugar, high salt, and unhealthy eating habits. Those with this type of nail need to avoid high fat, high sugar and high salt diets.

Chapter 6

NAIL ANALYSIS BY CONDITION

Now that you know the distinct nail characteristics to look for when doing an analysis, let us categorize these characteristics under the different bodily systems and health conditions.

Cardiovascular problems

Short, wide, reddish nails (Figure 2A, Picture 1a) signal cardiovascular problems including high blood pressure, atherosclerosis and the possibility of stroke or brain hemorrhage.

If the tops of the nails are wide while the bottoms of the nails are much narrower, this could be indicative of the possibility of stroke and other cardiovascular problems. Stroke is also possible if the lunulae are oversized and appear on all fingers, including the pinkies (Picture 2g).

If there are less than 8 lunulae on all the fingernails, then there is a problem with poor circulation. Patients exhibiting problems of this sort should take Vein Lite, Asparagus Extract and OxyPower to increase blood circulation and repair the lack of oxygen intracellularly. Nails with no lunulae altogether and a cloudy appearance overall (Picture 2h) are considered to be indicative of circulatory deficiency and a risk for cancer development in later life. If there are sharp horizontal ridges and/or lunulae on the pinkies, there may be a chance for heart attack.

Nail clubbing or drumstick fingers (Figure 1F, Pictures 1d and 1e) could also be a sign of a heart problem. Nails with a central canal that form a fir tree figure signal peripheral artery disease risk (Picture 3f). Heavy metal toxicity, which can affect both cardiovascular and liver function, is usually seen as dark discoloration around the lunulae (Pictures 3a and 4h).

Digestive and Liver problems

If the nail is flattened instead of being slightly curved in appearance, then this signals digestive problems such as chronic gastritis.

If the nail is blackish or yellowish in tone, then the patient may have a digestive problem (Figure 3A, Picture 2d). This problem may not necessarily be simply a fungal infection.

If the middle nail has a red elongated or circular spot in the upper corner, then this is possibly indicative of chronic gastritis (Figure 3B). Black lines and spots seen on the nail *that grow with* the nail are indicative of gastritis, intestinal or internal bleeding (Figure 2F, Pictures 2g, 4f, 4g). Stationary black spots seen in those of non-African heritage are suspect and should be further tested.

If the ring finger on the right hand has a black circular or oval spot in the middle of the nail, then this is indicative of liver problems, and even liver cancer (Figure 2F).

Liver dysfunction can also be signaled by half and half nails (Picture 1h) or Terry's nails (Picture 5a). In the case of the latter, there is a horizontal dark red band beneath the tip of the nails and the rest of the nails is pink, not opaque or white (Picture 5a) as opposed to Picture 2a where the rest of the nails is opaque (kidney problem). A yellow tint to the skin (jaundice) is also a sign of liver dysfunction (Picture 5b).

Bleeding

Black lines on the nail (Pictures 2g, 4f, 4g) indicate bleeding. Various reasons exist for bleeding. It can be just gum bleeding or hemorrhoids. You can use other markers to verify which part of the body may have some bleeding. For example, a cyst on the frenula (Pictures 6b, 6c and 6d) may indicate bleeding in the colon or intestines. If one has dark-colored urine, it may indicate kidney bleeding.

Respiratory problems

Nail clubbing (Figure 1F, Pictures 1d and 1e) and a surface that resembles rough glass in its opacity and texture point to respiratory problems such as emphysema.

If the colors of the different parts of the nails are reversed, with the lunulae being reddish (Picture 2e) while the rest of the nail is whitish, then the patient may have respiratory problems such as bronchitis.

Greenish or purplish colored nails signal a serious case of emphysema along with various other respiratory disorders. Ridges along the nails also signal respiratory problems (Pictures 2d and 3b), and perhaps are indicative of kidney problems as well.

Kidney Problems

Kidney problems can be manifested through the nails as well as other parts of the body. In the nails, transverse horizontal white lines indicate chronic kidney problems or low levels of serum protein (Pictures 4a and 4b).

Ridges, which can sometimes be blackish or colored, and white spots on the fingernail, indicate kidney problems and hormonal problems (Pictures 2d and 3b).

Opaqueness of nails along with a red horizontal rim at the tip of the nail is indicative of kidney disorders (Figure 1B, Picture 2a). Notice how this is similar to, yet distinct from, the appearance of nails which signal a liver disorder (Picture 5a). In liver problems, the nails are not opaque. Asparagus Extract, Bathdetox, Kidney Chi and Cordyceps Extract are recommended for kidney problems.

Hormone Problems

White spots on the fingernail indicate a hormone imbalance (Pictures 4a and 4e). There are more physical markers of hormonal imbalance (red dots on the tongue or cherry angiomas) that will be discussed in later sections.

If the nails are quite short naturally but are very wide, resembling a rectangle, with a normal color, then the patient may be infertile.

Arthritis

Nail beading (Figure 2C, Picture 3g) is indicative of osteoarthritis or osteoporosis.

Red lunulae indicate rheumatoid arthritis (Picture 2e).

According to a 2008 study in the *Arthritis & Rheumatism* journal, women whose index fingers are shorter than their ring finger may be twice as likely to develop osteoarthritis in the knees (Picture 5d). This finger length test also may indicate Hashimoto's thyroiditis.

Eye problems

If the thumbnails have gray colored markers and a wave-like appearance on the left side, then this is indicative of glaucoma in the patient. Vein Lite, Asparagus Extract and Juvenin are useful.

Parasites/Infectious diseases

Nails that are whitish, dull, and waxy looking are quite possibly due to the presence of tapeworms in the system or other parasites.

Besides anemia, spoon-shaped nails may also sometimes indicate parasites (Picture 1c).

Pitting in the nails may indicate fungal or tinea infection, if not psoriasis (Figure 1E, Pictures 4c, 4d and 5c). These nails may also be thick with a white or yellowish discoloration. Happy Skin Tonic is an effective topical application for this.

In those with suppressed immune function, such as diabetes or AIDS patients, thickening, discoloration and scaling of the nails are related to severe fungal infection (Picture 5c).

Osteoporosis

Nails that are atrophied, shriveled and thin, especially with ridges that look like beads on a string (Figure 2C, Picture 3g) is indicative of osteoporosis risk.

Blood and Bone Marrow Diseases

Spoon-shaped nails that are also pale in color signal anemia while triangular or shell-shaped or triangular nails indicate blood or bone marrow disease (Figure 2B, Picture 1c), such as polycythemia vera, leukemia, or lymphoma.

Lymphatic System problems

If the nail is slow growing, thick, and hard, with a curved surface area and dull luster, this is indicative of a problem in the lymphatic system. Cordyceps Extract, Reishi Spore Extract and Asparagus Extract can help.

If the nail is greenish, then the body is poisoned and the possibility of cancer is great. Take Asparagus Extract and Vein Lite.

Autoimmune/Idiopathic diseases

If the lunulae are red (Picture 2e) or bluish in color (Picture 3a) and rough, the center of the nail is raised, and the tip is curved upward (Figure 3C), then the patient may have an autoimmune disease such as lupus, rheumatoid arthritis, psoriasis, eczema, etc. Autocin or Psoricaid can improve this condition. This description is similar to the appearance in the case of respiratory disorders, where the nail is opaque, gray, and curling over onto itself while raised in the middle. This type of description is usually seen in patients with severe emphysema or cancer.

Nails with severe pitting, massive scaling and yellow crusting are most likely symptoms of psoriasis (Pictures 4c and 4d). Using Psoricaid/Autocin and Whole Skin Ointment can help.

Thyroid disorders

If fingernails are brittle and easily broken (Figure 3D), this is indicative of thyroid problems. Also, shoot-like growths from the lunulae also signal this problem (Figure 3E).

It is important to note that there are other physical symptoms which indicate thyroid disease, most especially low thyroid function. These will be discussed in depth in later sections.

Hashimoto's Thyroiditis

With the palm of your hand facing yourself, hold your thumb and your pinky together (as if you were forming the number 3) and keep your middle three fingers together. If your index finger is longer than your ring finger (Picture 5d), it may indicate a hypothyroid condition due to Hashimoto's Thyroiditis.

Please note that this finger length test should be used if the patient is exhibiting symptoms of low thyroid function such as hair loss, fatigue, weight gain, dry skin, cold hands and feet, delayed deep-tendon/knee-jerk reflexes and decreased mental capacity.

The finger length test may also be used to determine osteoarthritis risk in women.

Adrenal gland disorders

If the patient's fingernails have ridges and are easily split and torn, then this could signal some problem in the adrenal gland (Figure 3F). Chi Energy is excellent for this condition.

SECTION II

TONGUE ANALYSIS

Chapter 7

OVERVIEW OF TONGUE DIAGNOSIS

Tongue analysis is one of Chinese and Indian Ayurvedic techniques in relation to long-term disease prevention and good health. It has been used by the Chinese for thousands of years. As recently as the 19th century, Western doctors also looked at patients' tongues during examinations, though in a different manner in that it was used by the Chinese as a much more specific medical marker. The Western method of checking the tongue has since phased out but is actually a very important part of a general examination that should be reinstated in a modified form. Thus, both Western and Eastern thought can be incorporated to arrive at an exciting and remarkably accurate health analysis.

Generally, the appearance of the tongue can be a valuable guide concerning organ function. The tongue should be examined every day before or after brushing the teeth to inspect for problems. Many meridian lines run along the tongue, and thus the tongue is an important location of bodily function. When the body is not functioning correctly, it is reflected on the tongue. For instance, one will notice that during sickness, the tongue will appear duller and perhaps a different color and texture than when one is healthy. Similarly, the tongue may appear bloated when the body is experiencing disorders that cause water retention.

The tongue is the most visible internal organ of the body. The topmost layer of epithelial tissue is constantly growing and replacing old tissue with new. The entire layer takes only 2 to 3 days to become fully replaced. Since the regeneration is fast enough, the cells' metabolism must also be high, so any malnutrition or ailment in the body can be quickly seen on the tongue. The lack of necessary nutrients such as the vitamin B group, vitamin C, iron, and zinc all cause oxidation of cells and thus a change in the cells themselves. Taste cells also become atrophied as malnourishment progresses. Oftentimes, these changes are so immediate that they can be detected and followed before any other changes in the body occur.

Another reason why the tongue is so indicative of the body's condition is the fact that the tongue contains many blood vessels and thus reflects the condition of the blood in the body. If the constituents of the blood change even slightly, then this change will show on the tongue very clearly, resulting in a color change that is noticeable almost immediately.

We shall begin by clarifying the exact way in which to examine one's tongue. To begin, the patient should have a clean mouth that has been brushed recently but preferably not immediately prior to the examination. This way the tongue will not bear any temporary marks or color changes to the tongue surface, which may affect its normal appearance. The patient should not have eaten anything immediately prior to the examination as well, as this can also affect both the color and the texture of the tongue, depending on the consistency and the color of food eaten. The tongue should be extended out of the mouth evenly, with the tip pointed downwards, and a flat surface. The patient must be careful so as not to stretch the tongue so far that the blood flow is affected. The general quality of the tongue should be noted, including color, vitality, moisture, shape and coating. Specifically, if there is a coating, observation may be made regarding whether or not the coating extends over the entire tongue, or whether it is patchy, indicating a condition known as a geographic tongue. More detailed tongue characteristics must be examined next, noting symptoms of disorder such as bleeding, bruised spots, or lesions. The movements and facultative ability of the tongue must be noted as well.

When examining the tongue, one can determine a patient's health condition by analyzing the color, shape, vitality, coating, and moisture level of the tongue as well as examining the veins underneath the tongue.

Chapter 8

TONGUE VITALITY, MOVEMENT, AND MOISTURE

Vitality of the tongue

What is tongue vitality? Generally, dryness of tongue is a symptom of various internal disorders. Tongue movement is also indicative of this kind of vitality, which is closely connected to brain activity. Normally, the tongue is very flexible, supple and mobile. Any deviation from the proper ability to move the tongue signals deficiencies in coordination and brain function.

The general condition of the tongue must primarily be observed when doing the examination. Vitality and quality of tongue tissue must be evaluated first to see if any problems can be immediately noticed. A healthy tongue is firm and fits proportionately into the bottom of the mouth. It should make movements with fluidity and strength, and show a firm capability to facilitate speech and any other movement. If the tongue is too soft and contains no vitality (Picture 7d), the patient may be suffering from a secretory or chronic problem. The patient is lacking blood, fluid, or Chi (also called Qi, the Chinese term for overall bodily energy or strength). If the patient lacks energy and fluids, then the meridians are not balanced. The softness of the tongue can be related to any of these proposed circumstances: 1) the salivary glands do not secrete enough saliva, 2) the nervous system may be experiencing problems, or 3) the tongue muscles may be lacking in strength.

If the tongue is very stiff then the person's nerve transmissions are impaired and are thus unable to function properly. The stiffness of the tongue may be related to Type B meningitis, or if there is a high fever, then it may be related to liver coma or stroke. Patients with these symptoms must be treated right away.

Tongue Movement

If the tongue deviates to the side (Picture 7a) then the patient may be suffering from stroke, hemorrhaging, tongue or facial nerves damage, or Bell's palsy. If the brain, facial, or liver problems are too strong, damage to the nervous system will be detrimental. Deviation of the tongue from side to side involuntarily is a pre-stroke symptom, and should be examined by a physician for preventative measures immediately. A deviated tongue may also signal whiplash and heavy metal toxicity.

If the tongue perpetually trembles involuntarily (i.e., shivering gestures), then the patient is lacking tongue energy, Chi, and blood and has a poor immune system. The patients who suffer from tongue trembling have a hyperactive thyroid function and nerve damage. Old age can affect the nerves in the facial organs as well as the eyes, ears, nose, and mouth. Other causes of tongue trembling include poisoning by heavy metals such as mercury, manganese, barium, and chloride. Many heavy metals are found in the air we breathe, lead being the most obvious of these. Lead will cause headaches, insomnia, sweatiness and irregular periods as well. Mercury, also found in the air, can cause moodiness and gum problems with much saliva, and trembling in other parts of the body as well, including the fingers, eye, and legs. Many of the other heavy metals will cause such symptoms as hardening of the tongue, memory loss, and numbness.

Numbness of the tongue can be caused by methanol poisoning (which also leads to blindness) and/or thallium in the body, in the form of an acetate or sulfur derivative. These poisons cause peripheral nerve irritation, loss of body hair, and white coating on the nails.

A shriveled tongue impedes basic tongue functions. People with this symptom may have myocardial infarction. If the patient has no saliva at all, then the condition is very serious.

A limp tongue is a symptom of energy deficiency. A patient with this condition may be suffering from toxemia, septicemia, or a low thyroid gland output and function. The results of these conditions may be enlarged extremities or poor refractive abilities.

If the tongue is heavy because the veins on the underside protrude too much (Picture 7b, 11b, 11c), the patient may be suffering from liver problems, poor circulation, as well as heavy metal poisoning. Those with both protruding veins under the tongue and creases on the earlobe (Picture 6a) may have a very high chance of angioplasty or bypass surgery. Also, if the underside of the tongue exhibits noticeable venous branching, it signifies liver problems (Picture 11b, 11c). Very dark or black veins under the tongue point to a lung problem, most especially emphysema (Picture 11d). If the tongue moves slowly and appears to be curled under, then the patient may have trouble talking. This is also known as cerebral vessel accident caused by the after-effects of meningitis.

If the tongue cannot move in all directions quickly and lacks coordination, brain function is definitely impaired. People who have had a stroke may experience this type of inability to control the tongue movement.

Tongue Moisture

Tongue moisture represents body hydration. A normal tongue should be slightly moist. Dryness indicates insufficiency of fluids (Picture 7d), which also indicates stomach problems, while wetness is indicative of accumulation of fluids. The latter leads to edema, which can cause the tongue to enlarge and push against the teeth, creating teeth marks (Picture 7e, 7f). Smoking often produces a dry tongue, and this habit also tends to cause a general yellowish appearance of the tongue.

Under the Tongue

The underside of the tongue must be examined in order to determine the level of toxins in the body. This phenomenon is observed through protruding veins on the tongue's underside. Such symptoms reflect high levels of carbon dioxide and low levels of oxygen in the blood stream. In addition, dark veins increase acidity of the blood, a condition that makes people more susceptive to illness. Black or red spots under the tongue are due to accumulation of heavy metals such as lead, aluminum, mercury, etc. (Picture 7b). Additionally, dark, protruding and branching veins under the tongue also signal this condition (Picture 11b, 11c) since heavy metal toxicity can damage the liver. Metal Flush, Vein Lite and Asparagus Extract are recommended.

Chapter 9

TONGUE COLOR

Tongue color

The color of the tongue is a very important component of such analysis. This aspect of the tongue reflects what is known by the Chinese as the "Heat" of the system as opposed to the "Cold" characteristics in a person. If the tongue is dark red, Heat is associated with the condition. If the tongue is pale, "Cold" is associated. Heat is often related to heart diseases or heart trouble, while Cold is more often associated with cancer patients and people with poor circulation. You can sometimes easily tell if a person is "hot" if they appear to have a generally ruddy complexion, which is sometimes seen as redness throughout the body as well. Cold types, on the other hand, generally are seen as having sallow, pale complexions and are much more inactive than those that are considered in Chinese medicine to be hot. Hot and cold descriptions in Chinese medicine are very much related to the level of oxygen circulated throughout the body.

In a healthy individual, the tongue should have a solid, fleshy pink color (Picture 7g). A pale tongue (Picture 7h) is related to poor circulation and anemia. On the other hand, if the tongue is dark in color, with a red or even purple flare (Pictures 8c, 8d), then this may signal circulation blockages due to toxins in the system, or heavy metals in the body, which must be removed.

Color Distribution

Color distribution is a highly important feature of tongue analysis. If the color of the tongue spreads over into the front area, the patient is not seriously ill. If it spreads to the back, it is an inner organ disease due to excessive phlegm and poor digestive system. If it is only on the left side (when looking in), there is blockage in the organs. If the color is only on the right side, then the disease is throughout the body.

Color of the Tongue Tip

If the tip of the tongue is dark or reddish, this indicates that the heart is of the "hot" characteristic. Other possible causes of this condition could be worrying too much, nervousness, hyperthyroid activity, acute appendicitis, or the occasional symptoms of PMS.

Red spots on the tip of the tongue of a healthy individual may be a sign of blood stasis. Red spots on the root of the tongue indicates hormonal imbalance, particularly estrogen dominance.

Clinically, if patients show an extreme case of these descriptions, this is likely to be due to hyperthyroid activity, measles, scarlet fever, or a possibility of any number of infectious external diseases which necessitates immediate physician's examination. Extreme cases may also signify infection of the thoracic membrane, bronchitis or any other upper respiratory infection, or neurasthenia.

Different Tongue Colors

A normal tongue should be light red or pink in color with just a touch of moistness. If dry, then a stomach issue persists. If there is no coating, then there is a lack of blood or chi circulation.

While tongue color may be indicative of disease, it is used more for determining whether the condition is serious. Table 2 shows the correlation of the color to the severity of disease.

Table 2. Tongue Color vs. Overall Health			
Color	Minor condition	Moderate-serious condition	Sickness Ratio
Pink	81.40%	38.50%	47%
Red	17.50%	29.65%	170%
Dark Red	0.23%	15.35%	67%
Purple	0.87%	11.00%	1265%
Blue/Green	0	5.50%	Infinity

In some cases, tongue color may also be associated with certain diseases. For example, in Table 3, a purple/greenish tongue is more closely associated with Coronary Artery Disease (CAD), cancer and liver disease than diabetes.

Table 3. Correlation of Tongue Color to Certain Diseases			
	Dark red/light grey tongue	Purple/greenish tongue	Other
CAD		+++	++
Cancer		+++	++
Liver Disease		+++	++
Diabetes (type 2)	+++		++

Various tongue surface colors have been shown to be associated with different problems. The following is an outline of the symptoms and diseases that are associated with each of the different tongue colors.

WHITE/PALE

People with pale tongues (Picture 7h, 8a), not to be confused with having a white coating (see section on Tongue Coating), have this lack of color due to low or weak blood supply, which may be caused by anemia or malnourishment. A lung or large intestine problem is also associated with this tongue color. Parasites, renitis, edema, hemorrhaging, retarded adrenal cortex function, or unbalanced hormones could also cause this.

If the tongue is pale in one part and turns to red in other parts, this means that blood/chi circulation is impaired. Anemia may be associated.

If there is no coating and the tongue appears unusually wet, this points to a stomach problem. If the tongue appears to be slightly dry, then a lung problem may be the cause.

If the tongue is shiny (mirror-like) and small in size, there may be a risk for cancer of the spleen or stomach.

RED

The normal color of a healthy tongue is light red, signaling good circulation and a healthy blood supply. However, if one has a blood red tongue (Picture 8b), then most likely this abnormality stems from the fact that the person is of a "hot" type. A red tongue is usually associated with fever or a problem with the heart or liver.

If the tongue is red, large and has a slight coating, the fever is not real. Similarly, if the tongue is red, small, has no coating and has cracks, the fever is also not real.

If the tongue is red, spiky, and thick and has a yellow, gray or black coating, there is a real fever as well as a possible heart condition.

If the tongue is red and mirror-like, and the patient is thirsty, has chest heaviness and has nausea, this is associated with a stomach or gallbladder chronic disease (Picture 11g).

If the tongue is dark red (Picture 8c), this customarily means that the fever has already reached the blood. Usually this is associated with yin deficiency, and blood stasis has already occurred. If the tongue is dark red and appears wet, the condition may not be serious. If the tongue is dry and has cracks, then the condition is serious. Picture 11g is of a patient with serious gallbladder issues.

A tongue tip that is a darker red than the rest of the tongue may be caused by a heart problem. If the sides of the tongue are reddest, this signifies a liver and gallbladder problem. If the whole tongue is red, and if there is no coating or the patient experiences dry mouth, then it is a stomach problem.

Redness in the tongue may also be due to bacteria (21% related to infections), which could have infected the blood and caused an acute infectious disease, pus in the blood or organs, a hyperthyroid condition, hypertension, diabetes, tuberculosis, hypermetabolism, or post-operative dehydration. Bodily nutrition is confused and dehydration is rapid, so blood cohesiveness is higher, showing up on the tongue as possible spikes or lesions, or blood spots. The tongue could have an upside down T-shaped or lambda-shaped cracks (Picture 11f). If the patient is experiencing dryness of the mouth, it is possible that blood will appear in the stool, and the patient will have small amounts of urine that is reddish in color, as well as stomach pains. If there is a spiked appearance on the tongue, the patient may suffer a possible liver and gallbladder problem. If tongue is red and cracked, a lung and stomach problem is possible.

A red spot on the tip of the tongue signifies that the patient is overworked and may be experiencing insomnia and stress. In fact, this patient may suffer from a deficiency of vitamins and nutrients.

If both sides of the tongue become red, this patient suffers from high blood pressure and a hyperactive thyroid gland.

If the symptoms are more extreme and the tongue darker in color, besides being possibly an acute bacterial infection or chronic disease, like tuberculosis or hyperthyroid and cancers, these patients may have dilated capillary blood vessels, causing inflammation leading to a thickening of blood, resulting in slow moving blood.

PURPLE

This color on the tongue is an extreme case of tongue redness (Picture 8d). Blood stasis causes the color change from red to purple. This could be due to a number of possibilities:

- Heart disease with lung infection, where the lung function is impaired, and thus the oxygen exchange process is blocked.
- Fever symptoms due to unsaturated hemoglobin and high blood viscosity; the patient most likely suffers from poor circulation.

- Red blood cells are denser when ill, there is oxygen depletion causing an irregularity in blood density and production, causing a green purple color. This problem is also seen in alcohol poisoning.
- Early stages of circulation problems; cold temperatures and surroundings.

If the tongue is purple and dry, kidney or lung problems may be the cause.

If the tongue is purple, shiny and slippery-looking, this indicates a stomach, kidney, or lung. In some cases, this signals a serious condition, possibly cancer.

Internal trauma may also be the cause for purple or blue spots to appear on the tongue, as opposed to the whole tongue being a certain color. If the tongue has been dark red or purple for a long time, this patient should immediately see a doctor about the possibility of preventing cancer. Out of 12,448 cancer patients, a majority of these patients were seen to have symptoms such as these, especially patients with esophageal and sphincter cancer. Leukemia and lung cancer patients also proved to have the same tongue symptoms as those mentioned above.

If the tongue appears to have a purple hue, this also could be caused by poor circulation in the patient's membrane vessels. This symptom may be caused by ailments such as chronic bronchitis, certain lung diseases, or heart failure diseases. One must understand that this color can also be a sign of gynecological and gastroenterological diseases. This purple hue may also be due to old age, as the blood tends to slow down in old age.

A purple tongue body may also be due to a nitro or ammonium group binding with other nonreactive substances and the formation of a purple color has replaced one or more hydrogen atoms on a normally nonreactive phenyl constituent in the bodily system. People who work closely with pesticides, printing presses, plastics, textiles and/or explosives should be aware of this appearance.

YELLOW

Yellowness of the tongue signifies a problem in the stomach and spleen. Patients with yellow tongues generally have poor digestive systems, so the stomach contains a lot of carbon dioxide from anaerobic fermentation. If the patient has recently eaten a lot of food with sulfur in it, after digestion, hydrogen sulfide will be exposed in the tongue reflected by a yellowish tint. Such a tint is no cause for concern. The worst case is if the surface develops a thick white coating, signaling that the lymphocyte levels have increased, due to the presence of an array of possible infections and disease. If the liver and gallbladder are problematic, it will also show up as a greenish yellow or blackish yellow color, with abdominal bloating and pain upon pressure; nausea and constipation will also be prevalent in patients with this type of tongue color.

Yellow, sticky-looking tongue surface:
People with yellow surfaces generally exude malodorous   breath and have dulled taste buds. If conditions are extreme, there may be cracks in the tongue due to high temperatures in the body and the heat resulting from cell metabolism. This leads to fast production of epithelial cells, also quickly sloughing off old cells, forming cracks. There are some variegated symptoms of a yellow tongue.

Light yellow, moist-looking tongue surface:
These patients are often thirsty, always warm, and sometimes experience light coughing. People with this tongue color often also experience the discomfort of a bloated abdomen and chest area.

Yellow, sticky-looking tongue surface:
Patients will feel pain upon pressing the abdomen. They will have dry mouths but may not necessarily feel thirsty.

Yellow, dry-looking tongue surface:
These patients like cold drinks. Their bodies are generally warm and sweaty. People with this color surface have a congested upper body.

Yellow, slimy-looking tongue surface:
Patients will feel dry but not thirsty. People of this type will feel that their bodies are warm, faces red, chests congested.

GRAY

A tongue with a gray hue signifies that the patient's condition exceeds that of a yellow-colored surface in degree of severity and that the person is in the advanced stages of disease. These people are of yin power and have long-lasting colds, weakened livers and spleens. In more extreme cases, there may be spikes and cracks on the tongue, or the color may turn black. Infection by fungus (yeast or candida) will cause hydrogen sulfide production causing yellow and finally a gray color. These people have been shown to have a tendency to overuse broad spectrum antibiotics, causing resistance.

Gray, sticky-looking tongue surface:
These patients suffer from heavy spells of chest congestion and may feel waves of heat pass over them. They often feel very nauseous, quite thirsty and may drink a lot of water. Although they may sweat a lot, they generally do not feel the urge to urinate frequently. These conditions usually stem from respiratory system problems.

Gray, slimy-looking tongue surface:
These patients have bloated abdomens, a sallow complexion, and are generally fatigued. They generally do not have a lot of urine, and experience cold shudders, especially in the extremities.

Grayish-yellow colored surface:
Patients will feel their chest congested. They may also feel nauseous but experience no vomiting. They are also easily annoyed and may have dark, dense urine and a dry mouth but not be overly thirsty; diuretic action is strong.

Grayish-black tongue:
Patients may be feverish and experience headaches; the heart, lung, spleen and stomach are all in an unhealthy condition. Those with this tongue color also tend to be irritable, hyperactive and always thirsty. They also tend to have a combination of ruddy complexion, dry mouth, and swollen throat.

GREEN/BLUE

A green tongue has been shown to be mostly due to the later stages of a circulation problem. Reduction of hemoglobin amounts results in the overall lack of oxygen. The body's veins become narrow and clogged due to poor circulation and the blood will run with high viscosity and high counts of red blood cells. This condition is seen in patients suffering from alcoholism, pigment settlement, extremely cold temperatures, increase in enzyme activity and blood clotting kinase activity, increased nitrates, pulmonary heart disease, liver cirrhosis, hepatitis, coronary heart disease, gallbladder problems, edema, and uterine problems.

A blue tongue is associated with a pancreas problem (Picture 8e). Once the tongue turns into this color, the condition is serious. If there is no coating, then it usually means the patient is in the terminal stage.

If the tongue sides have green/blue stripes, or if it is stiff, then this patient may be suffering from liver problems and has the possibility of liver cancer.

BLACK

Patients are in their latest and most severe stages of disease if the tongue is black. The patient will have symptoms including shallow breathing, dizziness and heaviness of the head, cold extremities and a weak pulse.

This color represents the final stages of disease if transgressed from yellow to gray to black. They are the most dangerous stages of physical disorder. At this stage, the kidney is in poor working condition, and both hot and cold characteristics are in the worst, most extreme condition possible (the liver, stomach and lungs could also be in a serious situation). The tongue is usually darkest at the back of the tongue and lighter up front. Tongues that are black are usually fuzzy-looking, as if covered with mold.

Black, slimy, sticky surface:
The patient will be feverish, congested, have diarrhea and loose stool. These people generally do not like to drink water, and have cold chills throughout their bodies.

Black, dry surface:
This usually signals the extreme stages of lung disease; the kidney is very weak and debilitated. The yin and yang components are both virtually empty by this stage. The patient will feel immensely thirsty and nauseous, but be unable to vomit, as well as hot and feverish all over the body. She or he may be easily annoyed and have a weak pulse.

Black, dry, burnt-looking tongue with fuzzy growths, spikes or cracks:
This is often associated with liver problems (Picture 8h). These patients may feel constipated and terribly uncomfortable, as they are in their very last stage of disease. Other symptoms seen in patients include unclear, raspy voice and speech, thick, heavy breathing, and much heat throughout the body.

One must also check the coloring of the uncoated areas and the sides. Normally, the tongue is an even light-red color. But when the patient is ill, blood contents and concentration changes and the patient's tongue color will change accordingly.

Chapter 10

TONGUE COATING

The coating of one's tongue can say much about the person's health as well as whether or not their health is improving. A healthy person should have a thin, clear looking moist film over their tongue. Coating should not be too thick, too glossy, or too sticky. Changes in coating signify changes in the body. If one is ill, and the coating gets thicker, this means that the illness is becoming worse.

The color of the coating can also determine the degree of illness (Table 4). A black coating, for example, is more commonly found in those with an intermediate to a severe degree of illness.

Table 4. Tongue Coating vs. Degree of Illness			
Color	Normal – Slightly ill	Intermediate- Serious Condition	Ratio
White	86.70 %	54.00 %	56%
Yellowish-White	7.87 %	23.60 %	300%
Yellow	1.35 %	5.68 %	420%
Green-Grayish	1.12 %	2.25 %	200%
Black	0.89 %	2.25 %	250%

Normal coating should be a bit moist (not too wet, not too dry). This means that disease has not mixed with body's fluid system. If moisture is overproduced, this is a yang deficiency, usually found in the "cold" type and coexists with edema.

Do not use a tongue scrubber to try to scrub off the coating because this will hurt the tongue and mask any signs. Use a soft brush instead to prevent damage to the taste buds.

When looking at a person's tongue coating, you must evaluate these three characteristics: coating color, coating distribution and coating quality.

Coating Color

A white coating all over the tongue is usually a sign of low immunity or lung problem. A thicker white coating signifies that the condition is more serious (Pictures 9a, 12c). In the case of Picture 12c, the patient is a smoker and has tuberculosis. After a month, improvement is seen: the white coating has reduced and the tongue is healthier-looking overall (Picture 12d). A yellowish or white coating signifies fever and a local inflammation, possibly the stomach (Picture 9a).

A thick, yellow coating over the tongue is a sign that the patient has gastritis, digestion problems, or stomach ulcers. The darker the yellow, the more severe the condition (Picture 10c, 10d).

A grey film coating the tongue in the root area may be caused by several types of bodily weaknesses such as frequent fevers, but are mostly due to kidney problems (Picture 10h). If the coating turns to brown or black (Picture 8g), this also points to a kidney problem. If this symptom is not related to poor kidney function, and the tongue coating still appears to be brown or black, then this may be a sign of trouble in the intestines (may be related to constipation). It may also be caused by overuse of broad spectrum antibiotics (Picture 9b). Broad spectrum antibiotics kill the tongue's natural bacteria allowing fungus to grow and, thus, accounts for the dark brown or black film over the tongue.

A black coating can represent respiratory, digestive problems or kidney problems (Pictures 8f, 15b). It may also indicate high fever, dehydration, or chronic infection. A black, dry and spiky coating signifies liver problems (Picture 8h).

If a patient notices a black film over his tongue that is present only in the mornings, he should not worry. The patient may experience frequent fevers that arise from ailments such as stomach, lung, or esophagus cancer. A patient who is highly nervous can also acquire symptoms such as these. If the root of the tongue is covered with a spiky, fur-like substance, then the patient is over-stressed and needs to relieve his tension. The yellow-brown film covering the tongue can also due to kidney-related hormone problems such as impotence, especially if there are red star-like spots on the tongue anywhere besides the tip. Later stages of this problem may turn the tongue coating black (Pictures 8f, 8h, 15b).

If the coating of the tongue appears to be white and thick at first, then yellow, then brown, and finally black (Picture 8f), then one has an extreme illness, which should be examined immediately. If the color of the tongue appears to be changing from black to white, this signifies that one's health is improving.

If the tongue has no coating, this signifies that the patient is lacking protein and is often cold because he does not have enough fluids. If the tongue appears to be a purple color then the patient must avoid septicemia. If the patient is elderly and has thick blood vessels, this signifies that the patient has cardiopulmonary disease. If the tongue has no coating and has a glossy appearance, this is possibly indicative of iron-deficiency anemia or pernicious anemia, vitamin B-group deficiency, or an absorption problem. This is also seen in menopause or pregnancy difficulties. Finally, if any systemic disease presents with this sort of tongue appearance, this is a more serious case.

Coating Distribution and Location

Normal tongues exhibit a thin layer of coating that spreads over the entire surface. A healthy coating should consist of a thin whitish layer starting at the root of the tongue and thinning out as it approaches the tip. If coating distribution is reversed (light to heavy from root to tip), the condition is more serious. No coating on the tongue at all signals a liver or kidney problem. A general rule to observe is that the thicker the coating, the more extreme the situation.

When you look at the coating distribution, note which part of the tongue is coated.

- If the coating is only on the tip, this is associated with the stomach and may be a mild problem only.
- If the coating is only on the root of the tongue, this signifies stomach and intestinal accumulation.
- If the coating is on the left side only, it is an inner organs problem and is very difficult to treat (Picture 9c).
- If the coating is on the right side only, the problem is with the external organs (e.g., muscles).
- If the coating is only on the center of the tongue, then this signals a digestive (intestinal) problem (Picture 11a).
- If the coating appears to be peeling off (Picture 10b), this means that the condition is very serious and that recovery from disease is not going well. When the tongue starts to lose coating, normally it starts from the tip to the root; however, when the coating is peeling off irregularly, as in Picture 10b, then this is not normal.
- If there no coating on the root (Picture 9d), this is a serious problem and may involve the stomach, kidney or spleen. This can be likened to grass with no roots. Without the roots, the grass cannot survive. On the tongue, normal coating should start from the root to the tip. If there is no root coating as in Picture 9d, this signifies a severe condition.

Generally, one should also be aware of the color of the tongue body itself, since tongue body color signals a more severe condition than that of the tongue coating.

The color of the coating should also be taken into consideration to determine which organ(s) may be affected. A yellowish coating signals digestive problems, while a dark brownish/greenish coating points to a liver problem. A dark green coating usually signals the accumulation of heavy metals such as francium oxide, which affects coenzyme A activity and sulfur amino acids. If the coating becomes bluish, then it is indicative of copper poisoning. Black coating that cannot be easily scraped off is indicative of severe liver and kidney problems (Picture 8f). It is important to examine the root, or the very back, of the tongue. A tongue with thick, white coating is usually indicative of respiratory problems or lung infections such as pneumonia.

Description of Coating

If the film over the tongue appears to be slippery, thick, and shiny, then this patient is often cold and may commonly experience edema of various kinds. Moreover, patients with these symptoms may very well be suffering from bronchitis, asthma, or emphysema.

A yellow-white spot in the coating of the tongue signifies that the patient has poor digestion and has insufficient salivary glands. If a patient used to have a coating over the tongue but the coating seems to have dried up, then this patient is suffering from stomach problems.

If the tongue is covered with little white chunks and appears to be greasy, then the patient is suffering from a respiratory problem (Picture 9e). For this condition, it is helpful to use OxyPower, Synergen, Chi Energy, Bamboo Extract, and Cordyceps Extract.

If the tongue appears to be spiky, then this person's body gives off heat, such as in a person suffering from scarlet fever. This type of person does not eat well and often suffers from fever or pneumonia. If the patient eats rough food, the tongue's coating will be irritated and will form tiny spikes.

If the coating of the tongue resembles the petals of a flower and has a thick coating, then the patient is suffering from a severe cold and an epidemic problem can arise.

A wrinkled tongue with no coating suggests that the patient has liver problems.

If the tongue is covered with a frosty fur-like substance, this is due to poor spleen and pancreas functions as well as digestive problems. Digestron, Asparagus Extract and Diabend can be used here for beneficial results.

Geographic tongue

The geographical tongue (Picture 9g, 9h, 10a, 16b) is named after its map-like, patchy-looking appearance due to loss of coating in certain areas. It should be distinguished from a tongue ulcer (Picture 14f), which is usually associated with burning, pain and soreness, especially while talking, eating and so on.

A geographic tongue has two types that relate to different problems. One type of appearance, in which there is a light, thin white patchy coating indicates respiratory, allergies, asthma or sinus problems (Picture 9g).

If the geographical tongue also shows cracking, with deeper cracks up to 2 to 3 mm deep and a yellow coating (Picture 10a), this is due to an autoimmune-related digestive problem, possibly colitis, Crohn's disease or irritable bowel syndrome (Picture 9h, 16b). This type of tongue coating may also be due to iron-deficiency anemia or vitamin B-group deficiency. The worst for both cases is if the coating is mainly in the middle of the tongue, none at the root. This indicates a more serious condition. In Picture 9g, both cases of geographical tongue are exhibited, so it can either be a lung or inflammatory digestive condition, or both.

If you have a geographical tongue, vitamin B12, thiamine, and folic acid supplementation in conjunction with OxyPower and Synergen for lung problems and Psoricaid and Digestron for colitis, Crohn's disease and IBS are recommended.

Tongue surface changes

The tongue must be splotched before recovery, from thick to thin, from dense to very sparse, as a path to healing. Gradual recovery is the only true form of recovery until the new surface is entirely re-grown. But if suddenly all the symptoms of disease are gone instantly, then the person's chi is seriously out of balance and the kidney is not functioning; this is definitely not the correct path of recovery.

Chapter 11

TONGUE SHAPE, SIZE, AND LENGTH

We define a "healthy" tongue as one that is medium to thin in width coated lightly with a translucent/white film. The tongue should be large enough to fit soundly into the area between all the teeth, and no larger or smaller than that. An individual with a small, thin tongue is weak. If the tongue is very thick and covered with a fur-like film, it signifies that the patient is prone to illnesses although physically strong.

If the tongue is light-colored and fat, then this is associated with obesity and hypothyroidism. If the tongue is thin and light red in color, this is associated with heart and digestion problems. A tongue that is thin, dry, and dark red in color is associated with late-stage illness or chronic illness.

A healthy person excretes just enough saliva so that the tongue is always moist. Not enough fluid intake or absorption may cause insufficient amount of saliva secretion. For instance, when a patient has diarrhea, the patient's tongue will appear to have a very dry and rough surface. Another cause of insufficient saliva secretion can be related to high fever. When a patient's body temperature rises, the fluids in its system become used up so the saliva glands secrete only a small amount of saliva to conserve the body water content.

Western medicine also takes note of the condition of the tongue. If a patient suffers from a severe case of constipation, diarrhea, or poor digestion, the tongue will appear greasy and swollen (Picture 16e). If a patient usually feels bloated, has diarrhea, and has a lack of coating over the tongue, this signifies that the patient has eaten too many oily foods and is now experiencing an upset stomach. A patient with these symptoms should relax and fast for a while until the symptoms subside.

If a patient wakes up in the morning with a thick tongue but gradually reduces after the patient's daily activities, there is no need to worry. If the coating over the tongue becomes thicker over the day's routine, this means that the illness is spreading deeper into the body. Another sign that the illness is spreading is if the mouth becomes very dry and the salivary glands cannot secrete enough saliva to keep the mouth moist. Recovery paths can be identified when the tongue turns from thick to thin, from dark to light, and from dry to moist.

If the tongue is swollen, marked and very moist, slippery with teeth marks caused by swelling of the tongue, these are all signs of spleen problems. The reason for this swelling is due to edema of the tongue tissue caused by water retention in the area. But there are some holistic doctors who feel that this swelling can be related to poor digestive functions. According to the five-element system, spleen and digestive function are interconnected.

Many people have these characteristics: large and puffy tongue that is light in color and has teeth marks. A reason for this could be too much accumulated water (or any bodily fluid). One needs to look at several organs:

- Stomach – may not be able to make stored fluid actively useful.
- Lungs – unable to move water (lymphatic system).
- Heart – water may have incorporated within the circulatory system.
- Liver - if impaired, it cannot remove and decompose metabolites. Accumulation of toxins may result.
- Kidney - if albumin is low, then water can enter into blood vessels, causing edema, ascites and pleural exudates.
- All of the above causes electrolyte problems. Therefore, kidney function must be improved to correct this problem.
- Late-stage disease needs to improve inter-organ system to promote electrolyte imbalance.

In the beginning, only the lung and stomach are involved with this kind of tongue. However, other factors may also be involved.

Unhealthy diet and eating habits can cause "movement" problems. Typical characteristics are people who stay in damp areas, like to eat sweets, do not exercise, or have stiffness/soreness in joints.

If patient also has dizziness, vision problems, edema, puffy face, chest heaviness, and a slow pulse and the tongue has a greasy coating, this condition is serious.

Swollen Tongue

If the rim (the area around the edges of the tongue) is swollen (Pictures 7e, 7f), and the body of the tongue is puffy with teeth marks on the side, then this person is retaining water. Tongue tissue is generally more sensitive to water retention than other areas of the body. This accounts for the puffy appearance of the tongue. The teeth marks may be due to hypoglycemia as well.

If the tongue is so swollen that it hardly fits inside the mouth, then, if the patient happens to be a child, this is due to low thyroid function. If the patient is an adult, this symptom could be due to the condition of either the thyroid or pituitary gland. In the case of the pituitary gland, the anterior pituitary may become overly excited and release too many hormones. This excess amount of hormones causes swollen extremities as well as layered growth. If the tongue is swollen and has a bloody red color, it signifies that the patient has liver cirrhosis.

Hammer-Shaped Tongue

Some patients may have tongues that bulge out in the front but are normal-sized the rest of the way back to the root (hammer-shaped tongue), indicating hormonal imbalance as well as kidney problems possibly derived from excess sexual activity or other habitual problems (Picture 10e). SXD, Chi Energy, Super-X and Cordyceps Extract are recommended in this case.

Tongue Size and Length

If the tongue is thin and flat, this patient has poor circulation. If the tongue is small and thin, it is related to cardiovascular and brain problems (13%), cancer (5%) and malnutrition. If the tongue is white and flat, then this patient has poor circulatory and salivary functions. If the tongue is light red, thin and flat, then this patient's cardiovascular and digestive functions are poor. In the case of a truly chronic digestion problem, the patient will also appear thin and suffers from a yin and yang deficiency.

If the tip of the tongue is elongated (Picture 10f), this indicates a cardiovascular problem

A large and wide tongue is associated with chronic bronchitis (40%), cancer (24%) and digestive problems (22%).

If the tongue is thick and wide, this is associated with a liver or digestive problem (Picture 10g).

Chapter 12

OTHER TONGUE MARKERS

By examining ridges, spots, and/or bumps that may appear on the tongue, one can pinpoint the organ afflicted with disease (see the tongue diagram). Generally, markings or deformities on the tip of the tongue point to the heart area, while those on the front sides show lung-related problems. Markings or deformities in the center of the tongue are related to gastrointestinal and spleen problems. The edges along the very back of the tongue direct to gallbladder and liver functions. There may be kidney, urinary, bladder, or sex hormone-related problems if there is any abnormality on the root of the tongue. The underside of the tongue can signal circulation and liver problems.

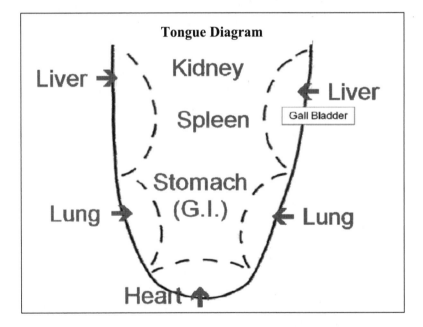

Tongue Diagram

Liver

Kidney

Liver

Gall Bladder

Spleen

Stomach (G.I.)

Lung

Lung

Heart

Perhaps the most important part to examining the shape of the tongue is noting the presence of teeth marks on the tongue, ridges along the side of the tongue which can point to spleen and other problems.

Teeth Marks

Teeth marks on the tongue are easily detected during diagnosis. For instance, indentations along the sides of the tongue are due to the imprint of the teeth onto the tongue, generally caused by water retention in the organ (Picture 7e, 7f). Water retention can be attributed to spleen/pancreas problems, signaling the need for improvement of the digestive system since the spleen and pancreas are both representative of and closely connected with the digestive tract.

Another close connection and probable cause for edema is the kidney. The excretory system may not function properly, and in this condition can result in water retention, especially in the face and throat areas. The tongue becomes swollen, forcing it against the teeth, creating teeth marks. Since the spleen has to do with immunity, and the pancreas controls much of digestion, this condition often leads to diabetes if left untreated. This type of condition is commonly seen with the lack of lunulae on the nails, signaling poor circulation and oxygen saturation levels. Patients are often prone to candida infections and cancer; in fact, a majority of cancer patients have teeth marks and lack lunulae.

Underside of the Tongue

Buildup of any kind can often manifest under the tongue. Any change of blood vessel consistency or change of color can be correlated to a change of bodily function.

The two veins found underneath the tongue are connected to heart, lung and liver functions. If these veins are not light pink or blue but dark-colored or purple and bulging, then these indicate poor circulation and increased acidity of the blood (the pH value of the central part of the tongue is normally 6.4 for males and 7.0 for females). The presence of red or black dots, spider-like (branching) veins and/or dark-colored veins indicate heavy metal accumulation and liver problems (Picture 7b, 7c, 11b, 11c, 16f).

The tables below present statistical figures which compares the number, thickness, width and length of veins underneath the tongue to different liver conditions. Characteristics that are common in most hepatitis patients include thin veins underneath the tongue with no branching and a thick tongue (Table 5). Furthermore, veins that are over 4mm are usually associated with either liver cirrhosis or liver cancer. Having three or more veins under the tongue is most likely associated with liver cirrhosis.

Table 5. Correlation between veins underneath the tongue and liver conditions

Condition		Hepatitis	Liver Cirrhosis	Liver Cancer	Fatty Liver
# cases		60	50	40	60
2 veins		90%	26%	45%	n/a
> 2 veins		10%	74%	55%	n/a
Thickness (cm)		5.21 ± 0.31	3.08 ± 0.27	3.10 ± 0.40	3.18 ± 0.27
Width (cm)		3.34 ± 0.21	3.78 ± 0.30	4.34 ± 0.21	3.18 ± 0.27
Length (cm)		5.45 ± 0.30	5.62 ± 0.10	5.63 ± 0.10	5.71 ± 0.42
Vein Diameter	≤ 3mm	99%	--	--	--
	≥ 4mm	--	80%	72.5%	--

In liver cirrhosis patients, there are more branched veins-- usually 4 of them -- and the vein diameter is thick. Liver cancer patients often have 4 to 5 large veins underneath a wide tongue (Table 6). For example, in Picture 7c, this liver cirrhosis patient has 4 branching veins. In Picture 11c, there are more than two veins; therefore, it is most likely due to liver cirrhosis or liver cancer. In Picture 16f, this liver cirrhosis patient has more than four branching veins.

Table 6. Number of veins under the tongue of liver patients

Condition	N	1	2	3	4	5	6	7
Hepatitis	60	58.4%	41.6%	--	--	--	--	--
Liver Cirrhosis	50	--	--	12%	46%	22%	12%	8%
Liver Cancer	40	--	5%	22.5%	32.5%	30%	10%	--

The dark, branching veins under the tongue may also be a sign of poor circulation in conjunction with heavy metal toxicity. Heavy metals like lead (most commonly found in tap water and paint), and mercury (found in the amalgam dental fillings for cavities), as well as aluminum (found in cooking utensils or cans) and cadmium (found in hair dye), are common contributors to heart diseases and mental disorders. These toxins, encountered in everyday life, in forms such as car exhaust and pollution, are potentially dangerous and must be removed from the system. If the veins on the underside of the tongue branch out and spread, a liver problem is the most likely cause and thus these people have trouble detoxifying. This would account for the indication of heavy metals under the tongue (Picture 7b). Thus, for those with liver problems, there is a heavy metal accumulation due to the decreased ability to detoxify the system. Metal Flush and Vein Lite have been used quite successfully for oral chelation, increasing blood circulation, and detoxification of blood.

Clinically, we can see that diseased patients have different appearances on the underside of the tongue in terms of size and shading of the main blood vessels that branch from the base of the mouth, where the tongue is attached. If there is any color deviation from the normal red color of blood vessels, this may indicate a problem in oxygen uptake by blood and a pH deviation in blood. The patient may have TB, chronic bronchitis, emphysema, hypertension or kidney/heart problems. This is illustrated in Picture 11d. The patient has emphysema, which obviously impairs oxygen uptake in the blood. OxyPower, Cordyceps Extract, Chi Energy, Reishi Spore Extract and Synergen are recommended for respiratory problems.

Spiky Tongue

If the spikes on the tongue are located on the tip, this is associated with a heart condition (Picture 12a). If they are located on the sides of the tongue, this is associated with liver and gallbladder problems. If located on the center, a stomach or intestinal problem may be present.

Roadmap-like Tongue

If seen in younger people, a roadmap-like tongue (Picture 11e, 15e) signals hormonal imbalance or blood disease. In older people, this type of tongue shows a digestive problem, particularly a lack of stomach acid or hypochlorydia.

Tongue Cracking

Cracks in the tongue body will correlate to different systems of the body depending on their location, and the depth of such cracks signifies the severity of the condition. Cracks that are deeper than 2 mm are considered to be associated with very severe problems, while cracks that are less than 2 mm deep tend to have to do with more acute situations that are not as dire.

If the tongue has cracks, this is due to chronic digestive problems along with Vitamin B deficiency as well as spleen and stomach problems.

Cracks may be vertical or horizontal or both, but if the problem is inherited, then these may not be of concern. Usually the lines appear directly related to the stomach and spleen, weak chi energy and metabolism, and poor absorption. Stomach, duodenal and cardiac sphincter cancers are all closely associated with the lines on the tongue. If a patient has stomach problems and cracks are later found on the tongue, then there may be a chance of cancer.

Cracking on the center of the tongue toward the back is due to poor kidney function. Cordyceps Extract, Asparagus Extract and Kidney Chi should be taken. Cracking closer to the front of the tongue, down the center, is due to gastrointestinal or stomach problems and is also known as fissured tongue (Picture 11f).

Deeper cracks are associated with more severe the stomach or gastrointestinal tract condition (Picture 11a). For example, in Picture 13f, this stomach cancer patient has deep cracks especially in the center. In Picture 13g, this esophageal cancer patient has a crack towards the root of the tongue, though it is not readily visible as it is covered by a brown/yellow coating.

If there are cracks running horizontally across the tongue in the middle area, it may also be a kidney problem, and if there is a crack along the edges, this signal spleen dysfunction. These disorders can be improved with the use of herbal products such as Asparagus Extract, Digestron, Diabend and Vitamin B complex. Any crack over 2 mm deep should be considered a serious condition and given attention immediately. Also, the condition is serious if the tongue has an upside down T-shaped crack in it.

Mirror-like Tongue

When the coating looks like it is peeled off and the tongue looks shiny, this is a mirror-like tongue (Picture 15a). This signifies blood and chi deficiency and that the disease is serious. Even if the disease is treated, the results may not be desirable.

A mirror-like tongue can also mean a number of things: serum albumin is low (as in Picture 15a), tongue cell metabolism may be retarded, poor food or electrolyte imbalance.

If the tongue is red in color and the patient feels thirsty, chest heaviness and nausea, then it could signify a stomach and gallbladder condition. In any case, a mirror-like tongue is usually associated with a serious condition.

Tongue Pain or Burning

Tongue pain or burning may be caused by many things but is most often due to a deficiency of the B vitamins. If, after taking a Vitamin B supplement, the pain and burning persists, then the problem may be due to iron deficiency. This symptom may occur in those with anemia. For those with Vitamin B complex deficiency, a folic acid supplement such as Asparagus Extract will be beneficial. For those with anemia, an iron supplement may be taken. I must issue a warning here, however concerning vitamin and supplement usage. One must be sure of their vitamin deficiencies and body types before taking any vitamin supplements. Oversupplementation can create problems. For example, taking too much iron has been known to increase the risk for colon cancer. Chi-F is an herbal supplement recommended for anemia. It doesn't contain any iron but is very effective in enriching red blood cells and platelets.

Chapter 13

TONGUE ANALYSIS BY SYSTEM

With time and practice, one should be able to find correlation between tongue appearance and organ dysfunction. Tongue diagnosis results are grouped into the five main systems of the body below, so that one can confirm the correct general conditions upon checking the following categories.

Heart Problems

Heart problems are easily detected by examining the tip of the tongue, which will appear thin, red and elongated (Picture 10f). If the tip of the tongue is especially red or spotted (Pictures 12a, 12b, 14e), this indicates a heart problem such as pulmonary heart disease or coronary heart disease. A crease on the earlobe (Picture 6a) indicates a heart condition, most likely congenital. Heart and artery problems may also be indicated by a purple or red, stiff tongue with little to no overall coating and a mirror-like appearance. The pulse may be faint, even when felt under some amount of pressure. Other symptoms include fever, perspiration, thirst, dizziness, aversion to cold, coughs, confusion, joint pain and headaches. This condition requires detoxification of toxins including heavy metals and calls for a reduction of heat and improvement of respiration and oxygen levels. Vein Lite, Asparagus Extract, Metal Flush, Wine Extract, Hypertine, OxyPower are excellent products of choice for these symptoms, for their oral chelating properties and ability to increase blood circulation.

Lung Problems

If the patient has pulmonary and/or respiratory problems, the area of the tongue on the side just behind the tip will be red or spotted like a strawberry, with a thin, white coating and/or and geographic tongue (Picture 9g, 9h, 14c). The front side of the tongue surface may be raised due to swelling (Picture 12e) or there may be detectable raised red points, which are related to allergy, asthma, or bronchitis. The pulse felt will be faint. Other symptoms include fever, aversion to cold, cough, and headaches, and calls for a reduction of heat and improvement of the respiration and oxygen levels, a problem that can be improved by taking OxyPower, Chi Energy, Cordyceps Extract, Reishi Spore Extract, Bamboo Extract Synergen.

Kidney/Hormone Problems

Poor kidney function causes the tongue to be light red and the coating thin and dry, especially in the root area, which will turn from yellow to black. Teeth marks (Pictures 7e, 7f) are also a sign of kidney problem, which causes water retention. The pulse is usually faint in kidney patients. Their complexion is also ruddy, and the body and face will feel hot with a ruddy complexion. Other symptoms may include fatigue and hot palms/feet. Therapy calls for improvement of the kidney/hormone balance and cleansing of the blood, through use of Asparagus Extract, Bathdetox, Kidney Chi and Cordyceps Extract. In Chinese Medicine, kidney function is also related to hormonal balance, and problems with the kidneys often indicate an imbalance in bodily hormones.

Red spots on the tongue indicate hormonal problems (Picture 12g). Sometimes the fingernails will have white spots (Picture 4e) to support this indication. This condition in teens is typical since they are still in the development stages, but for a grown male this could signal impotence or prostate problems, while for a female it is definitely a hormonal imbalance. Use the MIT to treat the lower back and abdominal areas for this condition, and Myomin can also help.

Digestion- Stomach/Spleen Problems

If the patient has stomach or digestive problems, the tongue will be thick and yellow with a spiky coating in conjunction with dry mouth syndrome. The pulse will be strong, and other symptoms may include fever, perspiration, chest congestion, wheezing, rash, and constipation. This problem calls for the reduction of heat and excretion of waste, by taking Digestron, Diabend, Liver Chi, CFC and Asparagus Extract.

Spleen-related conditions leave the tongue a purple-reddish color, with a thick, yellowish coating that has a greasy appearance (Picture 12c). Most important is the presence of teeth marks, which indicates spleen problems (Picture 7e). The pulse will be felt upon medium pressure, and other symptoms include congestion, vomiting, heat, and a urinary condition where there are only concentrated, small amounts of urine. Treatment calls for the use of a diuretic and the reduction of heat, effectively accomplished by taking Asparagus Extract. Digestron and Liver Chi will also help in spleen function and overall digestion.

If you see a cyst on the top portion on the frenula under the upper lip, it could be mostly related (71%) to having polyps (Picture 6b) in the small intestine. If you see a cyst on lower part on the frenula, it could mostly be related (74%) to colon polyps (Picture 6c). Overall only a 32% is related to irregular bowel movement problems (constipation). CFC, Asparagus Extract and Liver Chi can help.

Liver Problems

Liver problems leave the tongue dark red with bruised edges, called blood stasis spots (Picture 11h, 12f). One should also look underneath the tongue for branched veins (Picture 7b, 7c, 11b, 11c). If liver function is compromised, there is a detoxification problem, and toxins and heavy metals can accumulate in the body. People with liver disorders tend to have bloated stomachs, dry mouths with a generally bitter taste. Other symptoms include heart problems and a general feeling of warm discomfort. Dizziness and confused thinking may also be present. Treatment calls for the adjustment of liver functions and detoxification (of such toxins as heavy metals, etc.). Metal Flush, Vein Lite, Liver Chi, Vein Lite and Asparagus Extract are recommended.

Manifestation of Clinical Diseases on the Tongue

The following are general tongue characteristics associated with certain diseases.

Table 7. Diseases and Related Tongue Characteristics	
Condition	**Characteristics**
Anemia	■ 76% of anemic patients have tongues that are very pale in color ■ 61% have a yellow-white coating ■ The sides of the tongue may also be shiny
Coronary heart disease	■ 70% of cases have a white tongue coating ■ 35% have red tongue ■ 30% have red or dark spots ■ 73% have dark protruding vein(s) under the tongue
Chronic Bronchitis	■ White greasy coating (About 80% of these cases may be due to a cold) ■ 60% of those with yellow coating are related to an infection ■ A tongue with yellow coating has more bacteria than a tongue with white greasy coating
Diabetes	■ 64% of diabetes patients have a tongue that is red in color. About 68% of them also have swelling, dryness and some teeth marks.
Digestive Disease	■ Tongue is pink and swollen with a light white coating and cracking in the center. ■ Patients with inflammation in the digestive system have red tongues. ■ In stomach and colon cancer patients, the side of the tongue may be red or green/purple in color. The center of the tongue represents stomach and digestion. The side or edge of the tongue represents the gallbladder.
Duodenogastric Ulcer	■ Light red or light green tongue with a greasy white or yellow coating. ■ In severe ulcer cases, the tip of tongue may be red, shiny, with no spikes but has a thick greasy coating
Emphysema	■ In the early stage, tongue may be red with a

	▪	thick white or yellow coating
	▪	About 94% of patients have very dark and protruding veins under the tongue.
Gastritis	▪	Light red tongue with light white coating.
	▪	Approximately 69% of chronic gastritis patients have red or a dark purple tongue with thick yellow greasy coating.
	▪	If tongue has dark brown spots, the condition is more serious (atrophic gastritis).
Heavy Metal Toxicity	▪	Dark branching veins under the tongue
	▪	Dark/red spots under the tongue
	▪	Metallic taste in the mouth
	▪	Gums may have dark blue lines or deposits
Hepatitis	▪	Active hepatitis manifests as a thick yellow coating with the tip or side of tongue to be red.
	▪	Chronic hepatitis has a dark-colored tongue, thick yellow-white coating sometimes with red/dark spots (blood stasis) on and/or around edge of tongue. The underneath of the tongue has two or more dark, protruding, branching or varicose veins.
	▪	In the late stage, tongue loses coating and becomes mirror like. Sometimes there are cracks and red spikes
	▪	If a chronic hepatitis patient's tongue has a thick white (or yellow) coating for a long period of time, this could mean progression to liver cirrhosis, especially if the edge of the tongue shows a dark red and purple color and blood stasis spots appear.
	▪	White crystals (uric acid) on a liver cirrhosis patient's tongue mean liver and kidney complications.
Hypertension	▪	About 70% have light white coating
	▪	50% have red tongues
	▪	In 30% of cases, tongue may be swollen
	▪	About 30% of cases have red or dark spots (blood stasis) on the tongue
	▪	Tiny or fine white spots throughout the tongue (Picture 16d)
Hyperthyroidism	▪	80% have red tongue with light white coating
Hypothyroidism	▪	Swollen pale tongue, mostly with teeth marks

Liver Cancer	<ul><li>Liver cancer patients have purple tongues that are large and wide with blood stasis spots on the side of the tongue.</li><li>Underneath the tongue, there are dark, protruding, branching veins</li><li>Teeth marks are also present.</li></ul>
Kidney	<ul><li>Acute nephritis patients have a light red tongue with light coating. However, those who have hypertension as well may have a red tongue with spikes</li><li>Chronic nephritis patients have a swollen white tongue with teeth marks</li><li>Kidney failure patients usually have a thick greasy coating. When it turns to a brown/dark black coating, this means the condition is serious</li><li>Sometimes white crystals exist (uric acid)</li></ul>
Lung Cancer	<ul><li>In the early stage, a geographic tongue or red/black spots around the edge of the tongue.</li><li>When tongue becomes mirror-like, the condition is serious</li><li>Dark, protruding, branching veins are also present under the tongue</li></ul>
Myocardial infarction	<ul><li>White greasy coating or yellow-coated tongue</li><li>Dark colored tongue with red/dark spots. If a yellow greasy coating does not disappear within a short period of time, it means the condition is serious.</li><li>In late stage: Green-purple or dark red tongue without coating</li></ul>
Pneumonia	<ul><li>Thick white greasy coated dry tongue.</li><li>Serious when tongue has thick yellow greasy coating and is red, especially on the tip</li></ul>
Prostatitis	<ul><li>Red dots are present on the tongue.</li><li>Tongue may be light white or red with a yellow or white greasy coating.</li><li>Teeth marks signify a urinary problem.</li></ul>
Stomach Cancer	<ul><li>About 70% of stomach cancer patients show a purple colored tongue with 35% of them having blood stasis spots.</li><li>In the late stage, tongue is white with lots of red/black spots.</li></ul>

> ▪ About 60% of stomach cancer patients have tongues with thick coating and lots of cracking and teeth marks

Tongue Characteristics Associated with a Severe Condition

There is a group of tongue markers and characteristics that indicate a condition is in a very serious stage:

1. Tongue looks like a pig's kidneys (purple shiny color).
2. Mirror-like tongue (Picture 15a).
3. Tongue is rough (like sand), dry and has cracks.
4. Tongue is shrunken and dry (sometimes has cracks).
5. Tongue coating is black (or brown) in color, which indicates a severe kidney, digestive or respiratory condition.
6. Small, skinny tongue with no coating.
7. Tongue curls (wavering, trembling).
8. Tongue is stiff, causing difficulty in movement and speech.
9. Purple tongue with a white snow-like coating (Picture 9f).

SECTION III

OTHER PHYSICAL MARKERS

Chapter 14

EXAMINING OTHER PHYSICAL MARKERS

While the tongue and fingernails show very clear manifestations of health conditions, it is also worthwhile to look at other physical markers elsewhere in the body. Certain distinctive signs correlated with certain diseases, so you must be careful not to overlook them.

Biological Clocks

To test one's health, it is often appropriate to examine one's bodily rhythms or "biological clock." Melatonin serves as a factor when adjusting one's biological clock.

What, exactly, is a biological clock? Every earthly species has a rhythm by which members of that group live their lives. This cycle controlled in a time-clock is known as the biological clock. This clock controls even humans, the most evolved species.

Our bodily functions and substance levels are maintained via internal and external factors. Everything from your pulse to your behavior can be regulated by the biological clock. An example of this is a woman's monthly menstrual cycle, during which her uterine and vaginal linings, mucous membranes, body temperature, secretions, and many other things, are changing in response to her cycle.

From 11 pm to 5 am in the morning, human cells are dividing at a faster rate than any other time of the day, up to 8 times as fast as the fastest daytime rate. Thus, it is best to nourish the body during this fast-growing period. Between 6am and 7am is the time of the peak for cortisol in the blood. Also, metabolism slows down overnight, and so does your lymphatic system, causing swelling of certain weight-dependent tissues (e.g. around the eyes). Between 8 in the morning and noon is the time of the day where the skin has its most resilience, and the most secretions. From 1pm to 3pm in the afternoon, blood pressure and hormone levels are at their lowest points in the day, and thus one may feel at their lowest energy level at this point. From 4pm to 8pm, microcirculation increases its rate, and blood oxygen levels are at their highest. Pancreatic secretions are also at their highest at this point, and therefore it is the easiest time to absorb nutrients. Finally 8pm to 11pm in the evening is the highest production time for histamine. Blood vessel resistance is also at its lowest at this time, so blood pressure is decreased, and edema is more likely.

Human moods and stability correlate to the body's immunity level. The more stable a person's moods, the higher immunity that individual enjoys. Similarly, certain times of day relate to a strengthened or weakened immune response. This can affect the symptoms of different diseases. In rheumatoid fever, the fever tends to get worse in the evening. Similarly, for bronchitis and asthma, the coughing and symptoms tend to worsen as night sets. In this way, diseases are also affected by the biological clock.

Endocrinologists find that patients suffering from hyper adrenocorticosteroid function tend to have fewer problems in the daytime and more at night. Hence, doctors must be aware of the proper time to take a blood test for different diseases.

Coronary heart disease is at its worst in the early morning, a point that I shall refer to as its "peak". Heart attacks peak at mid-morning, cardiac arrest in the early morning as well. At these peaks, the death rates for these diseases are at their highest.

In the morning, diabetes is at its worst and the anti-insulin hormone is at its highest level, thus, the patient's blood sugar will be very high and most serious in the morning. Rheumatoid pain is also high at this time. Understanding one's biological clock can help one prepare for these peaks and alleviate the symptoms.

Scientists have learned of over 100 different rhythms in the body. There are daily, monthly, seasonal, and even annual rhythms. Also, research has found that the body's natural rhythm controls mainly three areas of bodily function: 1) energy, 2) mood, and 3) intellect.

Each person has a cycle upon birth for each of these main groups. The cycle for bodily energy goes once every 23 days. Moods and temper cycle once every 28 days, and the intellect cycles once every 33 days. At the point on the cycle that all 3 points are at their highest, one will feel their best and most energetic, with acute memory and stable moods. It is said that the midpoints between these cycles are the points where there is the most danger of contracting diseases, or for diseases to get worse. One can determine the point they are at in their biological cycle by assuming that when they are born, they are at the midpoint of the sine wave-like cycle just before the incline to the maximum. Then all you need to do is divide the amount of days you have been alive by the length of each specific cycle to find out where you are in it.

The ancient saying goes that one should get up with the sunrise to start working and go to bed upon sunset. There is some logic to these rituals. Biological clock specialists note that people's bodies are like clocks. Behavior is regulated precisely according to these clocks, and any deviation will result in serious problems. Chronobiology experts say that besides the five senses, we also have a sense of time that our biological clock runs on. The liver, small intestines, mucous membranes all have specific functions; even the smallest cells have time-related functions.

The organ most sensitive to the time sense is by far the brain. The brain's biological clock function allows for regular, restful sleep as well as vigorous thought and exercise drive and motivation. Even one's appetite is controlled by a biological clock via brain function. In a society where everyone has professional and social obligations, everyone is following their watches. This is the price of modernization of our society: the need to synchronize. The best time to think is about 10 in the morning, when your alertness is peaking and short-term memory is at its strongest. So meetings during which brainstorming is necessary will most productively occur at this hour. Many people need vacations in the summer but the body is actually most relaxed annually toward the end of February. Hence, the coming of the Chinese New Year brings with it a time of rest and relaxation, as it happens at the end of February on the Western calendar.

Cherry Angiomas

Cherry angiomas are a manifestation that estrogen attacks peripheral blood vessels, causing an aneurysm. Therefore, hormones are a major factor of cherry angiomas.

The location of these angiomas is very helpful in determining which organ has the problem. It may be found on the abdomen, the head or neck area, the arms or the thighs even. If you see cherry angiomas on the abdomen, first look for a liver problem. It could be hepatitis or an alcohol-induced problem. Then look for hormonal problems. Excessive hormones can also burden the liver. So in some cases, abdominal cherry angiomas could signal both hormonal and liver problems. Abdominal cherry angiomas in men signal liver, prostate, or reproductive organ problems (Picture 12h). In women, they signal liver, breast or ovarian problems (Picture 13a). Cherry angiomas on the head, hairline area or head indicate a stroke or aneurysm risk (Picture 13b).

You can always look at secondary markers to confirm which organ is affected. For example, check for dark, bulging veins under the tongue, bloating, fatigue, bitter taste and dry mouth when suspecting a liver problem. Also look for spider veins on the abdomen as these can signal liver issues (Picture 13c).

Look for red dots on the tongue or white spots on the nails if a hormone problem is suspected. The presence of red dots on the tongue is normal during puberty; however, some women as young as 16 years old may already have endometriosis.

I saw a 31-year-old chiropractor in Dallas a few years ago. He had many red dots on his tongue. I told him that he may have a present prostate or reproductive organ problem. He should not wait until he is 50 years old to check his PSA level. He said it is too late that he had testicle cancer at age 26.

At anti-aging meeting in Las Vegas in December 2000, I told a 48-year-old doctor from the US Virgin Islands that he has a high chance of getting prostate cancer. He had many red dots on his tongue. He is also African-American, which puts him at greater risk for prostate cancer. Two weeks later, he found out his PSA is 108.

On another occasion, I saw a 24-year-old woman from California who was overweight, had red dots on her tongue, hair on the arms and rough skin (Pictures 15d, 15c). I told her that she may have Polycystic Ovarian Syndrome (PCOS). She confirmed that she does have it and that in only a matter of minutes, I was able to determine her condition.

In February 2009, I saw R.L., a 58 y/o/m from Minnesota. He has more than 50 cherry angiomas on his abdomen and more than 10 cherry angiomas on his face and head (Picture 13b). I told him that the angiomas on his abdomen signify a risk for elevated estrogen and prostate problems. The angiomas on his face/head signify a risk for aneurysm or stroke. He says that he already had a stroke twice, a year ago and 5 years ago, respectively.

Frenula

After checking the rest of the tongue, it is important to look at the frenulum, the piece of tissue that connects the upper lip to the upper gums. If this piece of tissue has cyst-like growths on it, it signals digestive tract problems. If the growth is on the upper part of the frenula, this signals problems with the upper digestive pathway such as the small intestine and the upper colon (Picture 6b) having a 71% correlation to intestinal polyps. Growths on the lower frenula signal problems further along the digestive tract, such as in the large intestine and colon (Picture 6c). These have a 74% correlation to colon polyps. Check first for hemorrhoids or anal fissures in the case of the lower frenula cyst. If the patient has no hemorrhoids or fissures, then there is definitely a colon polyp problem. Overall, 30% of cases are related to irregular bowel movement problems (constipation). If the cyst is white in color, then the condition is chronic. If it is pink and soft, the condition is in its early stage. If there is more than one cyst on the frenula, then the condition is more serious (Picture 6d).

Xanthomas: Yellow Cholesterol Deposits around the Eyes

With excessive levels of cholesterol in the blood, some people are prone to xanthomas, in which cholesterol is deposited in tissues right beneath the skin. Usually this occurs in the delicate tissues around the eyes (Picture 13d), at the knuckles of the fingers and the elbows and knees. These physical manifestations, especially if found in those younger than 25 years old, indicate seriously high levels of serum cholesterol, a problem that needs to be addressed immediately.

Pale yellow patches on the upper corner of the eyebrow also signify that the person's blood lipid levels are high. Wine Extract and Vein Lite are excellent for this condition.

(An interesting thing to note in this type of examination is that, by examining Da Vinci's *Mona Lisa*, one can see that the subject of the painting, because of the obvious portrayal of yellow patches on the eyebrow, actually had heart disease.)

Earlobe Crease

An earlobe crease is a superficial line going diagonally across an otherwise smooth earlobe (Picture 6a). The presence of a crease on one or both lobes may predict future cardiovascular events such as heart attack or bypass surgery. According to a study in *The American Journal of Medicine*, a crease on one lobe increases the risk by 33% while a crease on both lobes increases the risk by 77% after adjusting for other known risk factors.

Over 30 studies have found that the presence of an earlobe crease is associated with increased risk for a heart attack. One study was conducted on 1,000 hospitalized patients. Of 373 patients with earlobe creases, 75% developed heart disease while 16% of those without creases developed heart disease.

Having both the earlobe crease and chest pain predicted heart attack 90% of the time. Without the ear crease, it only predicted 10% of the cases.

It is theorized that the ear creases, rather than having a genetic basis, result from age-related chronic circulatory changes that allow blood vessels in the earlobe to collapse, producing the crease.

Patients with this thin, diagonal line on the earlobe have a markedly high death rate. Within eight years, 75% of the patients tested with this line die, whereas only 57% without this line die. If the ears contain visible blood vessels, then this patient has heart disease such as myocardial infarction, coronary heart disease, or coronary dilation weakness or incapacity. Thin earlobes usually suggest that the patient has poor kidney function or diabetes.

Ears

Clinically, the ear has the most pressure points so any symptoms that the body shows will be most likely manifested on the ear and changes will appear. There is a problem if the outer ear (auricle) thickens or if there is a growing lump or wrinkle (Pictures 15g, 15h). This can be due to a stomach, liver or esophageal problem. Clinically, it is found that the outer ear has the most to do with lungs. If the ear is thick or has lumps, then it follows that lips and nails are purple. If the tongue has purple markings inside or if the underside is bloated, in cancer patients, it will signify an extreme condition and the ear changes slowly.

Over the years, many doctors around the world have studied the relationship between the ear and the body. Recent studies have shown that the larger the size of the ear, the healthier the person. Big earlobes signify a healthy kidney and body. The skin around the ears should be smooth and supple, not dipped or bumpy in any way. For instance, patients who have liver cirrhosis have a knot in the center of their inner ear. Bumps in the lower inner ear may suggest that the patient suffers from chronic bronchitis. If the lining of the outer ear has ridges or bumps, then the person may have a bone spur or neck pain.

Hair

As many people are already aware, the purpose of hair is not only to provide protection to the scalp. Hair accurately reflects the status of your health. It is made of corneal protein, 10 trace elements, and has more than 20 amino acids and derivatives, including zinc, iron, and copper. Measuring trace elements helps to reveal disease symptoms. Hair and other constituents have continued metabolism.

There are around 100,000 hairs on every adult head. Each hair usually lasts 3-4 years, and grows 0.2-0.3 mm per day. Normally, 90% of an adult's hair is growing while 10% is falling out. An average adult loses 60-100 hairs a day, but because an adult normally has an abundance of hair, this daily loss of hair usually goes unnoticed. If a person loses more than 100 hairs a day, the hair loss will soon become apparent and the person will be experiencing a balding effect.

Reasons for balding include:
1) Hormonal imbalance
2) Autoimmune conditions (alopecia)
3) Pathological diseases-pneumonia, tinea, anemia, tumor
4) Genetically inherited baldness

Hair growth and hair loss relate to renal system issues. Energetic people with healthy hair usually have strong kidney systems. Likewise, a person with good kidney function will have strong and healthy hair. If the kidney function is impaired, on the other hand, then the hair will turn white earlier and the person will age more quickly. If white hair appears and the patient is not too old, the problem may be either genetic or of neurological origin, or it may be due to diseases such as tuberculosis, digestive problems, anemia, or atherosclerosis. If hair that is not naturally dark turns dark suddenly, then it could be due to such extreme conditions as melanoma. If the person's hair is falling out, it could be due to zinc deficiency. If hair is brittle and easily broken, this is indicative of a thyroid problem. If there is relatively little hair and the hair is dry and shriveled-looking, then the kidney system must be checked. Hair loss in men is associated with poor kidney function. In women, organ deficiency is indicated by similar balding or patchiness.

Hair loss at the top of the head may be due to chronic problems, those relating to the gallbladder and bile. If there is bodily hair loss as well as balding, this may be indicative of a hormonal imbalance. Anytime hair seems to fall out more readily than normal, or hair loss is noticed, one should be aware of possible problems associated to the condition. Lily Hair Tonic, Vein Lite, and Juvenin are recommended for hair loss. For women specifically, add Pro-Metabolic. For men, add Prosta Chi.

As males reach adulthood, if the scalp becomes oilier, with a tendency to result in dandruff, this may also be a sign of possible future hair loss.

Face Color

A person's general facial complexion can say a lot about their health. Eyes should be clear and bright. Even if the patient has an acute condition, yet still has a normal complexion and clear eyes, the condition is in an optimistic stage for improvement. However, if the face color has no vitality and is ruddy and dark in complexion, along with having bright eyes and being energetic, then the disease is probably chronic and much harder to treat.

If the face has a greenish color, then the patient may have a liver problem. If the face is reddish, then the patient has a heart problem. If the face is yellowish, then there is a liver, stomach or pancreas problem. If the face is pale white, then there could be a lung problem. A blackish complexion signals a kidney problem.

In more detail, the following can be said about a person with a reddish complexion: possible high blood pressure, high risk of fever, possibility of tuberculosis. These patients may exhibit symptoms of lupus such as the typical butterfly-shaped patch on the lower cheeks. Any other patch-like appearance on the lower cheek will signal a heart problem.

There are several reasons why one would have a yellowish complexion:
1) If the patient eats vegetables, certain types may invoke a yellowish appearance upon digestion, which should return to normal after a while.
2) If not caused by the pigments in vegetables, it could be jaundice, which is due to hepatitis, which can be detected by looking at the eyes to see if the whites of the eye (sclera) are yellow in color along with the rest of the body.

Eyes

Poor eyesight is sometimes attributed to Vitamin A and B deficiency. If a person is middle-aged, and suddenly develops poor eyesight, then it could be due to diabetes.

If one is farsighted due to old age, but suddenly feels that she or he is able to see better for a temporary period of time, this could be due to an onset of cataracts. Cataracts cause initial swelling of the lenses, so that eyesight is temporarily repaired. If one cannot see well at night, it is due to a lack of retinal, a form of vitamin A, which works the on rod function for nighttime vision. For eyesight, Vein Lite, Chi-X and Juvenin are recommended.

The area under the eye has numerous blood vessels. If this area is dark or black, this could be due to hormonal imbalance, diabetes, nervous system disorder, neurasthenia, adrenocorticotropic hormone (ACTH) problem, or capillary blockage or kidney problems.

Sclera

Sclera, the whites of the eye, should be unspotted and totally white. Any deviation from this normal color and quality could indicate a problem.

Pregnant women or children who exhibit sclera coated with a blue tint may suffer from anemia. Scleras that are covered with green spots indicate that the patient has poor liver function.

Patients who have yellow, jaundiced sclera suffer from liver or bile duct dysfunction. Sclera that appears to be jaundiced may be due to blood hemolysis.

Broken blood vessels that cover the sclera are often due to atherosclerosis and problems with the arteries in the brain.
Small, red spots covering the sclera are the result of broken capillaries and dilation.

Itching and irritation in the area along with redness of the area characterize pinkeye infection, a temporary infection contracted from unsanitary conditions.

Redness in the sclera can also be due to insomnia and poor sleeping habits. A person with poor heart function and hypertension may also exhibit redness in the sclera. These symptoms, such as hypertension, are precursors to more serious ailments such as stroke.

Redness in only one eye can be attributed to the fact that the patient may suffer from certain infection including genital infections.

Scleras that appear to be coated with blue or gray dots are often causes by problems in the intestines such as tapeworms.

Bulging Eyes

If one eye appears to bulge, this means that the patient has a brain tumor, which is pushing out within the skull. If both eyes bulge, this signifies that the patient suffers from hyperthyroidism and heart palpitations. Bright eyes may indicate thyroid swelling. Other causes of these symptoms may be due to high blood pressure, Parkinson's disease, leukemia, hemophilia, or Vitamin B or D deficiency.

Sunken Eyes

Patients who have sunken eyes are usually thin, emotionally upset, and have malaria, diarrhea, or diabetes. If eyes lack energy, the pupils would dilate and the entire face would turn gray.

Dry and dull (no luster) eyeballs generally signify Vitamin A deficiency and can result in blindness. Dark circles under the eye suggest that the person suffers from the lack of sleep. If the area around the eyes is completely dark, then this patient has a serious kidney and circulatory problem. A person may also have adrenocorticosteroid dysfunction or cardiovascular/microcirculation problem.

Puffiness underneath the eyes indicates that the patient has not had enough sleep. He may be suffering from heart diseases or nephritis as well. The distinction between heart conditions and renal conditions is that the kidney condition will result in only facial edema whereas heart conditions result in whole body swelling.

Droopy eyelids often suggest that the patient suffers from Vitamin B1 deficiency, brain vessel problems, or poor energy.

Nose

If the tip of the nose is very hard, then the patient suffers from atherosclerosis or high levels of cholesterol. A swollen tip often means that the person has a problem with his pancreas or kidney. If the nose is totally swollen and large, then the heart of the patient is also enlarged.

French doctors have observed and studied over 2,000 cancer cases and have discovered that patients who have aquiline-shaped noses (beak-shaped) have the highest chance of developing laryngitis and lung cancer. Patients with flat noses run the greatest risk of growing lymphatic tumors. Those with large noses have the greatest chance of getting pancreatic or colon cancer. Patients with sharp, well-defined noses have the highest chance of developing liver or breast cancer. Although repeatedly shown through many test cases, these statistics are not 100% accurate.

If the inside of the nose is rough, this patient is unhealthy for a variety of reasons ranging from chronic colds to prolonged drug abuse to respiratory infections.

If the barrier between the nostrils is rotted and rough-feeling, then this patient may have contracted syphilis.

A red appearance on the outside of the nose signifies that the person has digestive problems. If capillary blood vessels are apparent on the outside of the nose, then this person has a bacterial infection and may have had too much to drink.

Although nosebleeds often look worse than they really are, frequent nosebleeds may signal a more serious problem. When you have frequent nosebleeds as well as bruises, these can be early signs of leukemia. Have your blood checked immediately in this case. Nosebleeds may also be a sign of blood-clotting disorders and nasal tumors.

Lips

Lips that are easily cut and rough could be related to a chronic stomach or intestinal problem. If the problem happens to occur in a newborn child, then this symptom is due to the fact that the baby has inherited syphilis. Dry or cracking corners of the mouth usually indicate that the patient has a membrane inflammation.

If the lips are always dry and cracked, this person may be dehydrated or unused to the weather. This person is Vitamin B deficient and lacks a diet rich with fresh fruits and vegetables.

Healthy lips should be red, moist, and with a pale luster that is indicative of healthy habits and good circulation.

If lips are dry, flaky and cracked, the usual reasons are the following: fever, dry weather, dehydration, and intake of spicy or sour foods. If in addition the lips are swollen or have blisters/infection, this is related to chronic alcoholism, chronic gastritis, Vitamin B deficiency or not enough fruits and vegetables.

If both lips are pale or white, then this patient suffers from anemia or bleeding.

Greenish-white upper lips indicate that the person has a colon problem such as diarrhea or recurring stomach aches.

Greenish lips indicate a vascular disease, such as thrombosis or stroke.

Pale lower lips often suggest that the patient has stomach problems such as vomiting, diarrhea, and minor pains.

If the inner part of the upper lip is yellow, liver or gallbladder disease is usually associated.

Light pink or light red lips suggest that the patient is weak but not very ill.

If lips are dark pink, this may indicate a fever or a lung or heart problem.

Red, dark-colored lips suggest a fever or pulmonary heart disease. This means that the lips are not getting enough oxygen. If the lips continue to grow darker, become the color of cherries, and are shiny, then this person has carbon monoxide poisoning.

If both lips are dark green or blue, then it is a circulatory problem and the patient should exhibit acute symptoms. If there is also a lack of oxygen, the lips can turn purple in color and shortness of breath is associated.

Completely dark lips, even the inner lips, suggest that the patient has a kidney failure. The darker the color of the lips, the more extreme the case. If the lips are also dry, the condition is even worse. Dark lips can also be attributed to insomnia, digestive problems, headaches, and a poor appetite.

Many lips have black spots (color pigmentation) due to chronic hypoadrenocorticosteroid output. If the corners of the mouth are black spotted, the patient has a poor digestive tract.

If lips are black, this signifies a digestive problem. This is often accompanied by constipation, diarrhea, headaches, insomnia and loss of appetite.

Inside of the Mouth

The inside of the mouth should be of a pink color. If the mouth is covered with blue or black spots then the patient has adrenocorticosteroid deficiency. Blood spots usually suggest a Vitamin C deficiency. One should take note of red, white, or black patches.

White patches occur more easily in males while under stress. However, about 1-5% of these spots may become cancerous. Smokers have more spots than the norm. These white patches are hardened and protruding, causing future lesions.

Red patches are softer, brighter than and not as painful as the white patches. These red patches usually occur on the tip of the tongue, underneath the tongue, or the bottom of the mouth. These patches are less likely to occur but have a greater chance of getting cancer.

Black patches generally grow on the roof of the mouth. Men have the patches more than women at a 2:1 ratio. Almost 30% of these patches will become cancerous. Patients exhibiting these symptoms should be aware of their health and take immediate precautions against the worsening of the condition to the point that it becomes cancerous.

Gums

If the gums are swollen and red, this may be due to gastritis or fatigue. If the gums are bleeding, aside from gingivitis, the cause may be a stomach or intestinal problem. Discoloration of the gums (dark purple in color) signals heavy metal deposits (Picture 13e), usually of mercury.

Taste

Bitter Taste

A bitter taste is associated with liver and gallbladder issues, namely hepatitis or cholangitis. Foods with "dry" characteristics affect the liver and reduce saliva production, producing bitter taste. Only bile produces this bitter taste.

This bitter taste is also associated with cancer. Cancer patients sometimes lose their sense of taste to sweets and are increasingly sensitive to bitter taste. This is due to a diminished circulation in the tongue, and a changed saliva constituency, which results in a chronically bitter taste in the mouth.

Associated symptoms of bitter taste are red face, red eyes, a bad temper, and dry stool. The tongue may be red with a thin yellow coating. If the heart is bothersome, and urine is dark yellow or reddish, then this may be cholangitis. In this case, it may be very effective and helpful to take Liver Chi and Digestron.

Sweet Taste

A sweet taste is associated with the stomach and/or pancreas. This may be caused by an overproduction of salivary amylase. This is common among diabetics. Those who have this sweet taste may also have teeth marks on the sides of their tongue. Diabend, Digestron is recommended for this condition.

Salty Taste

As you may have guessed, a salty taste relates to kidney issues. People with this type of condition usually also are fatigued, with lower back and knee pain. They may have ringing in their ears and dizziness as well. Cold sweats and night sweats, including nocturnal emissions, are common, as well as the need to go to the bathroom a lot, especially if the tongue is fat with no coating.

Sour Taste

If the tongue tastes sour, the condition may be related to gastritis, duodenal ulcers, or gallbladder problems. Nausea and bloating after meals may also occur.

No Taste

If the tongue has no taste at all, this is usually when the sickness first starts or is almost better. This is common in cases of intestinal inflammation or a variety of gastrointestinal tract diseases. Post-operative patients also feel this, as well as those who are malnourished, or lacking in zinc and vitamins. Digestron and Liver Chi will be beneficial for this condition.

Fruity/Fragrant Taste

If the mouth has a fruity, fragrant taste, then this is indicative of diabetes. This has also to do with one's age. The young are more sensitive to this than the elderly.

Spicy Hot Taste

A spicy hot taste or numbness of the tongue may primarily be due to a lung problem. In some cases, it may be due to stomach problems.

Tangy Taste

A tangy taste in the mouth may be caused by four factors: (1) liver or stomach problems, (2) nerve problem, (3) reduction of saliva production, or (4) late-stage cancer.

Ammonia Taste

An ammonia taste is associated with kidney problems.

Greasy Taste

Besides as a result of overeating, a greasy taste may be due to colds or a trachea problem.

Neck

The lymph nodes on the neck are very indicative of a person's health. It is also important to note the thyroid condition. If a person observes irregular sized knots that are under the skin, then the person suffers from a chronic inflammation of the lymph nodes. If the neck becomes red, painful, and hot, the person is experiencing an acute inflammation of the lymph nodes. Bamboo Extract is recommended in this case.

A swollen, bumpy, and uneven-faced neck is often indicative of thyroid tumors.

Dark, wrinkly pigmentation (skin texture is like that of an orange peel) that goes across the back of the neck indicates diabetes (Picture 14d).

Finger Length

With the palm of your hand facing yourself, hold your thumb and your pinky finger together (as if you were forming the number 3) and keep your middle three fingers together (Picture 5d). If your index finger is longer than your ring finger, it may indicate a congenital hypothyroid condition. Along with symptoms of hypothyroidism (delayed deep-tendon/knee-jerk reflexes, decreased mental capacity, cold/clammy hands, weight gain, eyebrow-hair loss), this finger-length sign can mean that one likely cause of the symptoms is Hashimoto's thyroiditis, an autoimmune disease of the thyroid, which results in the symptoms of decreased thyroid hormone, described above.

Coughing

Coughs that are due to diseases may be caused by many reasons. For laryngitis and phlegm, use Bamboo Extract. For seniors with coughs, use Bamboo Extract, and OxyPower for best results. For emphysema, take Bamboo Extract, OxyPower, Cordyceps Extract, and Chi Energy.

Acute coughing may be caused by upper respiratory problems: bronchitis, pneumonia, or diaphragm inflammation. Chronic coughs may be due to chronic bronchitis, tuberculosis, emphysema, or lung cancer.

Generally, short, light coughs are due to pneumonia or pulmonary diaphragm inflammations. Loud, hoarse sounding coughs are due to acute laryngitis. Coughing spasms that are not reflex responses may be due to diphtheria, whooping cough, rubella, or asthma.

If coughing is accompanied by much phlegm, especially when there are strips of blood, this may indicate tracheal expansion, bronchitis, tuberculosis, and lung cancer. Rust-colored phlegm could be due to pneumonia.

Night or morning coughs may be due to chronic bronchitis. If coughing occurs every morning around the same time, the trachea is very weak. This is a sign of a chronic problem. Coughing in the daytime may also be due to bronchitis. If coughing occurs at night, this signifies a heart problem.

If coughing occurs after performing some activity, this means that the lungs are weak.

If the sound of coughing resembles barking, it could be a throat disease, tumor or bronchitis.

A high-pitched cough may be caused by a narrow throat. In this case, take deep breaths after coughing.

If sound is "broken" and hoarse, this can be either laryngitis or cancer.

Short, quick, light coughs, usually with pain, could be an infection in the pulmonary cavity chamber or pneumonia.

A metallic sounding cough is mostly associated with diaphragm cancer, main arterial angioma, or bronchial cancer. Tumors put direct pressure on lung tubes, causing the metallic sound.

Coughing and wheezing are most commonly associated with asthma.

Coughs with fever are due to flu, lung inflammation, or tuberculosis. If it is hard to breathe, the cough could be due to asthma or heart failure. If there is vomiting with the cough, it could be due to rubella and or chronic laryngitis. If the phlegm is bloody, then the cough may be due to acute bronchitis, or lung tuberculosis. If there is a lot of blood, then it may be due to later stages of tuberculosis or bronchial dilation. Coughing accompanied by severe weight loss is symptomatic of lung cancer. Revivin must be added with the other herbs mentioned earlier.

Phlegm/Mucous

If phlegm or mucous is white, it could be due to an upper respiratory infections such as bronchitis or pneumonia, or an overgrowth of candida yeast may be the cause. Use Bamboo Extract, Cordyceps Extract, OxyPower and Chi Energy for best results.

If phlegm is green-yellow, then this may be due to a secondary infection, a viral infection. Bamboo Extract is best for this condition. Yellowish chunks in the mucus signal a cold or bronchitis, or recovery from pneumonia.

Green phlegm signals pneumonia. Very thick mucus with yellow or green in it means that the lung has pus, or tuberculosis or late stages of lung cancer with infection.

Red or reddish brown phlegm signals blood in the phlegm.

If the phlegm is pink colored, then it could be due to acute emphysema. If IV infusions are necessary, they should not be administered too fast to those who have this condition because water may accumulate in the lung and the phlegm will be pink.

If the phlegm is rust-colored, then the patient most likely is in the more severe stages of pneumonia. The phlegm will usually be this color for 2-3 days, and then it will turn yellow.

If phlegm is chocolate-colored, it could be due to amoeba or protozoan infection, which may infect the liver, causing pus. It may also affect the lung and trachea. Gray or blackish phlegm may only be due to environmental problems.

Thin, watery mucus or phlegm with air bubbles signals more severe types of secondary bronchial infection.

If the mucus has fresh blood and plenty of fibrous blood in it, then this could be tuberculosis or laryngitis. Use Bamboo Extract and OxyPower for the best results.

Breath

If the breath smells like beer even though you had not been drinking, it is a lymph node condition. If it smells like garlic but none has been ingested, it could be due to phosphate pesticide poisoning. Breath that smells like fermented apples is caused by diabetes. Breath that often smells sour and foul can be indicative of digestive problems. Breath that smells like ammonia or urine could be due to kidney failure or renitis. Asparagus Extract, Cordyceps Extract, Kidney Chi and Bathdetox are excellent for kidney conditions.

Breath that has a moldy smell may be due to liver disease. If it smells like stool, it may be due to abdominal infections or constipation. For these conditions, use Digestron, Liver Chi and CFC.

Breathing Patterns

Is one's breathing regular? If you can hold your breath after inhaling normally for approximately 30 seconds, you have good lung activity. Each inhalation should inflate your lung cavity (pleural cavity) by 6 to 9 cm. Researchers have shown that a healthy capacity should be between 3500-4000mL for men and 3000-3500mL for women. Upon exercise, the maximum capacity may reach 5000mL. As people get older, their breathing capacity reduces. Every 10 years after adulthood is reached should see a lowering of tidal capacity by about 9-20%. Boston University Hospital conducted a study on 5,200 people for 2 years and found that those who exercise regularly maintain good lung capacity even after the age of 60. Among those over 70 years old, those who did not exercise regularly had an average lowered lung capacity of 20.64%. To improve this condition, use OxyPower, Bamboo Extract, Cordyceps Extract, Chi Energy, Synergen, and Sinus Chi.

Bowel Movement

There is normally certain regularity to bowel movements. If the rate of movement becomes varied, and the patient suffers from bouts of constipation as well as diarrhea, then this may be due to colon problems. If the patient has abdominal bleeding and/or pain in the area, with gurgling noises in the region and left abdominal edema, it could be due to colon problems. Patients with rectal inflammation or rectal cancer often feel like they never have a complete bowel movement.

Mucous-caused blemishes are due to impaction of feces in the folded villi layers of the small intestines. A sticky, mucus layer of material gets stuck in these finger-like folds, and with time, it forms a sticky plaque that deters absorption of nutrients and causes disease from the toxic uptake. The required treatment for this condition is fast, followed by use of CFC to clear out the intestines. Once the body returns to normal, all that is needed is the upkeep of the system.

Constipation

Constipation is a common symptom, but often, it remains unrecognized until the patient develops sequelae such as anorectal disorders or diverticular disease. The definition of constipation includes the following: infrequent bowel movements (typically only 3 times a week), difficulty in defecation (straining during more than 25% of bowel movements), or the sensation of incomplete bowel evacuation. The prevalence of constipation increases exponentially in persons older than 65 years.

This condition can result in various degrees of subjective symptoms and is associated with abnormalities such as colonic diverticular disease, hemorrhoidal disease, and anal fissures. The use of laxatives and enemas can sometimes help. However, the more they are used, the weaker the colon becomes, so that it can no longer facilitate the production of regular bowel movements. CFC can be used for constipation and it has no side effects.

If constipation lasts for more than 8 weeks even after taking medication, it may be due to hypothyroidism or colon cancer.

Why does everyone like natural foods?

Advanced civilizations will find that medicine is not as good as adjusting one's diet. One must know the characteristics of foods, such as whether they are acidic or basic, cold or hot. Generally speaking, all grains, nuts, fish and meat are acidic. Most vegetables and fruits are alkaline, especially Asparagus Extract. Asparagus Extract is an extract from the whole plant. Each 5 grams of extract is from a half pound of whole Asparagus. If you take 1 to 3 bags a day, your body's pH level will turn to alkaline.

Those that wish to maintain a lighter diet should eat foods composed mainly of alkaline foods, including cereals. Lighter foods mean better foods for your health, including usually only vegetarian entrees with very few, selected animal products.

Alkaline foods generally make people calmer. On the other hand, acidic food eaters are generally more active.

In today's society, food and air suffer from environmental contamination, and an excess of acidic food intake will cause our cells to become toxic. As a result, body fluid and acid/base chemistry will not balance. Diseases are more likely with acidic foods. For better health, it is best to eat less animal products and acidic foods, and depend more on alkaline foods for detoxification and recovery of the body's acid-base balance.

Alkaline foods, in order or their alkalinity, include the following: spinach, syrup, celery, carrots, green beans, cabbage, broccoli, beets, squash, mushrooms, cauliflower, pineapple, avocado, raisins, dates, tangerines, strawberries, tomatoes, yams, grapefruit, apricot, lemons, oranges, peaches, bananas, scallions, grapes, pears, apples, and watermelon.

Acidic foods, also in order from most to least acidic, include: clams, sausage, oatmeal, lobster, peanuts, soda crackers, spaghetti, peanut butter, chicken, crab, beef, turkey, wheat, lamb, pork, pecans, smoked meats, eggs, bread, dairy products, honey, shrimp, corn, sugar, oil, wine, coffee, and tea.

Stool

Things to look for in stool are form, color, consistency, digestion, mucus, pus, and blood.

Stool should be yellowish brown in color. The longer the stool stays in the intestines, the darker and drier it gets. This is why in diarrhea, the stool is yellow (it did not stay in the intestines too long). If there is blood in the stool (occult blood), this could be dangerous (piles, intestinal bleeding). If blood is not seen in the feces, an exam will determine if there is cause for concern. If there is mucus and pus in the stool, an infection is the likely cause (amoeba).

If stool is mostly watery with little foam, it could be due to intestinal inflammation, or poison of some form. If the stool is loose, this could be due to chronic cholangitis or eating excessive fatty or greasy foods. Liver Chi and Debile are best for this problem.

Stool that has a lot of mucus may be due to colitis. Stool that is dry and pellet-like may be due to constipation or tumors. The quality of the stool has a lot to do with colon problems. Stool may be thin and appears in strips, has blood or pus, dry, or sticky. Air bubbles in the stool signal problems in the small intestine.

A 55 y/o/m colitis patient from Phoenix, AZ, had taken high doses of Prednisone and Sulfazalizine for 10 years to no avail.

Fortunately, he met me two weeks before his scheduled surgery. I suggested that he use Liver Chi, Digestron, CFC and Asparagus. To the patient's surprise, his intestinal bleeding stopped after a mere 30 days. After 11 months, the patient was completely off Prednisone for the first time in 9 years. In addition, by ending his steroid use, the patient has minimized his diabetes to a type II rather than the insulin-dependent diabetes.

Occult Blood

Approximately 50% of ulcer patients have occult blood due to internal bleeding. Internal bleeding can also manifest as black lines on the nails (Pictures 4f, 4g). If internal bleeding has been treated for over one month, special care must be taken, as it may be symptomatic of a tumor. Digestive tumors include esophageal, stomach, and intestinal tumors. About 20% of patients with occult blood have colon cancer; 40% have progressive stomach cancer; and 25% of esophageal cancer patients have occult blood. Trace amounts as low as 2-4mL of blood can be detected in the feces as occult blood. In these conditions, one will sometimes concurrently detect a dark vertical line on the fingernails leading to a dark splotch (Figure 2F; Pictures 2g, 4f). This confirms the possibility of internal bleeding.

For people who cannot digest fats well, their feces may have small drop-like white fat particles or pellets. Slender All, Digestron and CFC will be excellent for this problem.

Gas

Excessive amounts of gas may be due to interdigestive problems or digestive ulcers. It could also be due to liver, gallbladder or pancreas problems. Excessive gas may also be due to an overconsumption of foods such as beans, potatoes, eggs, or ingested air. About 99% of gas has no smell at all. Gas consists of 80 percent nitrogen, two to nineteen percent carbon dioxide, and methane, hydrogen, and oxygen. Digestron is excellent to use for gas problems.

Gas can also be due to late stages of digestive tumor, ruptured tumors and bacterial growth there.

Water Retention/Edema

Anytime extreme or abnormal swelling occurs, a hospital examination should be done immediately. The swelling may not impede daily activities or cause discomfort. In this case, the description may be functional edema, and treatment would call for reduced salt intake and the possible use of diuretic agents. Asparagus Extract is an excellent natural diuretic agent for this purpose.

Males should beware of foot swelling while females should watch particularly for facial edemas, which are more dangerous than the rest of the edemas. Prolonged swelling of the foot can indicate heart disease, while swelling in the face and upper body area indicates kidney disease. Both of these situations call for immediate action toward treatment and regulation of edema. If the face, tongue, and lips have an elastic feel and are swollen, then these are indicative of an allergic reaction to allergens such as different foods, animal fur, pollen and dust, etc.

Cell membranes have a specific permeability to water that increases and/or decreases according to bodily regulatory mechanisms that balance osmotic pressure to the external and internal environments of the cell. If there is an imbalance, the cells may shrink or swell to dangerous levels. In the case of edema, the three main reasons for this are:

1) Kidney problems
2) Heart problems
3) Liver problems

Edema can be attributable to several external reasons, such as standing for long periods of time, which would cause foot swelling, or high temperatures, which might cause general swelling. People that are overweight generally also have problems with water retention, mostly in the leg and foot. Twenty-five percent of all American women experience edema during or before their period, along with insomnia, cramps, and mood swings. Pregnancy in its later stages may also see an onset of water retention.

Older people who suffer water retention often have heart, liver and kidney problems. Taking medicines such as cortisones, contraceptives, and antiseptic drugs all cause water retention.

Edema caused by kidney problems is the most common reason for water retention in people. If the leg or ankle is swollen in the morning, it is likely due to a kidney problem. Asparagus Extract, Bathdetox, and Kidney Chi are recommended for kidney function.

Water retention caused by the heart is often manifested in the afternoon. Vein Lite, Asparagus Extract and OxyPower are best for this condition.

Edema caused by liver problems, especially liver cirrhosis, usually starts from the abdomen and spreads down to the feet. The spleen and liver become enlarged, and liver function becomes impaired. Liver Chi and Asparagus Extract will be excellent for this condition. Malnutrition also causes this type of edema, such as that associated with TB and anemia.

Hypothyroid conditions can also cause edema. Pro-Metabolic is used in this case.

Urine

To determine kidney function, observe the color, concentration, smell and amount of urine as well as urination frequency. If any of these characteristics changes, then there is a possible kidney problem.

Ninety six to ninety nine percent of urine is composed of water. The rest is composed of waste, uric acid or inositols. Urine output for normal adults should be between 1 and 2 liters per day (1-1.5L for women; 1.5-2L for men.) There should be a grassy smell, as urine decomposes to ammonia.

Urine should be light yellow in color, clear, with little turbidity or cloudiness. If left outside for longer, the urine becomes darker. Excessive water intake can make urine lighter in color, even colorless. Since the body's metabolism is about the same, urine should be about the same color every day. It is clear in cool weather, darker in the summer. In children, urine is cloudy in the winter. This means that there is a lot of salt content and they must drink plenty of water.

It is important to note that if the urine stream splits in men, there may be prostatitis.

Diet affects urine color. If you consumed acidic foods or drinks, then urine color tends to be darker. If you consumed alkaline foods, urine color tends to be lighter. The color change usually occurs for a short time and normal urine color returns. In the following section, we will look at the different colors and characteristics of urine and what they signify.

Pink/Red Urine

If the urine is reddish, it means that it contains red blood cells. The body maybe hemorrhaging or it may be due to high blood pressure, edema, and urine protein.

Blood in the urine may also be a sign of kidney, bladder or urinary tract infection. About 85% of these cases are generally due to *E. coli* infection and usually occurs in postmenopausal women. In younger women, the infection may be tied to a sexually transmitted condition.

Glomerular inflammation and lupus patients may have this type of urine along with fever. Patients with kidney stones may have blood in their urine, as do prostatitis patients and those who have suffered regional trauma. Appendicitis or colitis can also sometimes make the urine red.

If you did not take any similar-colored food and there is no pain associated, it could be a sign of early bladder/kidney cancer.

If there is blood in the urine and none of the above conditions are present and if there is no pain in the kidney area, check for bladder or kidney cancer.

Blue/Purple Urine

Blue-colored urine is symptomatic of cholera, where there is high blood calcium and vitamin D poisoning.

Purple urine (like grape juice) may be due to lead or heavy metal poisoning causing hemoglobin biosynthesis blockage.

Yellow/Brown Urine

Yellow, dark urine may be due to dietary intake, one high in carrots and other similarly pigmented vegetable, for instance. Liver diseases or gallbladder problems could also cause it, since bile is passed along the intestines and through the urine, and if the intestinal bile is clogged, there is increased bile in the urine. Hepatitis is also known to cause a darkening of color in the urine.

Dark yellow urine may result from taking a Vitamin B complex supplement. Otherwise, it is due to a bile duct problem.

Black/Brown Urine

Black or brown urine may be due to chemical poisoning or melanoma. In the case of melanoma, high melanin content in the liver comes out dark in the urine. If, after a blood transfusion, the urine shows black/brown, then it means that the wrong type of blood was given (hemolysis).

Dark brown urine is most often due to acute renitis, kidney infection and hepatitis.

Black urine is often an acute hemolysis problem in the blood. This may be due to a serious malignancy or an extreme case of malaria. The serum has lots of free oxygen and hemoglobin, and the urine is often black due to this. The ingestion of dopamine for the treatment of Parkinson's disease also causes urine to turn black.

Urine Difficulty and Frequent Urination

In younger women, urination difficulty and/or frequency could be due to cystitis. If in older men, it could be due to prostatitis. As mentioned earlier also, a urine stream that splits is a sign of prostatitis. At night, getting up once to urinate is normal. Getting up more times than that is not. If trembling occurs when urinating, this is normal especially in the winter time. But if there is pain associated with it, and the bladder is difficult to empty, it could be a bladder infection (women) or UTI/kidney stones (men). If one has frequent urination, use Kidney Chi and Night-Dry. For men, add Prosta Chi.

Urine Bubbles

The presence of bubbles in the urine (Picture 13h) is most definitely a sign of kidney impairment, most especially proteinuria. This means that you are losing protein. These bubbles can be composed of phosphate salt, carbonate salt, and albumin. If you drink or eat too much (e.g., soda), you will most likely get phosphate or carbonate salt. If this is the case, then drink 2,000 cc of water or eat alkaline foods to eliminate the bubbles. If there are still bubbles, then they are made of albumin. If the bubbles are small and pile up, it is definitely proteinuria. It must be treated promptly. Kidney Chi and Bathdetox are best recommended for urine bubbles.

Proteinuria

Urine protein (or proteinuria) is an important signal in various conditions. About 7% of hypertensive patients have proteinuria while 30% of diabetic patients have it. A higher urine protein level doubles the chance of serious problems. The best time to check is the first urination of the day.

In normal people, there should be trace amounts of protein in the urine. There should be no more than 5mg/100mL of protein in the urine. Any more protein than that could signal a kidney disease or inflammation, drug poisoning, or high fever. With an impaired kidney function, protein is excreted out (proteinuria). Proteinuria is associated with diabetes and hypertension. If left untreated, this may develop into heart disease and stroke. Urine placed in a test tube and heated over a flame with a drop of vinegar should become clear as it boils. However, if there is protein presence, then the test tube will be cloudy as the proteins come out of solution. For proteinuria, should use Asparagus Extract, Cordyceps Extract, Kidney Chi and Bathdetox.

Cloudy Urine

If urine turbidity is cloudy, this is not normal. The cloudiness may be due to severe urinary tract infection or UTI (leukocytes causing the urine to turn milky). Cancer or tuberculosis can also cause turbidity because the lymphatic system and kidney system are tied together. In some men, turbidity may be normal if the urine contains sperm as a result of not ejaculating for a long time. If crystallization occurs, stones are possible.

If a woman's urine is cloudy, and a burning sensation is felt when urinating, then this is indicative of a UTI. Kidney Chi and Asparagus Extract are best for this condition.

If urine is white and cloudy, it could contain pus, which indicates an infection. This could also be due to parasitic activity. In children, this is sometimes normal as it can indicate the presence of sedimented salt. More water is needed to ease this condition.

Urine Output

Normal urine output is 250cc to 350cc. Once urine output falls below this volume, then kidney problem should be suspected. The kidneys are very important. So if there is something wrong with kidney function, then toxins, wastes, and poisons cannot excrete out. Besides the color, urine output should be closely monitored as well to determine signs of kidney impairment.

Chronic kidney failure is categorized into stages according to the amount of urine output per day:
Stage 1: >90cc
Stage 2: 60-89cc
Stage 3: 30-59cc
Stage 4: 15-30cc
Stage 5: <15cc

In many cases, kidney failure is asymptomatic in the early stages. Stage 1 and 2 patients generally do not have symptoms but sometimes there is scalp itching, fatigue, no taste, and nausea. Stage 3 chronic kidney disease patients already exhibit signs of anemia.

Pain

Many diseases cause or are associated with pain. However, in cases where there should be pain but none is felt by the patient, then the situation is dangerous. For instance, if a patient has blood in the urine but experiences no pain, then check for kidney cancer.

Stomach/Abdominal Pain

Chronic, sometimes intermittent, abdominal pain, especially on an empty stomach, can indicate chronic ulcer, chronic gastritis, ulcerative colitis, chronic hepatitis or early liver cirrhosis. It is often accompanied by bloating, gas, lack of appetite, fatigue, jaundice, slightly red tongue, and/or teeth marks. Use of a heating pad or application of pressure on the abdomen can sometimes provide relief.

Often upper abdominal pain is indicative of acute gastritis or another type of stomach problem. Pain in the upper right abdominal area could be due to a gallbladder problem, cholangitis or gallstones. If one experiences pain after eating greasy or fatty foods, this is most likely due to a gallbladder problem. Gallbladder pain is located in the upper right quadrant of the abdomen and is most likely caused by a gallstone in the main bile duct. The pain can occur half an hour to an hour after a meal. Liver Chi and Debile are beneficial for these conditions.

Pain that is above the navel is due to overproduction of gastric acid. Usually when the stomach is full, the pain goes away. When hungry, the pain comes back. Only a few cases may be due to stomach cancer.

If pain is in the diaphragm, this might be an indication of a heart problem.

Abdominal pain associated with liver cancer is most often felt in the terminal stage. This is because the liver itself has no membranes, only surface nerves. When the liver is enlarged enough, then it pushes against nearby organs, causing pain.

General abdominal pain could be due to hepatitis, or even pneumonia.

Lower right quadrant abdominal pain could be due to the appendix and/or intestinal problems.

Pain in the lower left quadrant of the abdomen is due to microbial infection or cholangitis (inflammation of the bile ducts).

Pain in the upper left quadrant is due to pancreatitis. Sometimes pancreatitis can be mistaken for stomach pain. Pancreatitis is common in some gallstone patients, especially if their triglyceride level is high, causing blood viscosity. The pancreas produces enzymes that are supposed to go into the intestines. However, if the blood is too thick, these enzymes get pushed back, causing the pancreas to be inflamed.

Lower abdominal (below the navel) pain can be due to many causes. If it is short-term, this may be normal, possibly from bloating. If there is dramatic pain with nausea and fever, and the pain is located in the lower right quadrant, then this is most likely from appendicitis. Otherwise, it could be from an ovarian or uterine problem in women.

Other causes of lower abdominal pain are ectopic pregnancy, pancreas problem, kidney stones, bladder infection, PMS pain, or urethral stone. If the area around the navel hurts, it could be due to the presence of tapeworms, or intestinal chyme impaction, mostly in the small intestines.

If localized pain spreads throughout the entire abdominal area, this signals that the entire abdominal cavity has become infected.

If there is sudden pain in the stomach or duodenal area, it could be due to an open late-stage ulcer in the area causing internal bleeding. This pain is generally felt most severely after eating. Similar pain can also be felt if there is a parasitic infection in the area.

How can one determine if the appendix causes abdominal pain? If one lays flat on her back, takes a deep breath, filling it, to capacity, then holding it in for 30-40 seconds and expelling it quickly, you may be able to feel an extreme pulling pain. This would signal acute appendicitis, requiring immediate medical attention.

Drinking or excessive exposure to cold can cause involuntary muscle spasms in the stomach or intestines, or even gastritis. Bingeing often results in acute gastritis or pancreatitis. Pain when the stomach is empty may result from duodenal ulceration or gastritis.

Young people who have stomach pains generally get them from ulcers and appendicitis. Those over middle age should be especially careful of the possibility of tumor growth if there is chronic stomach pain. Digestron is useful for this condition.

Gallstones are most commonly found in middle-aged, overweight women. Symptoms include sporadic pain lasting from a few minutes to a few hours. This is normally due to either urethra or gallstones, or impacted feces.

With acute pancreatitis, pain will worsen over time. It is important to get this condition examined by a physician immediately.

Knife-sharp pains caused by ulcers can be explained by the fact that the stomach is naturally acidic, while bile is alkaline. Thus, when the foods mix together, bile reacts with and ultimately neutralizes the acidic stomach conditions, causing pain if there are ulcers.

Slight, sporadic colon pain is a possible sign of colon cancer. If the patient is over 30 years in age and experiences this pain along with bloating and irregular bowel movements, then precautions should be taken toward the early detection and prevention of cancer.

If a patient feels pain with nausea and vomiting, it could be acute pancreatitis. Use Diabend and Digestron.

Stomach pain with diarrhea may be due to cholangitis. If there is blood in the stool, cholera or a tumor is possible. Pain in the area without bowel movements or flatulence could be due to the impaction of feces in the intestines.

Another symptom we can look for are white spots on the torso area, smooth spots that have no pain or lesion. These circular or elliptical pea-sized spots signify toxins in the body. Recently, we have found that of 800 cancer patients, 74% had these spots on the torso. The spots disappear when the cancer clears.

Headaches

Generally, people get headaches from colds, fever, or nervousness. These usually amount to small, minor headaches that will resolve by themselves after a certain amount of time. However, some headaches are worse and require special attention. Myosteo and Vein Lite are best for this condition.

Headaches in the middle of the forehead are caused by disease of the eyes, ears, nose, or throat. Those caused by the eyes will also affect vision. Similarly, a condition of the nasal passage may cause pain in the forehead along with pressure and pain in the nasal area.

Pain on one side of the head could be due to an ear infection, a nervous disorder, a migraine or a brain tumor.

Sometimes a GI tract problem causes headaches but they are not frequent. If, after taking painkillers, the pain does not alleviate, then the most likely cause is hypertension or vertebra problem.

If the headache gets worse after lying down, it could possibly be due to a brain tumor.

Those above 60 years of age often experience aches in the temple area. This is possibly due to artery inflammation in the area that can irritate and cause headaches.

Headaches felt on top of the head are caused by neurasthenia and tension. Headaches spanning to the nape of the neck in the back of the head (the occipital) may be caused by high blood pressure, kidney problems, meningitis or seizures.

Headaches felt over the entire head may stem from meningitis, concussion, neurasthenia, or atherosclerosis. Meningitis or high blood pressure may cause severe head pain, such as that felt when experiencing a migraine headache.

Middle- or older-aged people with these types of headaches usually have other symptoms of stroke and need to be extra careful. Scientists find that patients who experience brain blood vessel hemorrhaging that lead to massive bleeding and death often have prior symptoms including sporadic sharp pains. Warning signs in middle- to older-aged people include acute headaches but not fever, nausea, or vomiting, or headaches that are severe mainly in the morning. Sometimes stroke can be triggered by any excessive exertion of the body, such as a forceful bowel movement or heavy drinking, in which the patient experiences excruciating pain. Other stimulating experiences and activities can also trigger stroke.

If you experience a headache while exerting yourself physically or mentally, you should lie down flat immediately. Do not simply take medicine, unless it has been previously prescribed or the pain is prolonged and severe. Do not massage intensively or shake the head in any way that could make the condition worse. If nausea is also experienced, lean back against something but do not lie down completely in case of vomiting and choking. If there is intermediate pain but it is bearable, this could be indicative of a brain tumor or eye disease. If a light headache is accompanied by dizziness, then the patient may have anemia.

Pain in the back of the head that is especially painful in the morning and eases as the day goes on is likely caused by high blood pressure.

If a headache occurs approximately 3 hours after eating, it may be due to hypoglycemia, especially if dizziness and sporadic pain accompany it.

Patients with brain tumors and parasinus conditions are likely to experience pain in the morning hours mostly.

Diseases of the eyes that cause headaches usually occur in the afternoon or evening.

Headaches that are experienced late at night that are caused by excessive pressure in the eye, even after rest, are likely to be caused by an infection of the iris.

Sudden sharp pain could be due to hemorrhaging and the bursting of blood vessels.

If one or both sides of the head has throbbing or pulsing pain, which lasts for hours or days, accompanied by nausea, vomiting, and fatigue, it could be a migraine headache. Women experience migraines more than men.

When headaches occur with throbbing and pressure, dizziness and worsening with shaking, it is caused by high blood pressure.

Pain from within the head, causing the sensation of a heavy head, always starting from the same point and expanding with time, could be due to the presence of a brain tumor. This generally feels worst from late at night until dawn and worsens when certain positions are taken.

If a headache or migraine occurs with nosebleed, stuffy nose, and ear ringing, this could mean a risk for nasopharyngeal cancer. If the migraine occurs in the same area but there is no nosebleed but there is blurred vision and ear ringing, do not ignore these signs. These could point to a brain tumor.

Severe, pulsating pain that travels from the forehead to the eye area, lasting between a few seconds to several minutes, could signal a seizure.

If the head is swollen with a throbbing pain and the patient experiences insomnia and excessive dreaming during sleep, dizziness and fatigue yet does not have any disease prognosis, this person may have what is called a functional headache.

Chest Pain

Organ problems, fractures, inflammation, or chemical or physical stimulation could cause chest pains. The exact cause is better diagnosed according to the area of pain.

Chest pains are most often associated with heart problems. However, in some cases of heart problems, there is no pain. An example would be among elderly people with a history of myocardial infarction (MI). About 52% of older people with MI have no pain, and approximately 20% of middle-aged people with MI have no pain. This is because older people have less sensitivity to pain.

Angina pain is normally localized in the heart area, and can be felt both in front of and behind the rib cage. Pain may irradiate to the left arm and the elbow area.

Acute pulmonary diaphragm infection or lung infection usually causes chest pain on only one side of the body.
Some pain is caused by pinching of rib nerves, leading to irritation in the area.

Myoplagia and other pains cause progressive muscle pains in the chest area.

Chest pain that does not span the mid-length of the chest area is generally due to herpes zoster. There could also be chest pain experienced in the case of esophageal or digestive cancer, and eating will be difficult.

If the pain sears like that of a knife wound or pinpricks, along with soreness in the area, it could be due to acute esophagitis or angina. Those with angina will also experience pressure in the area as well as breathing difficulty.

Chest pain with fever is often indicative of a respiratory problem such as pneumonia or tuberculosis-related pulmonary diaphragm infection. Chest pains with coughs and phlegm with blood, along with a feverish condition, usually signal tuberculosis or a bronchial condition.

If the patient has difficulty swallowing and is rather thin, then it is possibly a case of esophageal cancer. If there is chest pain with difficulty breathing, this could be a warning sign of emphysema. Chest pain that occurs with low blood pressure, pallor of the complexion, the tendency to have cold sweats, cold feet and hands, and even coma, could be due to heart attack.

If chest pain and fever is experienced along with fatigue and difficulty in breathing, it is due to an epicardium inflammation.

All of these symptoms, since they relate to probably serious conditions, should be checked immediately by a physician.

Numbness

When there is numbness in the limbs, it is almost always due to a circulation problem. Peripheral circulation may be impaired. If both hands are stiff when waking up, also check the blood sugar level. Hyperglycemia patients may have this symptom, a sign that high blood sugar has caused peripheral artery deterioration. Stiffness and numbness may also be a reaction to some drugs.

Dizziness

Dizziness is often caused by anemia. In addition, it could be due to an inner ear balance problem, vision problems, cardiovascular condition, hypoglycemia, or, at worst, a brain problem.

Sleep Patterns

A 1996 article in *Nature* states that we sleep best around midnight, if there is no light. If the light is always on, then the best time to sleep is between 4:00 and 5:00 am. Thus, sleeping in a darkened room allows for better rest and a healthier daily rhythm. While sleeping, it is best to avoid any light sources. Relaxin is recommended for sleep.

Sleeping positions may also be associated with certain conditions. If one sleeps on their stomach, then it is due to a weak liver. If one sleeps curled up in a fetal position, then this points to a kidney problem. If one sleeps spread-eagle on her or his back with an open mouth, then it could be indicative of a lung or bronchial weakness. If one sleeps spread-eagle on her or his back with the mouth closed, it is a circulation/heart problem. If the body is turned to the left but the head faces upwards, it is a stomach and intestinal weakness.

Body Temperature

Normal oral body temperature is between 36.2 to 37.2 degrees Celsius. There is typically a 1 to 1.2 degree fluctuation, so when the body temperature fluctuates to more than 37.3, or rectally 37.6, then this is not normal.

Temperature changes reflect changes in metabolism, so when one is eating or exercising, the temperature increases. Inversely, when one is hungry, the body temperature drops. Children generally have a higher temperature than adults, and the rectal temp is usually 0.5 degree higher than the oral temperature.

Fever

Fevers can be a sign of any number of diseases. The most common cause of fever is chronic infection (e.g., kidney infection, chronic tonsilitis, sinusitis, intermediate ear infection, heart membrane infection, pelvic infection, enlarged trachea, amoebiasis). If the fever is not associated with infection, then it may due to tuberculosis, anemia, pregnancy, menstrual period, liver cirrhosis, rheumatoid arthritis or hyper-adrenaline function.

A seasonal fever may also occur, usually because of body's inability to release heat (e.g. after summer).

Fevers that last for 1-2 weeks are typical and can be caused by acute diseases such as chicken pox, measles, scarlet fever, an upper respiratory infection or the flu, food poisoning or sun poisoning.

Any fever lasting over 2 weeks is due to long-term cholera, TB, toxemia, leukemia, cancer, and so on.

If the patient has a fever with phlegm and heart pain, then it is related to a respiratory problem.

Fevers with abdominal pain, nausea, and vomiting are due to digestive and liver problems. In the case of chronic bile duct infection, fever is accompanied by loss of appetite, nausea, vomiting, right upper quadrant abdominal pain, gallbladder attack, and liver enlargement. In chronic hepatitis, fever is accompanied by bloating, loss of appetite, a skinny build, fatigue, right quadrant pain, liver enlargement, edema, heavy sweating, and insomnia.

Fevers with frequent urination and bladder pain indicate excretory problems.

Fevers with lymph node swelling and pain in a localized area are due to an infection in the locality. If lymph nodes on the entire body are swollen, then it could indicate TB or blood diseases such as lymphoma.

If headaches, vomiting, and dizziness occur with the fever, it is due to a central nervous system infection. Meningitis or viral infection can also cause this.

If one has a fever and there are bruises beneath the skin, this is due to meningitis, or it is a blood disease or lymphoma.

If the liver area is swollen, it may be due to cholera, malaria, or acute parasitic diseases.

Skin

Look for skin changes on the forehead, wrinkles on the sides of the eyes, pale face, dark and spotty skin, as well as dry, cracked and wrinkled lips. Lips must be smooth, nice color, elastic and tender. If otherwise, then it means fatigue. A Vitamin B complex is needed as well as a diet with more unrefined grain.

If skin is very pale, it may not necessarily indicate anemic conditions in a patient. In this case, one should also check the gums and lips and the sclera of the eyes. Abnormalities in these areas, such as pallor or pain, can signal an anemic condition.

If there are white, bean-shaped spots that are clearly defined on the skin and spots where there is loss of pigmentation, this may be due to the effects of aging, if experienced in older people. However, loss of pigmentation may be due to genetic inheritance if it is experienced in younger people and may not be a genuine health concern.

If skin and the eyes are both yellow in color, then the patient may have cholangitis, pancreatitis, or gallstones.

If the skin is reddish, then there is a heart, liver, or intestinal problem. If the skin is bluish, then there may be a lung problem. Many blue lines in the abdominal area signal a lowered amount of adrenocorticosteroid production. If the skin has black spots, this is an even stronger indication of a problem.

If skin is dark and rough, then the patient must watch for stomach cancer signals. Patients with stomach cancer often start with the darkening or roughening of the skin as one of the precursor symptoms, occurring mostly on the sides of the body, inner thigh, and around the naval. In certain instances, the face and the palm will also be darkened.

As people age, their skin will naturally develop brown or black spots (age spots). This is a reflection of bodily changes. This type of pigmentation is also occurring in the organs of one's body, and can cause atherosclerosis if accumulated in the blood vessels, or fibrocystic disease. When these pigments are accumulated in brain cells, they cause loss of memory and senility. Those who are at this point in their lives must ensure that they are getting enough water, selenium compounds (such as those found in Asparagus Extract), Vitamins B and C, cysteine, and Vitamin A. These can be found in foods such as yeast, citrus fruits, honey, seaweed, milk, beans, eggs, and liver. Using Vein Lite and Asparagus Extract will have good results. Washing the face with Rainskin will also help lighten the age spots.

If the cheeks have spots or skin discoloration (Picture 14g), this indicates a hormone problem (pelvic infection, mastitis, cervical problem) or poor liver function. These cheek spots also mean that blood and chi are not normally functioning in the upper body.

If skin growth is observed and it is either painful or itchy, check for skin cancer. Skin color does not matter. Even if the shape is not irregular, there is no lesion or no color change, check for skin cancer. Moles that grow continuously and become irregular in shape should be checked immediately in the case of a malignancy.

Purple-colored spots on the skin signal a platelet deficiency. Skin or membranes that have blood spots or bruises that do not change colors upon touch could be caused by meningitis.

Bright patches that show up on different parts of the body like dermatitis could be a pancreas problem.

Itching

Itching can be a direct result of cold and dry weather as well as insect bites and allergic reactions. However, it can also signal far more severe conditions. In this section, we explore the various causes of itching.

In the winter, itching is common, usually from the calf to the back. Spicy foods, tea, and friction from clothes can worsen itching.

If the skin is itchy over a lengthy amount of time, one can normally see the area that is affected since it is inflamed and reddish.

If itching is generalized (affecting the whole body) and there are visible signs associated with it such as a rash, it could be associated with diabetes, liver disorders (liver or bile duct blockage), chronic kidney conditions, uremia, leukemia or cancer of the bladder, liver, kidney, lung or thyroid. In lymphoma, an increase in red blood cells causes the itching. Water baths do not relieve this type of itching, especially in older people. The underlying cause must be addressed in order to relieve this type of itching.

Scratching causes tinea type spots and pigmentation type spots, sometimes leading to infection.

If the area around the female genitalia is itchy (in the vulva folds) and there is a lot of discharge, the woman may be suffering from trichomoniasis or a vaginal yeast infection. Vulvar itching may also be a sign of amenorrhea or ovarian problem. If pregnant and with jaundice, yellow sclera, and no diarrhea/bloating/digestive problem, this can be very serious and may cause harm to the fetus if not immediately checked.

Itching is also common during pregnancy, usually in the second half of the pregnancy. This affects the abdomen to the upper thighs.

Rectal itching may be due to piles/hemorrhoids, fistula, parasites, and even colon tumors.

Acne

The location of an acne breakout can indicate its underlying cause. If the acne is mostly located on the forehead, this means that the liver has many toxins. High sugar intake can also cause this. Acne in the temple area may be caused by refined ingredients in food that block the bile duct in the gallbladder. Acne on the cheeks and sides of the nose means that circulation is poor in these areas. To correct this type of acne, improve circulation, cut down on oil intake and increase zinc and Vitamins B2 and B6. If acne is concentrated on the chin and jaw area before the menstrual period starts, this is related to the ovary and lymphatic system.

Sweat

Heavy sweating occurs in 1 out of 500 people worldwide. Even in winter, hands or palms may sweat. Sweating is controlled by the sympathetic nervous system. The body has 500 sweat "glands," two-thirds of which are in the palm.

We normally produce 500-1000mL of sweat per day. About 98-99% is water, and the rest is composed of urea, uric acid, and other inorganic salts. The constituents of sweat are similar to those of urine. It can help control and adjust body temperature, body fluid, and excretion of bodily waste. It can also help maintain skin pH to avoid bacterial infection. It is expectedly common in the summer. Not sweating in very hot weather is detrimental to the body. But if excessive sweating occurs in the winter, especially when eating or even with just a little effort, then it evinces some sort of condition or disease. In this case, it is a sign of a sympathetic nervous system disorder.

Heavy sweating is sometime characteristic in those who are dying. Perhaps this is a sign of release for the body.

Sweat that changes the color of clothes may be a sign of jaundice, especially if the sweat occurs on the thighs, underarms and breast area. This type of sweat is difficult to evaporate. If it smells like urine, then check for disease. Yellow stains caused by sweating on clothing can indicate the excessive urea content in the sweat, but it may also indicate liver cirrhosis if it has a fishy smell.

Constant sweating can signal many disorders:
1. Hyperthyroidism – may also occur with heart palpitations.

2. Septicemia – cold sweats that smell
3. Hypoglycemia – dizziness, fatigue, and hunger pangs may also occur
4. Toxicity caused by excessive medicine intake, heavy metals or pesticides – Phosphates, lead, mercury, and arsenic all cause the tendency to sweat.
5. Hormonal imbalance – puberty-related

Generalized Sweating

Sweating throughout the body is most commonly caused by heat/fever, catabolism, and mental factor. Other causes include:

- Hypoglycemia - Low blood sugar also causes paleness in the face, cold sweats, chills, and limb tremors.
- Hyperthyroidism - A person who has this condition usually has palpitations, does not like heat, has increased appetite but gains little or no weight. There may also be increased bowel movement, palpitations and nervousness.
- Diabetes - This eventually hinders the automatic/involuntary nerve system, causing increased sweating. It also causes the patient to eat more, drink more and urinate more. There is also reduction of weight.
- Chromium-enriched tumor - characterized by constant heavy sweating for longer periods, palpitations, tremors, cold limbs, and very high blood pressure when sweating.
- Hypertension
- Postmenopausal syndrome

Localized Sweating

- **Sweating around the nose.** This happens in those with rhinitis/allergy and low immunity. These people can easily catch cold. Those with sweating around the nose are characteristically very nervous, emotional, gets tired after working a long time, and talkative.
- **Sweating on head or forehead**. This is common in those whose body has high heat and those with liver or stomach problems. Digestive function is also very active.

- **Half body sweating (upper/lower, left/right).** This usually occurs in younger people with brain disease, hypertension caused by kidney disease, stroke, and paralysis.
- **Sweating on chest, between breasts.** Those with this symptom are typically very sentimental, very jumpy, easily worried, think too much, and are very sad. This may occur in educated people who think too much.
- **Genital/Perineal sweating.** This occurs in women with vaginitis and itching. Often the sweat smells. In men, it occurs when there is infection in the genital area.
- **Underarm sweating that smells.** This means that the sweat glands are overactive or may be infected. This is more prevalent in the young or middle-aged and occurs more in women than in men.
- **Sweating on one side of head/face or on the area on the left or right side of the nose.** This occurs in both men and women who have not fully recovered from a severe illness and who immediately engage in vigorous activity such as sex. In this condition, the body is not balanced yet and can easily catch cold. This is common in those with sinus, lung or allergy problems.
- **Excessive sweating on the hands and feet.** This is usually a sign of a spleen/stomach/kidney problem.
- **Palm/Sole sweating.** This is common in nervous, excited people, especially when making a public speech. It also occurs in teenagers or young adults who get stressed due to a lot of inhibitions or restrictions. If this type of sweating is year-round, then it points to a stomach or blood problem.

Night Sweats

Night sweats that include weakness, cough, chest pain, and loss of appetite are symptoms of disorders such as tuberculosis. It may also be due to adenolymphoma (tumor in the lymph system), hyperthyroidism, or autonomic nervous system abnormality. If the night sweats cease upon waking, then this is associated with chronic or long-term illness, especially TB.

Day Sweats

Sudden heavy sweating during the day for no apparent reason is not healthy. This means that the skin has no control over it and the body does not have enough chi.

Cold Sweats

When the nervous system is suddenly excited, cold sweats are sometimes triggered. In extreme cases, this is due to heart disease or heart failure.

If only one side sweats, this may be symptomatic of pre-stroke conditions.

If cold sweats occur with chest heaviness, pain and pressure in the ribcage, and poor appetite, this signals cardiovascular or brain problems.

Body Smell

Body odor/smell is usually associated with the respiratory or digestive system. The following smells are associated with certain health conditions.

Table 8. Smells and Associated Health Conditions	
Smell	**Possible reason**
Garlic smell	If not eating garlic, there are phosphate components in the smell. This could be due to agricultural poisons such as pesticides, rat poison, etc.
Rotten apple smell	Ketosis or diabetes
Chicken feather smell (slightly sweet smell)	Measles
Toasted bread smell	Typhoid fever
Stale beer smell	Lymphoglandulitis
Rotten or sour smell	Food accumulated in the stomach
Acidic smell in sweat	Rheumatoid condition
Halitosis	Poor oral hygiene

Fungal smell in the mouth	Liver condition
Bloody smell in the mouth	Along with yellow-colored sweat, may be liver cirrhosis
Pus kind of smell in the mouth	Nose infection or lungs may have pus
Bloody smell	Mouth, nose, upper respiratory, or bronchial bleeding
Vomit has fecal smell	Intestinal or colon blockage or an infection in the abdominal cavity
Ammonia smell	Nephritis, severe edema, kidney failure, abnormal metabolism, high BUN and creatinine
Urine smell in mouth and sweat	If there are also crystals on the skin (uric acid), this may be due to uremia
Sweat smells like underarm odor	Genetic. This occurs more in women than in men

Lymph Nodes

Enlarged lymph nodes usually need to be around 0.5 cm in diameter to be detected superficially. Otherwise, they are not noticeable. Lymph nodes may be found in the neck area or under the jaw, underarm, collarbone or groin.

The location of the lymph nodes is helpful in determining which part of the body may have a problem.

If you see some swelling under the jaw or in the neck area, there may be a problem in the mouth area. Examples would be tonsillitis or gingivitis.

If you see lymph nodes in the neck area arranged in a line (like a string), check for trauma in the area.

-s in the armpit indicate a problem in the arm or breast.

If the lymph nodes are in the groin, there may be an infection or inflammation in the lower limbs, hips or buttocks.

Body Weight

Weight change is related to thyroid function, especially in older people. If body weight changes in one month for no reason, then this signals a problem. For instance, if there is a sudden weight loss of 10 lbs or more without any drastic changes to diet or lifestyle or if there is no obvious severe illness causing it, check for cancer.

If a gradual weight loss occurs with palpitations, this may be due to hyperthyroidism. If weight gain occurs with fatigue, depression and cold limbs, then this may be due to hypothyroidism.

It is important to understand that it is very unhealthy to be underweight. If the patient has a digestive ulcer, then he or she may appear to be thin. If this patient does not have an ulcer, the thinness may be due to cancer. An average person above 60 years of age may be usually thinner than normal. This is okay, as it is a normally part of aging. Typically this may be because the patient has not had enough nutrition or sleep. A patient's weight loss can also be due to chronic mild diarrhea, gastritis, digestive ulcer, or non-specific colon inflammation.

A patient who is elderly and is overweight, but steadily loses weight, may have chronic diabetes. Besides this, the patient may also suffer from a chronic contagious infection, such as tuberculosis, parasites, and hepatitis. If a patient is treated for any of these illnesses and is still thin, and if the weight loss is rather sudden and significant, then check for cancer.

Female Disorders

Irregular menstruation, or spotting in between periods, is most likely due to a hormone imbalance.

Vaginal bleeding that occurs in postmenopausal women, even with no pain, can be a sign of uterine, cervical or ovarian cancer. This is especially true in those who are obese or those who have late-onset menopause and a family history of cancer. Women should be especially watchful of this.

If the nipples secrete a clear, sticky fluid, this could be a sign of breast adenocarcinoma. Nipples that secrete a yellowish fluid signify a mammary duct problem but it does not necessarily signal a cancerous condition. If the discharge is brownish or reddish in color, then this definitely needs to be medically examined immediately, as it may be cancer in its late stages. About 75% of women who have these symptoms after menopause have carcinomas.

Women between the ages of 50 and 60 should be especially careful of abdominal pain, poor digestion, and abnormally fast weight loss, as it may point to ovarian cancer.

Vaginal Discharge

Estrogen stimulates egg maturity and cervical gland secretion of sticky mucus. So changes in vaginal secretion (sticky, dry, or thick) after woman's period can determine when ovulation occurs as well as reproductive problems and even cancer.

If cycle is imbalanced and there is a sticky discharge in the transition and ovulation periods for less than 4 days or there is no sticky discharge at all, infertility is possible. If the patient has premenstrual syndrome, then check for endometriosis.

If the cycle lasts for more than 38 days and there is intermittent discharge, there might be a chance of Polycystic Ovarian Syndrome. Sometimes a cervical inflammation or vaginal infection may be the cause

Dry periods should be before and after menstrual bleeding. If dryness lasts less than 9 days, then there may be progesterone deficiency. If the patient becomes pregnant, it may result in premature birth or miscarriage. Intermittent or irregular dry periods (the infertile phase) are also associated with an 80% risk for breast cancer.

Postmenopausal vaginal bleeding

Postmenopausal vaginal bleeding can be caused by many diseases. It may be due to a problem with the vulva, vagina, uterus, ovary and fallopian tube.

A tumor in the reproductive system is the most likely cause of postmenopausal vaginal bleeding. Over 40% of postmenopausal vaginal bleeding is related to cancer, such as:
1. Endometrial or uterine cancer
2. Cervical cancer. Usually the bleeding is not thick and heavy. Rather, the blood is watery.
3. Ovarian cancer
4. Endometriosis, myoma, uterine polyps, benign ovarian tumor, cervical dysplasia, vaginal polyps, or vaginitis

In older women, vaginal bleeding is usually caused by vaginitis. This may be accompanied by pus, foul smell and spotting.

An intrauterine device (IUD) may also be the cause of bleeding. Some women fail to take out the IUD when they get older. This can push into the muscles, causing bleeding.

High estrogen has also been associated with vaginal bleeding. Pollen is said to be rich in estrogen, so women who are exposed to this may be a risk for vaginal bleeding.

Minor causes of vaginal bleeding include systemic blood disease, hypertension, diabetes and atherosclerosis.

Chapter 15

DIAGNOSTIC WHEEL FOR NAIL AND TONGUE EXAMINATION

The creation of the preventive diagnosis kit is the result of years of analysis and training. Under my father's guidance, I reviewed over 10,000 cancer patients' cases and determined distinct markers in the lunulae and tongue. Such observations allowed me to develop categories for 7 different groups of abnormality. The kit provides various suggestions for treatment using herbs and other natural remedies. The following is a comprehensive overview of the diagnostic kit, which I first introduced to the public in 1994 as a way to detect problems before CT scans or blood tests come back, before problems worsen.

To use the disc, one first finds an appropriate description of the person to be tested on the outer disc or disc B. Once the person's outward fingernail appearance has been found, turn the inner disc or disc A so that the color or the characteristic matches on both discs. The corresponding tongue description should match the person characteristics as a confirmation. Now read the paragraphs beneath the disc A cutaway opening onto the outer disc for possible symptoms and directions for improvement. If one has more than about 50% of the symptoms listed, then he or she is probably in the right category of description, as not everyone will have *all* the symptoms listed.

Nail matrices take about 3 months to grow up to the point of regular nail growth, and then one must allow another 6-8 months (in adults) for complete nail growth. A normal, healthy person should have 8 lunulae; four on each fingernail and none on the pinkies. Lack thereof indicates poor intracellular oxygen levels, and can lead to symptoms such as cold hands and feet, numbness, memory loss, and fatigue. In this condition, the patient may have higher risk of cancer and candida yeast infection. If one hand has fewer than eight lunulae or the lunulae are smaller than the other hand, then this indicates a circulation blockage on that side of the body. The lack of lunulae and the absence of markings on the tongue signal cardiovascular problems.

There should be no teeth marks on the edge of the tongue. Teeth marks indicate problems in the spleen and pancreas. Spleen function is related to the immune system, while pancreas function is necessary for digestion. Teeth marks on the tongue can indicate the possibility of diabetes, especially if it already runs in the family. If both markers are present (teeth marks and lack of lunulae), then the patient is in what I hypothesize to be the high risk category for cancer. If the oxygen saturation is low, and immunity is low, then cancer has the chance to invade. Also, if it is already in the family medical history, the patient must be especially careful. If only the thumbs have lunulae, and there are teeth marks on the tongue, the patient may already have early stages of cancer, which may not yet be detectable by other tests. In fact, by the time blood tests or CT scans can detect cancer, it may already be in later stages and difficult to stop. Teeth marks on the inner cheek can also be of this indication.

There are also three different groups of abnormalities, which can be described as the cold group, the hot group, and the hot/cold mixed group. Each of these three main categories also has beneath them three subcategories:

If the lunulae are barely noticeable, smaller than 1-2 mm, or if there are less than eight on both hands (between 3 and 7), this person is considered to be of the cold type. These people are also likely to have teeth marks on the tongue and inner cheek if the condition is extreme. She or he will often feel very cold, like warm climate and foods, and have occasional poor digestion. This condition calls for some fresh ginger in the diet and red or fermented tea along with Vein Lite, OxyPower, Asparagus Extract, Chi Energy, Digestron and CFC. Usually, for each lunulae missing, one needs to take 3 months of Vein Lite, Asparagus Extract and OxyPower for the lunulae to come back.

If the patient has lunulae only on the thumbs, they are in a more extreme cold condition and will most likely have teeth marks along the edge of the tongue and the inner cheek. She or he will feel weak, drowsy, cold in the extremities, have poor digestion and low immunity. This situation calls for a diet rich in fresh ginger, warm, spicy foods, along with Vein Lite, OxyPower, Asparagus Extract, Digestron and Chi Energy.

Patients that have no lunulae at all are in the most severely poor condition and are considered to the extremely cold types. These patients are at a high risk for cancer, and will often have very pronounced teeth marks on the tongue and inner cheek. Cancer patients have been seen to have differences in their blood composition and flow. Research at the Shanxi Tumor Research Hospital has shown that cancer patients and hypertension patients have a lower and higher mean corpuscular hemoglobin and whole blood viscosity, respectively. In cancer patients however, plasma viscosity increases and thrombin time decreases. Clotting time is also shorter, especially for those in later stages of cancer. Many patients may die of internal blood clots, or embolisms, either of blood or of tumor. Thus, the presence of lunulae is particularly important. They will appear sallow-complexioned and pale, weak and may be overweight. They may experience insomnia, poor immunity, the frequent need to urinate, cold extremities and poor digestion with loose stool. Females may experience severe menstrual cramps and heavy discharge. Other symptoms include chronic sinusitis, oral hygiene problems, gastroenteritis, hepatitis, and renitis. We recommend taking fresh ginger, red tea, spicy foods, Asparagus Extract, Vein Lite, OxyPower, Digestron, Revivin, Chi Energy, and Slender All.

Patients with large lunulae that are undefined may often feel hot in the torso area but cold elsewhere. People in the hot/cold mixed group generally begin from the hot characteristics and become more cold as a result of insufficient body care. There are three stages to this condition. In its early stage, the boundary between the lunulae and the flesh of the fingertip begins to cloud up, but is not conspicuous and may even fall in the slightly hot category. Cold has only partially entered the body, so it may not be easily noticed. During the middle stages, the boundary between the lunulae and flesh becomes quite hazy resulting in coldness in the extremities. At this point, teeth marks begin appearing. Indeed, the lunulae are barely distinguishable from the flesh on the fingertip beneath the nail, and the cold claims a good portion of the body during the final stages. The cold may even have spread to the kidneys and all over the torso. It is at this dire point that cancer can grow, and spread very quickly. To prevent this, care must be taken early on, and the early stage of the condition calls for lots of fresh fruit in the diet, Vein Lite, Chi Energy, and Asparagus Extract.

If the patient has small lunulae on every nail on the hands including the pinkies, or even if one hand has less than the correct number of lunulae while the other has a lunula on the pinky, she or he faces into one of these hot categories. In the slightly hot subcategory, the patient is in overall good health, but may also experience dryness in the mouth, occasional dizziness, constipation and poor digestion. Those with such symptoms should alter their diet by eating more fruit/vegetables and minimizing the quantity of spicy foods ingested. Patients should also take CFC, Asparagus Extract, Vein Lite, OxyPower and Diabend if necessary.

If the patient has rather large lunulae on the nails, or more than 8 lunulae total, he or she is considered "hot", and may experience anxiousness, restless, and experience dry mouth often, along with dizziness and constipation. These patients should not eat spicy foods and should eat more fruits and vegetables, and take Asparagus Extract with Vein Lite, Hypertine, CFC, Relaxin, Diabend and OxyPower.

If there are large lunulae on all the fingernails, this person falls in to the very hot category on my kit and will have other symptoms such as redness of the face, high energy to the point of hyperactivity, a loud voice and a big temper. These people definitely need to eat plenty of fruits and vegetables, take Asparagus Extract, Oxypower, Vein Lite, Diabend, Hypertine, Chi-Happiness, Relaxin and CFC.

It is apparent through reviewing cancer patient files that approximately 80% of all cancer patients are of the cold category of varying degrees. This does not mean that only those in the cold category are at a risk of this disease, or does it guarantee that hot types never get cancer. Of course, there are deviations. However, this does not say that cold types are generally at a higher risk of cancer than hot types, and thus care must be taken to prevent it from happening.

I will here clarify that even if the rest of the fingernails have no lunulae, if there are lunulae on the pinkies, then this still indicates heart problems. One does not necessarily have to have a hot condition to have heart problems. Indeed, cold types may suffer from heart problems as well.

SECTION IV

FINGERNAIL, TONGUE AND BODY ANALYSIS: A COMPREHENSIVE LOOK

Chapter 16

COMPLETE FINGERNAIL, TONGUE AND BODY ANALYSIS

In the previous sections, we looked at individual characteristics to look for in the nails, tongue and the body. Some of these characteristics are so unique that they can be used to detect certain conditions independent of other signs and symptoms. A cyst on the lower frenula, for instance, is almost always a sign of a colon problem. However, many other signs need to be cross-checked with other signs in order to find out the real underlying condition.

In this section, we combine everything we have learned so far to get a comprehensive look at the different health conditions and associated symptoms. Like many diagnostic techniques, looking at one or two symptoms may not be enough to get a complete picture of a person's health condition. Cold hands or feet, for example, may be a sign of poor circulation or, perhaps, a low thyroid function. In this instance, it is important to look at other symptoms to pinpoint the major problem.

CARDIOVASCULAR SYSTEM

There are plenty of reasons why the Fingernail and Tongue Analysis should be aptly put into practice. However, for those with Coronary Artery Disease (CAD), this preventive method may mean the difference between life and death. Even with the numerous innovative, technological advancements in the medical field, clinical signs of CAD are still elusive. While risk factors exist including hypertension, obesity, etc., these factors are not necessarily indications of CAD.

Many people may not even be aware that they have poor circulation or are at risk for CAD unless they take certain laboratory tests. However, barring any symptoms such as chest pain or breathing difficulty, many will not even have the reason nor the desire to have their blood drawn or have imaging tests done.

With the Fingernail and Tongue Analysis method, there is a way to tell if you have poor circulation without undergoing any of these tests. All you have to do is observe certain physical signs indicating that your blood may not be flowing as smoothly as it should or that you are not getting enough oxygen in your cells. In many cases, these signs appear very early in the progress of the disease, even if laboratory results do not show it yet.

Problems with your cardiovascular system can impede normal blood flow. Ideally, it takes 2.4 seconds for blood to travel from the heart to the toes and back. If your cardiovascular system is compromised, however, there is no practical way to measure the blood's travel time. The good news is that there are physical signs that represent poor circulation, such as the following:

- Ear crease (Picture 6a)
- Lack of lunulae (Picture 2h)
- Cold hands/feet
- Limb numbness
- Dark protruding veins under the tongue (Pictures 7b, 11c)
- Red spikes or dark spots on tip of tongue (Pictures 12a, 12b)
- Nail clubbing (Pictures 1d, 1e)
- Lunulae on the pinkies (Picture 2g)
- Vertical ridges on nails (Picture 3b)
- Central nail canal or ridge (Picture 3f)
- Cherry angiomas on the neck/head (Picture 13b)
- Xanthomas (Picture 13d)

Vein Lite, Asparagus Extract and OxyPower are recommended to improve circulation and cardiovascular health.

Ear Crease

A diagonal ear crease (Picture 6a) is a widely known indicator of cardiovascular disease risk, particularly stroke. Approximately 89% of ear creases are related to a heart problem. In fact, at the 2004 World Stroke Conference, researchers presented clinical evidence that patients with an ear crease had higher levels of arterial plaque, more severe narrowing of the carotid artery and higher risk of transient ischemic attacks and cardiac arrest. If a person has an ear crease and a lack of lunulae or has a lunula on the pinky, the chance for cardiovascular disease is even higher.

Once the cardiovascular problem is addressed and treated, a shallow ear crease may disappear. However, if the crease is deep, it may be permanent.

Lack of lunulae

As discussed in an earlier section, the lunula is the white, crescent (or half moon) shape at the base of your nails. The lunula indicates the level of oxygen saturation in the cells. Normally, you have one lunula on each fingernail except on the pinky. Each lunula should take up to no more than ¼ of the size of the fingernail. Having less than eight lunulae or having very small lunulae (Picture 2h) signifies poor circulation and deficiency of oxygen. Lack of oxygen is often mistaken for shallow or difficulty breathing. This is not necessarily so. It means that there is circulatory or lymphatic blockage that needs to be cleared to prevent further damage.

Lunulae should reappear once the condition improves, as these cases illustrate:

E. Cole, DC from AK: "I have several patients who suffered from numbness of the limbs, to whom neurologists had suggested surgery. I used Vein Lite and their limbs returned to normal due to tremendously improved blood circulation."

Dr. Cobra in Florida reports, "After using Vein Lite for half a year the lunulae came back on my fingernails."

L. Steffensmeier, DC from IA, notices that when he is not feeling well, his lunulae disappear. So he uses Vein Lite and OxyPower. The lunulae reappear and he feels much better.

On the other hand, lunulae (especially large ones) on all fingernails, including the pinkies (Picture 2g), signify cardiovascular disease risk.

If the nails also exhibit vertical ridges, there is an added risk for atherosclerosis.

Red spikes or Dark Spots on tongue

The tongue also shows signs of poor circulation. A red- or purple-colored tongue indicates blood stasis (Pictures 8b, 8c). Red spikes on the tip of the tongue can indicate heart problem or hypertension (Picture 12a). Dark marks on the tip of the tongue indicate coronary heart disease (Picture 12b).

Dark, protruding veins under the tongue

The presence of dark, protruding veins underneath the tongue is again an indication of blood stasis (Pictures 7b, 11c). The dark color means lack of oxygen and more carbon dioxide. When both an ear crease and dark veins are present, the chance for bypass is very high. It is therefore important to address the problem immediately. Dark, protruding veins under the tongue can also signify heavy metal accumulation, leading to cardiovascular problems. To eliminate heavy metal toxicity, Metal Flush is recommended with Vein Lite and Asparagus Extract.

Nail Clubbing

Nail clubbing is primarily an indication of lung problems (Pictures 1d, 1e). In some cases, though, it can be a sign of heart disease. According to the *Journal of the American Medical Association* (June 2005; 52(6): 1020-28), unilateral nail clubbing is associated with hemiplegia and infective endocarditis. In 87 patients with hemiplegia, or paralysis of half of the body, 13.8% of them had clubbing on the affected side. Of 60 patients in infective endocarditis, or inflammation of the heart lining, 50% had bilateral clubbing.

Central Nail Canal or Ridge

A "fir tree" abnormality on the nail (Picture 3f) is associated with peripheral artery disease.

Cherry Angiomas on the Forehead

When cherry angiomas are located on the forehead (Picture 13b), there is a chance of a stroke or aneurysm. As discussed in various sections of this book, cherry angiomas signal elevated estrogen, both in men and women.

Some studies have demonstrated that high estradiol (the harmful form of estrogen) is linked with an increased risk of coronary artery disease or atherosclerosis (*Aging Male*. 2004; 7(3):197-204). This was confirmed by another study which explained that elevated estradiol promotes atherosclerosis risk factors in men with CAD. Furthermore, excess estrogen increases the chance of a thrombus or abnormal blood clot in both men and women. Conversely, those who are suffering from myocardial infarction or who have had a heart attack have higher estradiol and lower testosterone levels (*Neur Lett*. 2007; 28(2): 182-186).

Therefore, the presence of cherry angiomas on the forehead is already an early warning sign and should not be taken for granted.

Lunulae on the pinkies

If there are lunulae on the pinkies (Picture 2g), this may be a sign of a congenital heart problem. In those with this sign, 80% have either a parent or a grandparent who has or who has had a history of heart problems.

Xanthomas

It is also important to look for xanthomas around the eye area (Picture 13d), as these can signify elevated cholesterol, a strong risk factor for atherosclerosis.

Stroke

There are many misconceptions regarding stroke that may be putting some of us in harm's way.

Myth 1: If you have normal or low blood pressure, you will not get a stroke. This is false. Stroke has many other risk factors (cholesterol, etc.) so having low or normal blood pressure does not necessarily mean you are not at risk for stroke.

Myth 2: Skipping medication is fine. Taking medicines or supplements must be done on a regular basis. Just because you feel good today does not mean that it is fine to skip your medicine. For example, if you are taking an anti-coagulant, you need to take it daily.

Myth 3: Prescribed medicine must be taken for life. This is not true in all cases. You must have periodic checkups to determine if you still need to continue taking a medicine or supplement or if the dose needs to be adjusted.

Myth 4: Skinny people are not at risk for stroke. Again, this is false. There are many fit and slender people who have risk factors for stroke although they are unaware of them.

Myth 5: Stroke is only for old people. While stroke may be more common among older people, it strikes the younger ones, too. Therefore, prevention must be practiced early.

Cardiovascular disease (CVD)

Hypertension, high lipids, and high glucose are three of the main factors of CVD. Chronic inflammation (throat and nose inflammation, chronic colitis) also increases the risk. Research has found that among chronic colitis patients, their C-reactive protein (CRP) is high, which increases their risk for CVD. In one study on 300 CVD patients, the top 52 patients with the highest CRP all died within 5 years.

Case reports:

R.L., 58 y/o/m from MN, underwent a Roux-en-Y procedure (gastric bypass) to lose weight. After the surgery, he weighed 228 lbs. When he was checked, there were more than 10 cherry angiomas on his face and head (Picture 13b), signifying a risk for aneurysm or stroke. He says that he already had a stroke twice, a year ago and 5 years ago, respectively.

A.V., 72 y/o/f from CA, has no cherry angiomas but has a belly fat (no fibroids, cysts, etc), has moons only on thumbs, has an ear crease and a cherry angioma on the forehead, all indicating aneurysm risk. She says that she had a stroke two years earlier due to an aneurysm. Her memory is also poor and she has cold hands and feet.

S. M. from FL has cherry angiomas on the forehead and abdomen, making her at risk for aneurysm, stroke or an estrogen-related problem. She revealed that five years ago, she suffered from a stroke/aneurysm. Her estrogen is also high, affecting her liver and breast.

R.H., DC from TX, has a 39 y/o/m patient who was found to have a high risk for cardiovascular problems and colon polyps through Fingernail and Tongue Analysis. About a month later, he suffered from a heart attack and had to have a triple bypass.

R. Motley, a 54 y/o/m DC from CA, relates that he had a crease on one earlobe and was told in August 2004 about a possible heart problem. About 2 months later, he had a heart fibrillation. After that, he developed a crease on the other earlobe.

J. Blair, ND from NJ, has a 75 y/o/m patient who was analyzed in 2006. He had less than 4 small lunulae on the right hand and only one lunula (on the thumb) on the left hand, suggesting poor circulation especially on the left hand side. Now he found out that he has 74% blockage on the left side of the body.

M. Stewart, DC, has a 49 y/o/m patient who had lunulae on his pinkies, indicating heart disease. After taking Vein Lite for more than a year, the lunulae on his pinkies disappeared. He has better circulation and normal blood pressure.

E. Williams, DC from TN, shared with us that a few years ago, an analysis showed he had arterial blockage and high cholesterol and was told he may need an angioplasty. Then he started taking Vein Lite tea. About 3 months later, the blockage completely cleared. He said that without Vein Lite he would probably be dead by now.

W. Meredith, DC from NH, has a 65 y/o/f patient who, in 2001, was found to have a cardiovascular problem through F&T Analysis. But she didn't take the herbs. In 2004, she had a heart attack and underwent a bypass. Now she wants to start on the herb program.

R. Reiner, DC from FL, has a patient found to be at risk for a heart problem through F&T analysis in 1999. At that time he weighed 167 lbs, worked out regularly and had no history of heart disease so he didn't believe it and threw his paper away. Six weeks later, he had a heart attack. His angiogram showed two of his arteries were completely blocked while another 2 arteries were halfway blocked. He subsequently had a bypass operation.

D. Eggett introduced the Fingernail and Tongue Analysis method to physicians at the Utah Valley Health Assoc. Expo. One doctor had dismissed his warning of a heart condition and had ended up in a hospital (just over one month after the analysis!), undergoing a double bypass operation.

L. Eberting, DC from MO, had a 65 y/o/f patient whom I saw during the Las Vegas Parker Seminar. I explained to her that she was highly at risk for atherosclerosis and would possibly need a bypass operation. Incredulous, the patient felt her current state of health was stable. In April of 2001, she had a bypass operation. In 2003, she had another bypass operation.

J.C., a 60 y/o/m from FL, reports that he had lunulae only on the thumb and two pinkies, signifying that he has circulation problems and a congenital heart disease. He has genetic mitral valve prolapse. He then took Vein Lite, OxyPower and Asparagus Extract. Two months later, all his lunulae are starting to reappear.

R. Lorenat, DC from IA, had an ear crease and lunula on the pinky, signifying that he had a chance of getting heart disease early. He verified this, saying that he had a heart attack just a few months earlier.

One 45-year-old chiropractor from FL had clubbing nails, no lunulae, and very white nails, indicating either a heart or lung problem. He was so surprised. He said that 2 years before, he had open heart surgery. Now he wants to be on the herb program right away.

R. Hicks, DC from TX, has a 41 y/o/m patient who was found to be at risk for a cardiovascular problem in 2005 through the F&T analysis. Two months after that, he had a heart attack and had a triple heart bypass.

M.S. from NY has a lunula on his pinky and horizontal indentations on his nails, indicating a cardiovascular problem. He thought his symptoms were only due to digestive problems. However, at the end of June 2007, he was taken to the hospital for heart problems. It was discovered that he has stage 1 mitral valve prolapse.

J. Fowler from FL has a 68 y/o/m client who was found to have circulation blockage or heart problem two years ago through fingernail and tongue analysis. Then he later found out that he did have some blockage. After two years on the Chi program, circulation on the left side of his body is up to 93% while circulation on the right side of his body is now up to 87%. Circulation through his carotid artery has vastly improved as well.

L. Jordan, DC from IN, h as a 64 y/o/m patient who was analyzed in 1998 and found to have early markers of a cardiovascular problem. After a stress echocardiogram, his doctor determined that he did not have any problem. However, in 1999, he suffered from a heart attack.

HEAVY METAL TOXICITY

The accumulation of heavy metals can lead to behavioral, mental and physical disorders. We are exposed to heavy metals such as mercury, lead and cadmium on a daily basis is common and from sources as common as toys, kitchen utensils and exhaust. Awareness of the dangers of heavy metal toxicity is just the first step. Having yourself checked for heavy metals is even more important.

Conventionally, a blood, urine or hair analysis will help determine heavy metal poisoning. An easier and quicker way is to look for physical signs indicating heavy metal toxicity:

- Blue or black protruding veins under the tongue (Pictures 7b, 11b, 11c)
- Black or dark-colored nails (Pictures 3a, 4h)
- Blue- or dark-colored gums (Picture 13e)
- Metallic taste in the mouth

If you possess any of these indicators and have been or are exposed to heavy metals, you may have metal accumulation in your system. Other symptoms include dizziness, fatigue, and loss of concentration. Children with lead poisoning generally exhibit hyperactivity, poor appetite, irregular sleeping habits, temper tantrums, and loss of concentration. Metal Flush is the best recommendation for heavy metal toxicity. Vein Lite and Asparagus Extract may be added for synergistic effect.

Case report:

M. Headlee, DC from WI, had dark, branching veins underneath his tongue, indicating heavy metal toxicity. After using Vein Lite and Metal Flush for 3 weeks, he felt much better and the dark vein under his tongue was much lighter.

To detect digestive issues, look for these signs:

- **Crack on the tongue.** When you check for digestive health, always look for cracking on the tongue (Pictures 11f, 13f), especially on the center. This suggests digestive issues, particularly gastritis. The number of cracks and the depth of the cracks correlate to the number and severity of GI tract or stomach problems, respectively. If the tongue is red as well, there may be inflammation in the body.

- **Black lines on the nails.** If the patient has black lines on the nails (Pictures 4f, 4g) and a crack down the center of the tongue, then these may indicate bleeding due to a stomach or duodenal ulcer. The stool will not often show if you have minor bleeding. Stomach bleeding may be caused by acid and pepsin secretion. If you have this condition, digestive enzymes should not be used.

- **Teeth marks.** Teeth marks on the tongue (Pictures 7e, 7f) may also signify digestive issues, specifically with the pancreas (hypoglycemia). Approximately 72.2% of digestive patients have teeth marks. If the tongue is red and has teeth marks, this is an indication of hypoglycemia. Because there is a chance of hypoglycemia developing into diabetes, and vice versa, it is important to regulate blood glucose levels.

- **Yellow coating on tongue.** A yellow coating on the tongue (Picture 9b) and bloating are also signs of digestive issues.

- **Roadmap-like tongue**. A roadmap-like tongue (Picture 11e) in older people signifies low stomach acid, or hypochlorydia. Other signs of hypochlorydia are vertical ridges, horizontal lines, and brittle nails.

- **Geographic tongue**. In some cases, a geographic tongue (Pictures 9g, 10a, 16b) is associated with inflammatory disease such as Ulcerative colitis, Irritable Bowel Syndrome or Crohn's disease. Any lung issues must first be ruled out.

To help improve digestive health, Digestron and GI Chi are recommended.

Case reports:

R. S., 67 y/o/m from CA, came in for an analysis and complained of abdominal pain. He couldn't even eat. Upon checking, he has a yellow coating and deep crack on his tongue (Picture 15f), indicating digestive issues. His tongue is also pale and has shiny edges. These two signs are usually associated with ulcers.

Since June 2007, he's had digestive issues: he had difficulty swallowing or eating. He also lost so much weight. At that time, he took Angiostop, Revivin, Digestron, and Liver Chi. Six months later, he can eat normally and gained his weight back. He continued Digestron and Liver Chi for a year.

Then when he drank 2 glasses of cognac and 9 beers, it caused extreme abdominal pain and his inability to eat (Drinking alcohol when you have an ulcer or digestive problem can cause abdominal spasms). His digestive problem from 2 years ago had recurred and he was very worried. He has started taking Digestron and Liver Chi again.

F. Akbarpour, MD from CA, relates that a 42 y/o/f patient was analyzed using the fingernail and tongue method and found to have a serious digestive problem. A lower and upper GI scope revealed no problem. However, an ERCP test found that she had early stage pancreatic cancer.

C. Chrencik, DC from AL, suffered from diverticulosis and anemia which could be identified by black lines running vertically along his fingernails and the presence of a cyst on his frenula. He had difficulty walking at that time. One year after being on Chi-F, Chi Energy, Asparagus Extract, Digestron, etc., he called our office to say that he no longer had any lines on his fingernails, his lunulae had returned, and his condition had much improved.

R. Welch, DC from CA, has a male patient in his who had a black line on his fingernail, signifying some kind of bleeding. He did not pay attention to it. Three months later, he told Dr. Welch that he had just gotten out of the hospital. Apparently he was hemorrhaging internally and was vomiting blood due to an ulcer.

K. Hajduk, DC from CA, has a patient who had short black lines on 3 fingers, indicating stomach bleeding. A test confirmed that she did have stomach bleeding.

Rabbi Gertner from NY reports on an 85 y/o/f who was being treated with prescriptions for hypertension but she still passed out. An examination using the Fingernail and Tongue Analysis found that she has digestive and liver problems. Then she started on Hypertine and Liver Chi. After a check-up one week later, she needed no more prescriptions.

Abby's Health and Nutrition in FL reports on a 36 y/o/m who had a very red tongue with a crack and thick white coating on the center (Picture 16a). He also had three nodules in the ear (Picture 15h), which represent a possible stomach, liver or esophageal problem. He later revealed that he has severe GERD.

COLON

A cyst on the lower frenula is a strong indicator of colon problems, most likely colon polyps (Picture 6c). It is important to check for this sign because more and more people under 40 years old develop colon polyps, and many of them do not even know they have the condition. Out of 65,017 subjects under 40 years old, 701 had colon polyps. A 2005 study involved 36,000 men and women under 35 years old. After a colonoscopy, 260 were found to have colon polyps. Of the 260, five were colon cancer cases, even in patients as young as 17 years old. The subjects had these symptoms prior to the colonoscopy: anemia, blood in the stool, constipation, diarrhea, abdominal pain, and lump above the groin area (on both sides).

Skin tags (Picture 16h) may also be an early sign of a colon problem and should not be disregarded.

Colon Polyps

Three factors influence the formation of colon polyps: (1) bowel constipation (1) excess bile from the liver and (3) excess estrogen.

1. Constipation can irritate the colon and cause the formation of polyps. It is important to get rid of bodily wastes because stool contains indoles, nitrates, and bile salts, which are toxic to the membrane of the intestines and colon if accumulated. When they stay in the colon or intestines too long, the membrane absorbs these toxins. As a result, the mucosal membrane of the intestines becomes inflamed and damaged. To improve bowel regularity, CFC is recommended.

2. Bile is produced from the liver. When a person eats meat or fat, the liver tries to produce more bile, which is then stored in the gallbladder. However, if a person eats too much, too fast, this sends a signal to the liver to produce more and more bile. If the gallbladder cannot store the excess bile, it gets accumulated in the colon or small intestines instead. Secondary bile salts are carcinogens, so if they accumulate in the colon, the risk for colon cancer increases.

3. Colon polyps start out as benign tumors but may become malignant and develop into colon cancer. One of the risk factors of colon cancer is a history of breast or genital cancer (which is well-known to be related to estrogen). One study found that women with breast cancer have an 18% chance of developing colon cancer within 6 months (*Family Practice*. Dec 2003). This is determined to be due to high estrogen levels. Estrogen may play a role in the development of colon polyps. This link has been evident in many cases where patients have both myoma and colon polyps. After taking Myomin, which reduces estrogen, both the myoma and colon polyps reduced or cleared.

A colonoscopy is typically employed to check for colon polyps, which is a strong risk factor for colon cancer. However, there are many missed diagnoses with this method of testing, as these cases illustrate:

A 39-year-old male from CA had a colonoscopy but no abnormalities were found. A year later, another colonoscopy found a 4.1 cm tumor. A 1-cm polyp takes about 5 years to grow.

Another patient in his 50s was found to have two colon polyps 3 years ago. Recently, a colonoscopy revealed that there are 4 colon polyps, one of which is 1.5 cm, apparently missed on the first colonoscopy.

These cases illustrate that sometimes we cannot rely on colonoscopies to detect abnormalities in the colon. A 1-cm polyp takes about 5 years to grow, so in the first case, a colonoscopy should have detected the 4.1-cm tumor well before it grew to that size. Similarly, in the second case, the 1.5-cm colon polyp should have been detected already but it was missed on the first test.

In a colonoscopy, a sigmoidoscope is used to check for abnormalities; however, sigmoidoscopes are sometimes not long enough to check the entire colon. The scope also 'floats' so it may not detect all of the growths along the intestinal wall. Therefore, another tool is necessary for detecting colon abnormalities as early as possible.

This is why watching for a frenula cyst is important. If the cyst is on the top portion of the frenula, 71% is associated polyps in the small intestine and/or upper colon. If the cyst is on the lower part of the frenula, 74% of the cases are related to colon polyps and/or rectal problems. Having multiple frenula cysts is obviously related to a serious colon or intestinal problem.

If both frenula cyst and abdominal cherry angiomas are present, then this means that a high estrogen level is affecting the liver and colon and may lead to the formation of colon polyps. Myomin and CFC are recommended.

In some cases of diverticulitis (inflammation of the colon), both frenula cyst and dark lines on the fingernails may be present. In this case, GI Chi, Digestron and Psoricaid are recommended.

Patients with colon polyps also have some or all of these symptoms: anemia, blood in the stool, constipation, diarrhea, abdominal pain, and lump above the groin area (on both sides). When fecal bleeding occurs, hemorrhoids are most often believed to be the cause. However, if bleeding continues after a week to a month of hemorrhoid treatment, the risk of colon polyps (and even colon cancer) is very high. Eating certain foods can sometimes cause diarrhea and/or constipation. Irritable Bowel Syndrome could also be a possible cause. However, there is also a chance that colon polyps may be the cause.

Constipation and/or irregularly shaped feces are also associated symptoms of colon polyps.

Pain and lumps in the abdomen may be indicators of colon polyps. Furthermore, blood in the stool, constipation, or irregularly shaped feces are all risk indicators of colon polyps.

For colon polyps, the recommended program includes CFC, Myomin, Debile, Liver Chi, and Reishi Spore Extract. Also avoid red meat in the diet and try to minimize or eliminate constipation

Case reports:

S. Green, DDS from FL, has relates that when he sees a cyst on the frenula, 100% of the time the patient has a colon problem. His knowledge of the Fingernail and Tongue Analysis has significantly changed his practice and concepts.

L. Ross, 53 y/o/m DC from FL, was found to have a high chance of colon problem in 2000. In May 2004, he felt severe pain in the lower left abdominal area near the groin. All in all, he spent about $12,500 for tests, but nothing was found. When he was analyzed using the F&T method, a big cyst was found on his frenula, he had no lunulae and there was a black line on his nail, all indicating he had a serious colon problem. He now uses herbs.

E.R., a 37 y/o/f from NY, shared that an analysis found she was at risk for colon polyps (she had a cyst on the frenula). Shortly thereafter, a colonoscopy and endoscopy revealed that she did indeed have a colon polyp.

R. Rozich, DC from IL, reports that while he was doing physicals at a school and implementing the Fingernail and Tongue Analysis method. One 9-year-old boy had bedwetting problems. Upon checking, he noticed a frenula cyst on a 9-year-old boy. So he asked the mother if he had any problems with the colon. The mother was very surprised. Her son's belly was hard and distended, most likely causing pressure on the bladder. So Dr. Rozich recommended CFC for the colon. After only one week, the boy had no bedwetting problem, confirming that it was the colon problem causing the bedwetting.

C. C., DC from AL, had black lines running vertically along his fingernails and the presence of a cyst on his frenula. At that time he was suffering from diverticulosis and anemia.

K. Wirtz, DDS from AZ, has a female patient who was analyzed in 2006 and found to have colon cancer risk. Six months later, she had surgery to remove a portion of her colon and intestine, along with a high grade glandular dysplasia polyp. Surgical biopsy revealed the cancer cells were forming. If she had waited three more months, the cancer would have metastasized. She writes: "I want you to know how deeply grateful I am to have listened to your recommendation. I am saved by this advice. "

J. Iannetta, DC from ME, has a female patient who had a cyst on her frenula, indicating a colon polyp risk. Tests showed that she had three colon polyps.

J. Stickel, DC from IA, reports on a patient with myoma and polyps in her colon. After taking Myomin for only 3 months, her myoma and polyps had completely disappeared.

L.B., a 50 y/o/f from NY, had 2 big cysts on her frenula and no lunulae in March 1999 (Picture 6d), signifying that she may have colon polyps or even colon cancer. Five months later, a colonoscopy showed she had 20 colon polyps. All were removed; one was found to be pre-cancerous. She started on Angiostop, Myomin, CFC, etc. In 2000, she reported that she had stopped with the program because her polyps were clear.

J.K., a 54 y/o/m from PA, had a chance of getting colon polyps because of the cyst on his frenula and had had bad digestion, evidenced by bubbles in his urine. At that time, he only took Asparagus Extract and the bubbles disappeared. In 2001, he found he had 2 colon polyps and another 2 the next year. Now he's on the Chi liver/colon program.

S.B., a 44 y/o/m from PA, had a PSA level of 7 that decreased to 3, still above the normal level. He had red dots on his tongue, a cyst on the frenula, and cherry angiomas on the abdominal area. He is also on the prostate and liver/colon program.

R.H., a 39 y/o/m DC from TX, was found to have a high risk for colon polyps through Fingernail and Tongue Analysis. He had his colon checked and they found 9 colon polyps.

All these cases demonstrate that estrogen affects the colon, liver, and hormone system. Reducing estradiol level, therefore, is very important.

HEPATIC AND BILIARY SYSTEM

Many patients have liver problems while their serum levels (ALT and AST) are still within the normal range; however, there are physical signs that can alert you that a liver issue exists even before blood tests.

Early symptoms of liver problems may include the following:

- **Dark branching veins under the tongue.** Liver problems can manifest as branching or varicose, protruding, and dark veins under the tongue (Pictures 7b, 7c, 11b, 11c, 16f). The darker the veins and the more branching there is, the more serious the problem. Tables 5 and 6 in Section II of this book enumerate the incidence of branching veins in liver diseases. For example, in Picture 7c, there are four dark veins under the tongue, which has a strong correlation with liver cirrhosis.
- **Red or dark spots on the sides of the tongue** (Blood stasis spots) can also indicate a liver problem (Pictures 11h, 12f).
- **A thick and wide tongue** may also indicate liver problems (Picture 10g).
- **Large cherry angiomas and/or spider veins** on the chest and abdominal area (Pictures 12h, 13a, 13c). This can be due to either liver metabolic or hormone (estrogen) problem. Too much estradiol has been proven to cause liver problems.
- **Dark or red bands on the tips of the nails** (Terry's nails) can also indicate liver issues (Picture 5a).

Furthermore, if you have typical liver symptoms, it may be a good idea to have your liver tested:
- Bloating after meals
- Loss of appetite
- Fatigue
- Acne
- Jaundice (Picture 5b)
- Bitter taste, dry mouth
- Bad breath

If you have these symptoms, use Liver Chi, Cordyceps Extract, and Reishi Spore Extract. Add Myomin to this regimen if abdominal cherry angiomas are also present.

Estrogen and the Liver

The biological effects of estrogen occur when it binds to two receptors, estrogen receptor alpha (ERalpha) and estrogen receptor beta (ERbeta), both of which are found in the liver and other tissues and organs. Since estrogen is metabolized in the liver, accumulation of too much estrogen can obviously affect liver function.

Case reports:

K. Swickard, Kansas City, MO, wrote. "In the most exciting case, six months ago, a man with terminal liver cancer and a very yellow face came in and said his physician told him he had two weeks to live. Six months later he is still alive, seems better, but I don't know how long he can survive, he is using Liver Chi, Asparagus Extract, Revivin, Cordyceps Extract, Reishi Spore Extract, and Vein Lite"

J.G., a 51 y/o/m from CA, had fatty liver and Hepatitis C which developed to late-stage liver cirrhosis. He had more than 4 dark branching veins under the tongue (Picture 16f). He also had edema, jaundice, and fatigue. Then he was recommended Liver Chi, Cordyceps Extract, Bathdetox, Asparagus Extract and Reishi Spore Extract. After only 3 days, he felt better and had more energy. A month and a half later, he had increased energy and mental clarity, his insomnia was gone, and his edema reduced. Before he started the protocol, he had lost 38 lbs. After 8 months, he has gained back about 15 lbs.

A 57 y/o/f with Hepatitis C for 17 years took Liver Chi, Vein Lite and OxyPower for 3 months. Her HCV RNA titer reduced from 1,440,000 to 460,000, a 68% reduction.

Gallbladder

The gallbladder's primary function is to store bile. When bile becomes concentrated and thickened, it can form into gallstones (cholelithiasis) or cause the gallbladder to be inflamed (cholecystitis). Gallbladder attacks result when the flow of bile from the gallbladder is obstructed. Attacks are usually manifested as pain in the upper right quadrant of the abdomen as well as nausea, usually occurring after meals. For gallbladder problems, Debile and Liver Chi are recommended.

RENAL SYSTEM

In 2002, the five-stage classification system for chronic kidney disease was established. This system is based on the estimated glomerular filtration rate (eGFR), which is calculated from the serum creatinine level and level of proteinuria (Source: "USRDS 2008 Annual Data Report" NIH 2008).

| Table 9. Kidney Failure Classification according to eGFR ||
Kidney Failure Stage	eGFR (%)
1	> 90
2	60-89
3	30-59
4	15-29
5	<15

Each stage is also associated with either more than 20mg/dl of urine albumin, an albumin/creatinine ratio of at least 30 mg/g, or other evidence of structural damage to the kidney. When kidney failure reaches Stage 5, kidney dialysis is necessary.

Studies show that terminal kidney cases are primarily associated with glomerulonephritis causing proteinuria (43%), diabetes (40%), drug reaction (10%) and hypertension (7%). Many kidney problems can be detected very early, even before eGFR rates are determined by a blood test.

The classification system may be useful if the patient has undergone a urine or blood test; however, there are numerous cases where a kidney problem goes undetected because a patient is unaware of symptoms that can signify kidney disease.

When it comes to kidney symptoms, urine is the first thing that comes to mind. Because urine contains the waste products from the body, it can be a useful tool in determining kidney failure.

Many people incorrectly believe that the more transparent or water-like urine appears, the healthier the individual. The purpose of urination is to expel bodily waste. Clear urine may be a sign that not enough waste is released. Yellow urine suggests normal kidney function. Urine that has noticeable air bubbles (foamy) generally contains an excessive amount of protein. If the urine has a rotten or sour scent, it may be a sign of kidney failure. Cloudiness and/or blood in the urine may also be signs of kidney problems.

Important signs that indicate a kidney problem:
- Puffy face when waking up
- Foamy urine (Picture 13h)
- Edema in legs and/or ankles (Pictures 14a, 14b)
- Teeth marks on tongue (Pictures 7e, 7f)
- Dark color and puffiness under eyes (eye bags)
- Solid vertical ridges on nail (Pictures 2d, 3b, 4e)
- Horizontal white lines or strips on nails (Picture 4a, 4b)
- Yellow/black coating on root of tongue (Pictures 8f, 8g)
- Half-and-half or Terry's nails (Pictures 1h, 2a)

Teeth marks on the tongue signify edema. Retained water can cause the tongue to swell and push against the teeth, thus creating the teeth marks. Foamy urine signifies that due to impaired renal function, your body is losing protein (proteinuria). Wait a few seconds after urinating. If the bubbles do not disappear, then this is indeed proteinuria.

Blood and urine tests are conventionally used to determine kidney function and kidney disease risk. High blood urea nitrogen (BUN) and creatinine levels often signify reduced renal function. A study from the Minneapolis Veterans Affairs Medical Center found that middle-aged men whose urine tests (dipstick test) detect more than a trace amount of protein in the urine had triple the risk of end-stage renal disease (ESRD). Those with abnormal readings on both dipstick test and estimated glomerular filtration rate (eGFR) were 41 times more likely to suffer from end-stage renal disease than those with normal results. The study evaluated data on 13,000 men aged 35-57 years old at the start of the study in 1972-1975. Follow-up occurred through 1999.

In many cases, blood/urine tests will not show abnormalities if either one of the kidneys has at least 30% function. Besides the symptoms already mentioned, the following are also signs of kidney disease:

- Soreness or pain in the lower back or waist area
- Low energy and appetite
- Color of urine is darker, sometimes pink or red
- Total urine volume at night is more than at daytime
- Anemia
- No strength in thighs when climbing stairs (~3 floors), even without carrying anything
- Lower back becomes sore after sitting for two hours
- Thighs and knees are weak or have no energy after standing and working
- Lack of concentration
- Hair loss when washing hair
- Difficulty sleeping even if you feel sleepy. And once you fall asleep, you wake up right away

The presence of the above signs can indicate kidney problems. Prompt attention is needed because although a blood or urine test may not indicate kidney failure, the problem may already be at the very early stage.

Hypertension is one of the major factors of kidney disease (and vice versa, especially in younger people. Diabetes (both Type 1 and II) is another. In fact, there is a strong correlation between the two. About 40% of those who suffer from diabetes have renal disease. If diabetic patients find traces of protein in their urine (bubbles or foam), this is usually a sign of stage 3 kidney disease. Stages 1 and 2 often are asymptomatic.

Some drugs may also cause kidney damage. Some examples are antibiotics, antifungals (calamycin, gentamycin), anti-inflammatories, diuretics and anti-cancer drugs. Dyes that are ingested for x-ray/imaging purposes may also be harmful to the kidneys. Herbs that contain aristolochic acid can also cause kidney damage.

A proper diet can always help reduce the risk of certain diseases. Supplements may also be taken to promote kidney health. Asparagus Extract, Bathdetox, Kidney Chi and Cordyceps Extract are supplements that improve kidney function.

Case reports:

E.W., 36 y/o/m from CA, has Focal segmental glomerulosclerosis, an autoimmune-related kidney disease. He had half-and-half nails (Picture 2a), proteinuria, a yellow coating on the root of his tongue and a minimal urine output. After 9 months on the kidney program, his BUN dropped from 34 to 15, his creatinine dropped from 2.5 to 1.5, his urine protein went from 3+ to negative, and his 24-hour urine output increased from 0.8 liter to 1.8 liters (normal).

W.H., 44 y/o/m from NV, had a gray/black area on his tongue a year ago, indicating a kidney problem. He later found out that he has high uranium and arsenic content, affecting his kidneys. After being on Kidney Chi, Asparagus Extract, Metal Flush, and Vein Lite, his tongue is much better and his kidney function has improved.

AGING-RELATED CONDITIONS

There are some signs signifying risk of some age-related conditions. For example, beaded vertical ridges signal osteoporosis or arthritis (Picture 3g).

For other signs of aging such as hearing loss, impaired vision, and thinning/graying hair, Juvenin is recommended to delay their onset.

Osteoporosis

As mentioned, beaded vertical ridges (Picture 3g) may signal osteoporosis. Thinning nails also signal osteoporosis. This can be confirmed by a bone density test or blood test (to check for BGP, PYD or DPD).

BGP (Bone Gla protein) or osteocalcin is a calcium-binding protein of osteoblast cells, which is used as a biochemical marker for bone formation. When BGP is high, the rate of bone formation is also high. On the other side are PYD (pyridinoline) and deoxypyridinoline (DPD), both bone loss markers. Elevated PYD or DPD levels mean that you are losing bone mass.

Case reports:

J.K. from NY was analyzed and found to be at risk for osteoporosis (she had vertical ridges on nails, beads on a string). Later, a bone density test revealed that she does have osteoporosis.

E. Schlabach, DC from OH, has a 74 y/o/f patient with severe osteoporosis and was already using high doses of Vitamin D and calcitonin. The patient was taking Youth Chi at 2 capsules, 2 times daily with Vitamin D and calcitonin and reduced her DPD by 26% (9.5 → 7). The patient discontinued Youth Chi, taking only Vit D and calcitonin, and her DPD level increased to 12 in October 2008. At that point, she went back on Youth Chi and her DPD level normalized with an 83% reduction in 7 months.

	Dec 2006	Mar 2007	Oct 2008	May 2008	Reference Values
DPD level	9.5	7	12	2	Healthy: 3.0-7.2 Std units Osteoporotic: >7.2 Std units

L. Jordan, DC from IN, has a female patient was analyzed and found to be at risk for osteoporosis. A couple of years later, she was diagnosed with osteopenia.

Hormonal imbalance manifests as:
- Red dots on the tongue (Picture 12g)
- Cherry angiomas on the abdomen (Pictures 12h, 13a)
- White spots on the nail (Picture 4a)
- Skin discoloration on cheeks (Picture 14g)

White spots are commonly seen on the nails of girls undergoing puberty. This is normal since the hormonal cycle is active during this stage. Red dots on the tongue or abdominal cherry angiomas are very good indicators of elevated estrogen. That is why the presence of these signs is associated with the risk of estrogen-dominant conditions such as cysts, fibroids, endometriosis, breast cancer, prostate cancer and others. It is very important to give prompt attention when you see these signs. Further tests may be done, if needed. But, in the meantime, estrogen level needs to be reduced in order to prevent exacerbating the condition.

Case reports:

S.B., 21 y/o/f from CA, found that she was at risk for fibroids/cysts due to the red dots on the back and sides of her tongue. Her mammogram then confirmed that there were 2 fibroids on her right breast and 1 in the other. After taking Myomin, the cyst fibroids in her breast disappeared.

J.P., DC from MT, has a 34 y/o/f patient with cherry angiomas on the abdomen and red dots on the tongue, indicating a risk for estrogen-related conditions. She said that she did have an ovarian cyst. But she didn't do anything about it. A year later, she found that her CA.125 is 16 (normal is < 3), indicating ovarian cancer.

T. Toole, DPh from KY, 45 y/o/m has red dots on the chest, signifying an elevated estrogen level. He found that his estrogen is twice as high as the normal level in men. His PSA is also high. Both sides of his family have a history of prostate cancer.

A.J., a 66 y/o/f from NY, had numerous cherry angiomas on the abdomen, indicating a high chance of developing a female organ and/or liver problem. She didn't do any preventative measures as suggested. Later on, she complained of abdominal pain and her lab test results revealed that she had elevated levels of liver enzymes, ALT and AST, indicating a liver problem. A pelvic ultrasound also revealed she had 3 fibroids in the uterus. There was also fluid in the endometrial canal, which needs to be further examined for possible cancer. Abnormal fluid vaginal discharge is a common indication of either ovarian or uterine cancer and should not be ignored.

D. Smith, DC from CO, has a 33 y/o/m patient who was found to have a high chance of a testicle or prostate problem due to red dots on his tongue and abdominal cherry angiomas. He went to his MD had found a hydrocele in his left testicle, removed through hydrocelectomy.

Hormonal Cycle

Knowing the female hormonal cycle can be helpful in ruling out certain symptoms associated with it. At the start of the menstrual cycle (first day of bleeding), estrogen and progesterone levels are at their lowest. The unfertilized egg is discharged.

During the following days, hormone levels start to rise. It is said that cognition and mental clarity are high on days 12 to 14 of the cycle. Women are at their most efficient during this time. On the 14th day, estrogen and testosterone will peak. Women may also experience some abdominal pain, irritability, vaginal bleeding or spotting, or high libido.

The first two weeks of the menstrual cycle is the time that the breasts are most relaxed. This is the best time for a mammogram to reduce false positive results. If there is some nipple discharge during this time, see a physician.

On week 3, progesterone increases, the endometrium starts to thicken, and libido decreases. It is at this time that women are most prone to a genital infection.

On week 4, progesterone is at its highest point. This is the worst time for asthma sufferers. This is also the most emotional period during the cycle. Concentration is usually not good at this time. Women may also have acne or tender breasts. If the egg has not been fertilized, the uterine lining starts to shed and another menstrual cycle begins.

Hormone Replacement Therapy

Several decades ago, hormone replacement therapy (HRT) was almost always recommended to women who undergo menopause, whether they are suffering from menopausal symptoms or not. Both estrogen and progesterone were usually prescribed to women to reduce menopausal symptoms and to supposedly delay aging. However, numerous studies have shown that the risks of HRT outweigh the benefits.

Studies have shown that synthetic hormones can cause many health problems ranging from heart disease to cancer. In fact, the National Cancer Institute listed estradiol as a carcinogen in 2002. Supplementing with progesterone also poses a risk of developing estrogen-related problems because progesterone is indirectly converted to estrogen. In fact, California's Prop 65 requires that "listed" chemicals should bear a warning label stating that natural or synthetic products may be carcinogenic or are reproductive toxins. Progesterone has been a listed substance since 1988.

A study published in the *Family Physician* on September, 2003 reinforces the concept that HRT causes health risks. The study revealed that if women used estrogen and progesterone together, there is a 66% increase of breast cancer cases (about 15,000 more cases every year). If only progesterone is used, there is a 22% increase. Furthermore, just because postmenopausal women do not produce estrogen from their ovaries does not mean that they cannot develop ovarian cancer. Studies show that these women actually have a 6% chance of getting ovarian cysts and a 0.2% chance of getting ovarian cancer within the first 5 years after menopause.

In 2007, another study adds to the reasons why HRT should be avoided if possible. The Million Women Study involved 948,576 post-menopausal women in the United Kingdom. Half of the women took HRT for at least 5 years. The study followed these women for 5.3 years for incident ovarian cancer and 6.9 years for mortality.

What researchers found out is that current HRT users were 26% more likely to die of ovarian cancer than those who had never used HRT (the never-users). Overall, for every 1,000 HRT users, 1.6 women died compared with 1.3 non-users. Incidence of ovarian cancer also increased with duration of use, although the type of preparation, components and mode of administration did not significantly affect incidence rate.

It must be taken into account that HRT also increased the risk of breast and endometrial cancer. When taken together, the incidence of all three cancers in the study is 63% higher in current users of HRT than in never-users (Source: *The Lancet.* 2007 Apr 10).

One important note in the study is that when women stopped taking HRT, their risk returned to those of the never-users, suggesting that HRT does play a significant role in ovarian cancer.

Some health risks are associated with contraceptives. Birth control pills are a synthetic form of estrogen and progesterone, so they are advised against those who have or are at risk for breast and endometrial cancer, among other conditions. If birth control pills are absolutely necessary, then take it with Myomin to reduce the risk of hormone-related conditions from occurring.

As an alternative to synthetic hormones, N-HRT cream and Chi-F may be used instead by women experiencing menopausal symptoms.

For those who have taken or are taking hormone supplements, even bio-identical hormones, or birth control pills, adding Myomin will help in reducing the risk for estrogen-related cancers such as ovarian, breast and endometrial cancer. It works as an aromatase inhibitor to reduce estrogen, and it competes with estradiol at the estrogen receptors.

Case reports:

K. MacDonald, DC from MN, has a 38 y/o/f patient who has been suffering from PMS for 3 years. So she started using bio-identical progesterone cream for it. Ten months later, a breast lump was found which was then surgically removed. She stopped the cream, used Myomin instead and is doing much better.

N. Brant, DC from NY, has a 54 y/o postmenopausal patient who took bio-identical hormones (progesterone, estradiol, estriol, and testosterone) and developed an ovarian cyst and belly fat. Now she is taking Myomin.

R. Feldstein, ND from CA, has a 55 y/o/f patient with red dots on her tongue, indicating a risk for estrogen-related problems. She said she had hot flashes, for which she was taking bio-identical estrogen and progesterone. She was also overweight and did have a 2-cm breast lump.

V. Jefferson, DC from NY, has a 58 y/o/f patient on bio-identical estrogen and progesterone. She has a fibroid and heavy bleeding. She's already had a 6-pint blood transfusion but was frustrated because she was still bleeding. She was so thrilled because only less than a day after she took Angiostop, Myomin and Revivin, her bleeding stopped.

J.M. a 41 y/o/f from CA, experienced heavy bleeding during her period. It was later found she had endometrial dysplasia. Both her MD and holistic doctor suggested she use progesterone for it. Seven months later, she developed uterine cancer and had to have a hysterectomy. At that time she was losing weight, had red dots on her tongue, and had no lunulae except on her thumbs. After more than 3 months on Myomin, Angiostop, Revivin, Asparagus Extract and Reishi Spore Extract, her weight has maintained, the red dots on her tongue are fewer and 5 lunulae have reappeared. Now her condition is normal.

B. Sanborn, DC from MI, has a 16 y/o/m patient with gynecomastia. His estradiol and DHT levels were both high. He has tried 8 different supplements, including DIM and indole-3-carbinol (I3C); however, they had no effect on him. After taking Myomin and Prosta Chi for two months, his estradiol level reduced from 300 to 70 and his DHT level reduced from 1,100 to 250. His gynecomastia also improved.

D. Smith, DC from CO, has a 62 y/o/f patient who was given progesterone and estrogen after menopause in 2000. A year later, a 2 ½ cm meningioma (brain tumor) was found. Around 2003, she had vaginal bleeding and was given more progesterone. The bleeding stopped but she developed a breast tumor. In 2004, her meningioma had grown to 5 cm. (Meningiomas have progesterone receptors which could account for the growth in tumor size.) Then she stopped taking the hormones and used Myomin instead. After a year, the breast tumor dissipated, and the meningioma has reduced to 2 ½ cm in size.

B.M., a 61 y/o/f RN from NJ, had red dots on the tongue, hot flashes due to hormonal imbalance and uterine cyst. On the advice of her physician, she started using estrogen and progesterone, which only made her feel worse. After using Myomin and Revivin, the 4.5 cm^3 cyst in her uterus cleared.

S. Whitaker, ND from CA, has a female patient who used Clomid, a fertility drug, in 1999 and Depo-provera but did not conceive. Later, fibroids were found in her uterus. In 2006, she used Clomid again as well as in vitro fertilization and a progesterone injection, still with no results. At this point, her fibroids have gotten bigger so she stopped the drugs completely. Instead she used Myomin and

Chi-F, which reduced her fibroids enough that she could conceive. Now she has twin boys!

D.C., a 68 y/o/f from NY, was given bio-identical hormones (testosterone, estradiol and progesterone) for her osteoporosis in the lower spine and hips. After 15 months, a tumor was found in her left breast. Now she is on Angiostop, Myomin and Revivin.

A woman in her 60s from CA relates that she has a very high estradiol level. Three years ago, she had breast cancer and had a mastectomy. But her cancer recurred. When she was young, she had a DES injection to prevent miscarriage. Now she has 2 children: her son (in his 20s) has testicular cancer and her daughter (in her 30s) has cervical cancer.

N.K., a 23 y/o/f from FL, has been using Depo-provera, a synthetic hormone that prevents pregnancy, for 8 years. She stopped last year when she was diagnosed with cervical pre-cancer. Depo-provera users are warned by the FDA about increased risk of irreversible bone loss. In preliminary studies, there is evidence that Depo-provera increases the chance for cervical cancer 9 times.

M.L., a 40 y/o/f from CA, had a family history of cancer and has been on long-term use of contraceptives (since 15 years old). She used Depo-provera for 2 years, temporarily stopped and used it again for 4 more years. In June 2004, she had to stop taking it again because a lump was found in her breast. In Jan 2005, it was confirmed that she had stage 2 cancer even though her breast cancer marker, CA 27.29, is only 21.9. The lump in her breast was 2.8x1.7 cm^2 in size. Now she is on Angiostop and Myomin.

RESPIRATORY SYSTEM

Respiratory issues may be determined through the following early markers:

- **Nail clubbing** (Picture 1d). This is the main early indication of lung problems. Section I discusses in detail the different lung diseases associated with nail clubbing such as cystic fibrosis, pneumonitis, etc. (Table 1).

- **Geographic tongue** (Pictures 9g, 9h). A geographic tongue may also indicate colon problem (e.g., colitis) if accompanied by digestive symptoms.
- **Vertical ridges on an opaque nail** (Picture 3b)
- **White coating** on tongue (Picture 9e, 12e)
- **Tongue is inflamed only around the edges** with red dots on the tip or sides (Pictures 12e, 14c).

Case report:

A. Barber, DC from AK, has a 79 y/o/f patient who had clubbing on her opaque fingernails, suggesting a respiratory condition. At that time she had a bloody cough. Dr. Barber recommended Bamboo Extract, Cordyceps Extract, Chi Energy, Reishi Spore Extract, Asparagus Extract and Synergen. A few weeks later, the patient no longer had the bloody cough but still continued to stay on the program for a year.

AUTOIMMUNE CONDITIONS

Autoimmune conditions are often manifested in the nails. Nail pitting (Picture 4c, 4d) is one sign of autoimmune conditions such as psoriasis, eczema or alopecia. Nail clubbing can sometimes also signify autoimmune conditions. Half-and-half and Terry's nails (Pictures 1h, 2a) are related to autoimmune-induced kidney disease.

A geographic tongue, while primarily a sign of a lung condition, may also signify ulcerative colitis (Pictures 10a, 16b and 16g), especially when cracks on the tongue are also present.

Case report:

M.V., 46 y/o/m from CA, complained of low energy for about 7 years. He often needs to sleep until 11am. He also has frequent urination and often uses antifungals and antibiotics. During the analysis, the following were observed:

- He has a geographic tongue (white coating on center) with a lot of cracking (Picture 16b). These symptoms indicate Ulcerative Colitis risk. He also has a small growth on his upper frenula, which is a strong indicator of a colon problem. His clinical data show that his red blood cells, hematocrit and iron levels are all low.
- He also has a red tongue, which signifies inflammation or infection. Lab results show that he has blood and pathogen overgrowth in the stool (*E. coli*, *Klebsiella*, and α-*Hemolytic streptococcus*). Furthermore, he urinates frequently, sometimes 3 or 4 times at night (prostatitis). His urine stream also splits, signifying a urinary tract infection. These are why he often uses antibiotics.
- Cherry angiomas (three of them) were also seen on his abdomen, which means that he has elevated estrogen. High estrogen has been linked to autoimmune conditions, including colitis. He confirmed that his luteinizing hormone (LH) level is high. In males, LH promotes the production of testosterone, which in turn is converted to estrogen

CANCER

Early detection of diseases such as cancer is very important. What you may not know is that every person has cancer cells. They occur 6 to more than 10 times in a person's lifetime. However, they do not show up in tests because they have not reached the detectable amount yet. Fingernail and Tongue Analysis is a fairly accurate way of determining your risk for certain types of cancer.

An early predictive marker for cancer is the presence of lunulae on the thumbs only (found in 80% of cancer cases), especially if you have had them before and they disappear and you also feel cold. It is important to note that you should not rely on these markers alone.

A hard spot two inches to the left of the abdomen may also indicate cancer. About 80% of cancer patients have this symptom.

An interesting symptom that seems to be common in many cancer patients is the appearance of white spots shaped like rice on the abdomen. In a 1964 study, 800 cancer patients were observed. Among them, 589 had these white spots. In 1978, a study on 200 cancer patients found that 166 of them had three of these white spots on the abdomen. Then a 40-year study followed 2,800 cancer patients. The study found that, with treatment, survival rate is higher among patients with fewer white spots.

Case report:

P.G., 54 y/o/f from FL, had lumps in the navel area. In 2000, a biopsy found no evidence of cancer. However, about a year later, a 2nd biopsy confirmed that she had 2 tumors and was diagnosed with Follicular non Hodgkin's lymphoma B cell type CD20(+). She found out later that 2 more tumors have grown with standardized uptake values (SUV) of 12 and 13.7, respectively. A high SUV indicates a high tumor grade. A 3rd new tumor was found in the left kidney area with a SUV value of 5.9. In Aug 2005, she started on Angiostop, Revivin, Asparagus Extract and Reishi Spore Extract. After 7 months, her tumor SUVs reduced to 9.8 and 11, respectively, while the 3rd tumor increased to 7.5.

In the following sections, we will look into physical signs that are unique to certain types of cancer.

BRAIN CANCER/ NASOPHARYNGEAL CANCER

Besides tinnitus and other conditions, ear ringing may also be due to a brain tumor (especially if it is only in one ear) or nasopharyngeal cancer. Headaches, dizziness and blurred vision may be additional symptoms of brain cancer. Also, many types of cancer metastasize to the brain.

For nasopharyngeal cancer, smoking is a big risk factor. Also those who have had the Epstein-Barr virus may be prone to nasopharyngeal cancer. A nosebleed can sometimes be an early sign of nasopharyngeal cancer as well as a lump in the neck.

Case reports:

Y. Dikansky, DDS from NY, has a 38 y/o/f patient who had headaches and dizziness. She thought her headaches were migraines. She later found out that she had a brain tumor.

A 60-year-old male from CA is a smoker. He also had a history of Epstein-Barr virus infection. One day he had a nosebleed after blowing his nose. He later found that he has nasopharyngeal cancer.

G. Dillague, MD from CA, has a 47 y/o/f patient with a brain tumor (35 mm diameter). She did not experience any progress after undergoing chemotherapy and suffered from severe weakness and cognitive impairment. She had given up on chemotherapy when she started taking Angiostop, Reishi Spore, Asparagus Extract and Revivin. After 3 months, the tumor reduced to 7 mm in diameter. Her energy also tremendously increased. Whereas she could hardly stand up and walk before, now she could attend church with a walker. Her mental processes have also improved so much.

BREAST CANCER

The presence of red dots on the tongue (Picture 12g) is the most important indicator of elevated estrogen, and therefore, the risk for estrogen-dominant conditions such as breast cancer. Large cherry angiomas (over 10 to 15) on the chest (Pictures 12h, 13a) also strongly indicate breast cancer (or liver disease) risk.

A study published in the *International Journal of Surgery* links probing surgery to increased breast cancer recurrence. The study involved 1,173 breast cancer patients treated with surgery from 1964 to 1980. Of these, 520 women relapsed. The researchers contend that removing the tumor triggers the release of certain growth factors involved in the healing process. These growth factors, in turn, trigger dormant cancer cells in other parts of the body to undergo angiogenesis (new blood vessel formation). This process causes the women to relapse early (Source: *Intl Journal of Surgery*. 12 Sept 2005).

Further investigation is warranted to definitely establish the link between cancer surgery and recurrence. However, this particular study is not isolated. In a 2002 article published in the journal *Lancet*, colon cancer patients who underwent traditional surgery had a significantly higher recurrence rate than those who underwent laparoscopy, a minimally invasive procedure in which only a small incision is used (*Lancet*. 2002 Jun 29;359(9325):2224-9). This study reinforces the idea that a major procedure such as surgery somehow triggers angiogenesis, causing cancer recurrence.

The risk of surgery-induced angiogenesis does not imply that women should forego surgery altogether. Rather, researchers suggest that the addition of an anti-angiogenic therapy (such as Angiostop) before and after surgery may be more beneficial to breast cancer patients and can minimize recurrence of the disease.

Case reports:

J. Hamsa, MD from CT, reports on a 56 y/o/f patient who was found to be at risk for breast cancer because of red dots on her tongue. She did not agree because she's a vegetarian, she exercises and she feels healthy. Then 3 months later a biopsy revealed she had ductal carcinoma in situ in the breast.

M. B. Obuseh, MD from TX, reports on a 50 y/o/f patient found to have a high chance of breast cancer (red dots on the tongue, lunulae only on thumbs, teeth marks). The patient revealed that she already had a lumpectomy and radiation 2 months before for breast cancer. She felt very weak and couldn't even walk. Then she took Angiostop, Revivin, Asparagus Extract, Reishi Spore Extract and Vein Lite. After two months, her energy returned. Seven months later the lunulae appeared on two fingernails on each hand. Teeth marks reduced and the red dots on the tongue had disappeared.

Y. Dikansky, DDS from NY, reports on a 49 y/o/f patient: "I used fingernail and tongue diagnosis methods on her and warned her that she is at risk of developing breast cancer. I suggested that she improve her health but she did not think the situation was serious.

A year and a half later she has breast cancer, confirmed by a biopsy."

R. Welch, DC from CA, has a female patient with ovarian cysts. She had red dots on her tongue and no lunulae. With these symptoms and the ovarian cysts, her breast cancer chance was very high. At that time she had no lumps in her breasts. Shortly thereafter, she went to Mexico for some tests but no sign of cancer was found. After a year and a half had passed, she was told again that her breast cancer chance was really high. Five months later, tests showed that she had stage 2 breast cancer and had to have a mastectomy on one breast.

A.O., a 31 y/o/f from CA, had missing lunulae and red dots on the tongue, indicating a risk for cancer in the reproductive organs. Later, she found out that she had Stage 1 ductal carcinoma in situ.

F. Akbarpour, MD from CA, has a 70 y/o/f patient diagnosed with breast cancer in 2003. She took Herceptin and underwent chemo. But despite that, the cancer still metastasized to the liver, lung and bones. Then she added Angiostop and Myomin. Two years later, only a small percentage of the bone cancer remained.

M. Myerowitz, DC from ME, has a 48 y/o/f patient with breast cancer that spread to her brain. After 2 years on Angiostop, Myomin, Revivin, Asparagus Extract and Reishi Spore Extract, the cancer has resolved completely.

B. G., a 71 y/o/f from PA, has found to have an increased risk for breast cancer in 2006 due to the presence of red dots on her tongue. She also has a family history of breast cancer. She had a lump on the left side of her breast at that time, which her doctor said was some form of calcification. Now she has been diagnosed with breast cancer.

Hormones and Breast Cancer

The use of hormones (synthetic and even bio-identical) can increase the risk of developing breast cancer and related diseases. A new study published in the February 16, 2009 issue of *Lancet Oncology* reports that an HRT drug called Livial (not available in the US) recommended for menopausal symptoms as well as osteoporosis increases the risk of breast cancer recurrence by as much as 40%. Among those who had a recurrence, 70% were distant metastases, which are usually fatal. These results were not surprising at all. We already know from the 2002 Women's Health Initiative study that synthetic hormones increase the risk for breast cancer, heart disease, stroke and blood clots.

The following cases further illustrate the risk involved with HRT, even bio-identical hormones. It is therefore beneficial to take Myomin with HRT in order to avoid hormone-related side effects.

K. M., DC from MN, had PMS and used bio-identical progesterone cream for it. Ten months later, a breast lump was found which was then surgically removed. She stopped using the cream, used Myomin instead and is doing much better.

R. Shemesh, MD from FL, has a 54 y/o/f patient who had very low levels of estrogen, progesterone, and testosterone 4 years ago (saliva test). At that time, she was given a bio-identical cream by her gynecologist. A year later, she developed ovarian cancer. Her Ca.125 was 499. After undergoing surgery and chemo, she is now on Myomin.

R. F, a 55-year-old ND from CA, had red dots on her tongue, indicating a risk for estrogen-related problems. She said she had hot flashes, for which she was taking bio-identical estrogen and progesterone. She was also overweight and had a 2 cm breast lump. It was suggested that she stop the bio-identical hormones and instead use Myomin, Slender All and Pro-Metabolic. After a year, she has lost 43 lbs (down 2 sizes) and no hot flashes anymore. Her breast lump reduced to less than 0.5 cm in diameter.

D.C., a 68-year-old female from NY, was given bio-identical hormones (testosterone, estradiol and progesterone) for her osteoporosis in the lower spine and hips. After 15 months, a tumor was found in her left breast. Now, she is on Angiostop, Myomin and Revivin.

CERVICAL CANCER

One of the first signs of cervical cancer is vaginal bleeding after intercourse. Other signs include irregular bleeding and an increase in white discharge (e.g., pure fluid becomes milky with a foul smell).

One of the main risk factors of cervical cancer is HPV (human papillomavirus) infection. Among sexually active young women, HPV infection is prevalent in about 80% of them.

If you have any of the above enumerated signs, you must have yourself checked for cervical cancer.

Case reports:

M.T., a 40 y/o/f from FL, was told years ago that she was at risk for hormone-related cancer (no moons, red dots on tongue). When she was 21 years old, she had uterine and cervical cancer. At 24 years old, she had colon cancer.

J. Wise, ND from OK, has a 48 y/o/f patient with cervical cancer cells. She used Myomin and Chi-F (and a high dose of folic acid) for 3 months and now her system is almost clear.

A woman in her 60s from CA relates that she has a very high estradiol level. Three years ago, she had breast cancer and had a mastectomy. But her cancer recurred. When she was young, she had a DES (diethylstilbestrol) injection to prevent miscarriage. Now she has 2 children: her son (in his 20s) has testicular cancer and her daughter (in her 30s) has cervical cancer.

R. St. Laurent, RPh from RI, has a 54 y/o/f patient who had a vaginal tumor the size of a marble. She had chemotherapy but to no avail. After 7 months on Angiostop, Revivin, Reishi Spore and Myomin, the tumor was completely eliminated.

Colorectal Cancer

It is important to look for early signs of the disease, such as the following:

- **Cyst on the frenula**. The frenula is the thin tissue connecting the upper gum to the upper lip. A growth or lump on the frenula signals a colon problem (Pictures 6b, 6c, 6d).
- **Only thumbs have lunulae.** Lunulae are white half moons on the fingers. If you've had them before and then they disappear, this signals a cancer risk. People who have this sign may also feel cold.
- **Baby hair on the cheeks**. This is normal in infants and typically fades as they grow older. However, if adults suddenly grow soft, light-colored hair on their cheeks like baby hair (Pictures 14h, 16c), this may signal colorectal (or lung cancer also). This means that their hair follicles have returned to the fetal/infant stage and may be a sign of malignant cancer (lung or colorectal cancer) risk in an internal organ. This cancer produces hormones that stimulate the growth of hair, starting on the cheek and spreading to the ear and forehead. In its early stage, the cancer may not be detectable by tests for a few months to a few years.
- **Chronic colitis**. The chance for colon cancer increases if you have been suffering from ulcerative colitis for many years without any healing.
- **Blood in stool**. Dark lines on the nails are early signs of bleeding. When blood does show in the stool, this indicates that the cancer has progressed to stage 3 already. The shape of the stool may also change, sometimes with bleeding.
- **Gallbladder removal**. Colon cancer risk also increases within 10 years after your gallbladder has been removed. This is because bile does not have any other outlet. Secondary bile

salts are carcinogens, so if they accumulate in the colon, the risk for colon cancer increases. In this case, avoid high fat diets and deep fried foods.

Colon polyps also increase the chance for colon cancer. There are three main factors contributing to the risk for colon polyps: bowel movement problem, excess bile from the liver and excess estrogen. These factors were discussed in the colon section within this chapter.

Larger polyps have a greater chance of being cancerous. Having multiple polyps also increases the risk of colon cancer.

A colonoscopy is typically used to detect colon polyps; however, there are many missed diagnoses using this test. A 1-cm polyp takes about 5 years to grow, so a colonoscopy should be able to detect a polyp larger than 1-cm. But, to reiterate, the test failed to detect a 4.1 cm tumor in a 39-year-old mail. In another patient, a colonoscopy did not detect all colon polyps on the first test. In fact, it missed a 1.5 cm polyp. It is true that no diagnostic tool is 100% guaranteed. Therefore, it is important to be aware of other signs, and not just rely on a colonoscopy, to determine the risk or presence of colorectal cancer.

Case reports:

K.L., 53 y/o/f from AZ, was diagnosed with thyroid cancer. Four months later, she came for an analysis. She had a cyst on the frenula and angiomas on her abdomen, indicating that her chance for colon cancer is high. She revealed that she does have a family history of cancer (her mother died of breast cancer that metastasized to the liver). She is also too thin for her height. Furthermore, she has had hair on her cheeks for about 5 years (Picture 16c), a sign usually indicating either colon or lung cancer. Twenty days after her analysis, she reported that she had colon bleeding. The abdominal cherry angiomas that she has indicate high estrogen (she does have a lump in the breast), which can also increase the risk of thyroid, breast and colon cancer. She is now taking Angiostop, Revivin, Myomin, Asparagus Extract and Reishi Spore Extract.

J. Fowler from FL has a 54 y/o/f client with a geographic tongue (Picture 16g) and a cyst on the frenula, both of which signal a colon problem, specifically colitis. She revealed that it has progressed to colon cancer already. She also has baby hair on her cheeks, signifying either colorectal or lung cancer. She said that she has lung cancer as well.

P. Gonzalez, ND from TX, reports in 2002, "I warned my patient 6 years ago that he may get colon cancer by using the fingernail and tongue method. He did not follow any of my prevention suggestions and he has recently died from colon cancer."

J. Kerin, DC from CO, writes, "In November 1998 I began to experience nausea and pain in my intestines. I had met Dr. Chi a couple of years earlier and was impressed with his accuracy in diagnosing people without even knowing their histories. Over the next two months I became more ill. I had an appointment with Dr. Chi, who told me I had a major problem with my intestine, and I should take care of it as if I had colon cancer. Two months later my physician confirmed that I had colon cancer. After 9 months following Dr. Chi's advice my colon was much better." She is now doing well.

K. Wirtz, DDS from AZ, has a female patient who has had consultations with me. She shared the following story: "I am writing to share with you 'my story,' in hope that this will inspire others.

In December 2006, we met once again to discuss the RA therapy. This time you were very emphatic, recommending I immediately order a colonoscopy, because you could see cancer in my body.

Today, I write to you, just one week out of surgery. They removed a portion of my colon and intestine, along with a high grade glandular dysplasia polyp, at the junction of my colon and cecum. My surgeon shared with me that the results of the surgical biopsy revealed the cancer cells were forming. If I had waited on your advice, just three months, I could be in a very different place in my life right now."

P. Peterson DC from FL, was found to have a very high chance of getting colon cancer. He checked and found he did have colon cancer. So a month later he had surgery to remove the cancer. Then he took Angiostop, Revivin, etc., and had good results.

S. Carter, PhD from CA, Assistant Director of Valley Cancer Institute, brought two people to see me on September 1, 2002. I found that the 14-year-old female had a high chance of getting a colon problem. It turns out that the girl was later treated for colon cancer at UCLA hospital.

D.M., a 50 y/o/m from MN, was found to have a high chance of developing colon cancer (missing lunulae, black line on fingernail, cherry angiomas in abdominal area). Three months later, he found that he had colorectal cancer (8cm size), which was also affecting his prostate.

J.S., a 38 y/o/m from CA, relates that he had no lunulae at all and had a large frenula cyst, both indicating a chance for a colon condition. After a year on the herbs, he grew lunulae on both thumbs. In April 2005, his father is diagnosed with stage 4 colon cancer that has metastasized to his lungs. Statistics indicate that the chance of developing cancer is genetically linked. In particular, the risk increases to 8 times higher if a first- or second-degree relative has cancer. Based on this and the symptoms that J.S. has, he is at risk for developing colon cancer. Although his progress is a bit slower than he wanted, he is glad that he has started on the herbs now, before his condition becomes worse as his father's had.

L. Frank, LCSW from NY, has a 50 y/o/m patient who had no lunulae. She told him his cancer risk is very high. A year later, he said he has developed colon cancer (4 inches of his colon were surgically removed). Sure enough, there is a big cyst on his frenula.

M. M., DC from FL, reports that in 1999 his friend had all the physical markers indicating colon cancer risk. However, he just disregarded it. Then 5 years later, he found that he did indeed have colon cancer and, by then, it had metastasized to his kidneys and liver. Sadly, he passed away that same year.

K.M., DC from MN, has a 51 y/o/m patient who had a lump on the frenula area. He also did not have any lunulae. Both of these signify a chance of getting colon problems. A biopsy later on revealed that he had Stage 2 colorectal cancer.

ENDOMETRIAL/UTERINE CANCER

Endometrial cancer is more prevalent among Western women. It is ranked as 4th among the different cancers. It usually occurs among menopausal or postmenopausal women. Only 5% to 8% of the cases occur in women younger than 40 years old. After 45 years old, a woman's risk for endometrial cancer increases, with the peak at 55 to 69 years old. The older you develop endometrial cancer, the harder it is to treat.

When vaginal bleeding occurs in postmenopausal women, 5% to 10% of the cases are endometrial cancer.

Risk for both endometrial and uterine cancer is high for women who are obese, consumes a red meat, high fat diet, has early menstruation or late menopause or are never pregnant. Hormone replacement therapy users also have a high chance of developing not just endometrial and uterine cancer but breast and ovarian cancer as well. The use of the prescription drug, Tamoxifen, has also been linked to increased endometrial cancer risk.

Unlike ovarian cancer which is usually asymptomatic, endometrial cancer can be detected early. Vaginal bleeding or discharge is an early sign of the disease. If the disease is still inside the uterus, then surgery can still correct the problem. However, if the disease has already spread through the uterine lining, the disease is most likely in stage 3 already.

The following guidelines can be used with vaginal bleeding as a diagnostic tool.

- If a woman is postmenopausal for over a year already with no bleeding, then bleeding suddenly occurs, chances are high that she has endometrial cancer.
- During menopause, if there is heavy or excessive bleeding, if the period occurs two times within one month, or if the bleeding lasts for more than a month, then check for endometrial cancer.
- In younger women, having irregular periods increases the risk for endometrial cancer later on in life.

In one case, a 56-year-old woman has already been postmenopausal for 4 years and suddenly had vaginal bleeding. A biopsy of her endometrium was recommended. They discovered that she has endometrial dysplasia, which later developed into endometrial cancer.

ESOPHAGEAL/THROAT CANCER

One sign that can indicate the presence of or risk for esophageal cancer is when you feel like food is stuck in the throat or it goes down very slowly. A growth in the esophagus may be causing the blockage in this case.

There are several factors that can increase risk of esophageal/throat cancer. Consumption of canned, smoked or preserved food can increase the risk. Preserved food contains nitrates which are harmful to the esophagus. Garlic helps stop the action of action of these nitrates.

GERD (gastroesophageal reflux disease) or acid reflux also increases the risk. Chronic acid reflux can eventually harm the lining of the esophagus. This also leads to Barrett's esophagus, a complication of GERD and another risk factor of esophageal cancer. A dark brown or yellow coating on the tongue as well as teeth marks (all pointing to a digestive problem) may indicate esophageal cancer risk (Picture 13g).

Case reports:

J. Florendo, DC from NV, has a male patient in his 40s with Barrett's disease. From March to May, 2007, two endoscopies found a tumor in his throat. He then started taking Angiostop. After 6 months, his physician said he has no tumor anymore.

R.S., 66 y/o/m from CA, couldn't swallow and had pain in his esophagus six months ago. He also had fainting spells. Then he started on Angiostop, Revivin, Digestron and Liver Chi. After 3 months, he had no difficulty swallowing at all. After 6 months, he had no more pain. This shows that the esophageal pain and his trouble swallowing were due to an abnormal growth in his esophagus.

K.S., a 69 y/o/f from NY, had a 3-cm benign growth in the throat. After using Angiostop, Asparagus Extract, etc., for 6 months, the growth is almost gone. She also was in a lot of generalized pain, like due to the many drugs she was taking before. After using Bathdetox 10 times, all the pain was eliminated.

KIDNEY OR BLADDER CANCER

Urinary bleeding can be associated with kidney cancer when the cancer presses on the blood vessel. If there is blood in the urine (dark or pink-colored urine) but there is no pain in the kidney area, this may be a sign of kidney cancer and not just an infection or kidney stone. However, before you jump to any conclusion, it is important to know the source of the bleeding.

The first time you urinate in the morning, measure the urine. If the first cup (~200-300 ml) has blood, this means the problem is in the urethra. If the second cup has blood, the problem is most likely in the bladder. If the third cup has blood, then the problem is with the kidneys.

As discussed in Section III, blood in the urine may also be a sign of kidney, bladder or urinary tract infection. Postmenopausal women are usually prone to *E. coli* infections due to severe dryness in the genital area. Younger women may be prone to urinary tract infections or sexually transmitted infections. However, if none of these cases apply, blood in the urine along with the absence of pain in the kidney area may be an early signal for kidney or bladder cancer.

Case reports:

R. Abraham, MD from CA, has a 60 y/o/m patient with kidney cancer. After he took Sutent, he still had a 2-cm tumor. Then he added Angiostop and Revivin. After 6 months, his 2-cm tumor reduced to 1 cm. A year later, the tumor cleared.

E.C., 63 y/o/m from CA, found blood in his urine but he had no pain about 2 years ago. He also had a very puffy face. He was already warned of his risk for kidney cancer. He had surgery to remove one of his kidneys and no other treatment. Then in May 2009, he fainted while walking up a flight of stairs. He found that his cancer has metastasized to the brain and lungs.

L. Lu, LAc from CA, has a 93 y/o/m patient with cancer in both kidneys (he had dark-colored urine with no pain). After 3 courses of chemo, he still had kidney bleeding. Then he added Angiostop and Revivin. A week later, the bleeding stopped. After 4 months, he is still doing very well.

LIVER AND GALLBLADDER CANCER

A history of Hepatitis B and C as well as fatty liver and liver cirrhosis increases the risk for liver cancer. Furthermore, it would be wise to watch out for these signs:

- Cherry angiomas on the abdomen, especially if there are 10 or more large ones (Picture 13c)
- Skin itching
- Spider veins on the abdomen (Picture 13c)
- Jaundice (Picture 5b)
- Thick and wide tongue (Picture 10g)
- More than 3 or 4 dark, branching veins under the tongue, this may be a sign of liver cancer already (Picture 7c)
- A lump, thickening or wrinkle on the auricle or outer ear may be a sign of stomach or liver cancer (Pictures 15g, 15h).

Liver cancer is usually associated with pain in the upper right and left quadrant of the abdomen.

Aflatoxin, a potent carcinogen found in peanut fungus, is associated with stomach and liver cancer risk. Also, a stone in the main liver bile duct increases the risk for liver cancer. If a liver tumor is located in this duct, it becomes very difficult to treat.

Gallbladder cancer is more uncommon and is also difficult to diagnose. The location of the gallbladder allows the cancer to grow undetected for a time. It also makes a gallbladder biopsy difficult and dangerous. Gallbladder cancer is mostly asymptomatic; however, if there is pain in the upper right quadrant of the abdomen that radiates to the back, then this is already an early sign of a gallbladder issue. If the gallbladder wall is thick and rough, gallbladder cancer risk is also high. Furthermore, studies show that about half of the ultrasound tests that reveal gallbladder polyps larger than 1 cm are already cancerous.

Case reports:

C.T. relates that his wife had yellow sclera (sign of jaundice), a wide tongue, skin itching and a deep crack on the tongue. All these point to a risk for liver cancer. Two months later, she found that she had stomach cancer, which has metastasized to the liver. A month later, she passed away.

R.F., 60 y/o/m, has many red dots on his abdomen and a sharp pain in the right abdominal area. He thought it was due to kidney stones but found that it was liver cancer (liver mass was 1 cm^3).

A.F., a 45 y/o/f from HI, has cholangiocarcinoma, or cancer of the bile duct. Her face had a dark complexion, she couldn't eat and she was in pain. After trying Angiostop and Liver Chi for only 2 days, the pain completely alleviated and she now can eat.

T.C., a 48 y/o/m from CA, had constant stomach pain for years, for which he took morphine. The pain was thought to be due to gallbladder disease, so his gallbladder was removed. But the doctors found nothing. Later, he found out that he had liver bile duct cancer (he also had a history of Hepatitis B). At that point was skinny, had no appetite, weak, jaundiced and had constant abdominal pain that radiates to the back.

J. Fowler from FL reports that she has a male client who has many cherry angiomas on his abdomen, showing a risk for either a prostate or liver problem. Now he has been diagnosed with liver cancer.

LUNG CANCER

Clubbing on opaque nails (Picture 1d) and with a chronic dry cough may be signs of a lung cancer risk. This risk is heightened especially if the patient has a history of smoking. Table 1 in Section I lists various types of lung cancer and the corresponding incidence of bilateral nail clubbing.

Soft baby hair on the cheeks (Pictures 14h, 16c) on adults is also another sign of lung cancer risk (as well as colorectal cancer risk).

Chest pain, coughing with blood, and unexplained weight loss are also important signs of lung cancer. However, when these symptoms appear, it means that the disease has progressed to a later stage. Please note that chest pain associated with lung cancer is usually located in the same area and occurs in smokers who are 40 years or older.

Environmental factors can definitely affect lung function. Exposure to asbestos, arsenic, radon, coal electromagnetic radiation and dust from mills increases the risk for lung cancer. Exhaust from automobiles and factories also contains harmful chemicals, again increasing lung cancer risk. Certain occupations also have higher lung cancer risk than others. For example, jobs that expose you to smoke (e.g., chef, baker, mechanic, etc.) increases your risk for lung cancer. Smoke from cooking oil especially is harmful especially with repeated and long-term exposure. Other risk factors include a history of chronic bronchitis, tuberculosis, and

Case reports:

R. Krary, DC from IL, said that two years ago her assistant was analyzed through F&T analysis and found to have a chance of getting lung cancer. Later on, an MRI revealed she did have lung cancer and subsequently had surgery to remove one of her lungs.

A 70 y/o/f client of Abby's Health & Nutrition in FL was very pale, had nail clubbing, had no lunulae, and had an ear crease, all indicating a high chance of heart or lung problem. One month ago she said she had chest pain and had to go to the hospital, thinking she had a heart problem. She had learned that she was scheduled soon for a lung cancer operation.

B. W., 54 y/o/m from NY, was analyzed and found to be at high risk for lung cancer (nail clubbing, opaque nails, and no lunulae). A CT scan found the lung cancer has metastasized to the brain. He's now on the herbs.

A.E., a 52 y/o/m from CA, is a heavy smoker. In 2006, I warned him that he might develop lung cancer. All his nails were very opaque with slight clubbing. His tongue had dry and yellowish-white coating. In late 2008, he was indeed diagnosed with lung cancer. He asked why I didn't tell him that he will *definitely* have lung cancer. Now he wants me to save his life. He had a tumor in the upper left lobe of his lung that was about 7cm in size. The doctors couldn't operate immediately because of the size. After taking Angiostop, Revivin, Reishi Spore Extract and Asparagus Extract as well as undergoing chemotherapy and radiation for 3 months, his tumor reduced to less than 1cm. It was surgically removed but he still continued with his therapy. He is doing well.

V. Rakitin, ND from IL, has a 50 y/o/m patient with small cell lung carcinoma that has metastasized: he had a 6-cm^3 tumor in his lung, a 6-cm^3 tumor in his pancreas and a 2-cm^3 tumor in his kidneys. After 2 courses of chemotherapy, his urine turned dark brown. This was attributed to his high bilirubin count of 14. After 2 weeks on the Chi program, his bilirubin reduced to 4 and his urine was lighter in color. Two months later, both tumors in the pancreas and kidneys were gone and his lung tumor reduced by 60%. His lung tumor reduced by 90% a month later.

K.O., 65 y/o/m from HI, was diagnosed with metastatic lung cancer earlier this year. There are 2 large lesions in his lungs, 7 tumors in his brain and tumors in his lymph nodes. Chemo for 3 months was not much help. Around May 2007, he started Angiostop, Reishi Spore, Asparagus and Revivin. Before the end of summer, he stopped the chemo and took only the herbs. After 5 months, the brain tumors are fewer (now only 2 tumors), the lung lesions have reduced in size, and all tumors in the lymph nodes have cleared.

LYMPHOMA/LEUKEMIA

- **Triangular or shell-shaped nails** (Picture 1b). Having triangular or shell-shaped nails may indicate a bone marrow or blood disease, particularly leukemia and lymphoma. Whenever you have these nails, check your hemoglobin, platelets, white blood cells and red blood cells. In some cases, nail clubbing is also associated with these blood diseases.
- **Nose bleeds.** Nose bleeds may also be a sign of lymphoma or leukemia.

- **Lymph nodes.** The presence of lymph nodes throughout the body is also a very good indication of lymphoma risk. It is important to distinguish lymph nodes that indicate infection and lymph nodes that indicate cancer. If there is no infection in the body and there are lymph nodes, then check for cancer. If the nodes are soft, it is not likely cancer. Cancer lymph nodes are very hard (almost like stone) with an irregular surface. There is no pain when pressure is applied on the nodes.

Location and the quantity of the lymph nodes can help determine which part of the body is most likely affected. Lymph nodes may be found in the neck area or under the jaw, underarm, collarbone or groin.

Table 10. Location of Lymph Nodes Associated with Certain Types of Cancer	
Location of lymph nodes	**Possible cancer(s)**
Groin	Uterine, Testicular or Rectal cancer
Neck	Nasopharyngeal cancer
Left collarbone	Liver, Stomach or Colon cancer
Right collarbone	Pleural (lungs, esophagus) cancer
Throughout the body	Lymphoma

Case reports:

R.P., a 46 y/o/m from CA, has triangular nails. He spent 3 months and about $24,000 on tests to find out that he has Non-Hodgkin's lymphoma. With the fingernail analysis, it only took minutes to determine that he has a blood disease.

A 30 y/o/f chiropractor from FL had nail clubbing, signaling a lung problem or lymphoma/leukemia risk. She said that she is a leukemia patient already.

M.D., a 35 y/o/m DC from UT, was found to be at risk for lymphoma. He said that when he was 4 years old, he had lymphosarcoma.

A.S., a 33 y/o/f from NY, has clubbing nails. She said that she had lymphoma in the spleen 2 years ago. (Her father also had lymphoma 2-3 years ago.) She also had red dots on the tongue, showing estrogen-related problems. She revealed that she just found out she has breast cancer.

P.G., 54 y/o/f from FL, had lumps in the navel area. In 2000, a biopsy found no evidence of cancer. However, about a year later, a 2nd biopsy confirmed that she had cancer (2 tumors) and diagnosed with diagnosed with Follicular non Hodgkin's lymphoma B cell type CD20(+).

V. Rakitin, ND from IL, has a 45 y/o/f patient with non-Hodgkin's lymphoma. She had tumors located in the armpit, neck and under the rib. She started on Angiostop, Revivin, Asparagus Extract and Reishi Spore Extract. On the 2nd week, she started 3 courses of chemotherapy. After 6 weeks, her tumors cleared. Her doctor says that normally it takes 6 months, not 6 weeks, to reduce the size of the tumors with chemo. Evidently, chemotherapy and the herbs have a synergistic effect, significantly shortening the treatment period.

OVARIAN CANCER

Ovarian cancer is the 5th leading cause of cancer deaths in women in the United States. In 2008, there were approximately 21,650 new diagnosed cases, with 15,520 deaths resulting from the disease (Source: National Cancer Institute). Usually in those diagnosed through ultrasound and CA-125 screening, 75% of the cases have already progressed to stage 4 and have metastasized, causing increased mortality (*Family Practice News*, January 15, 2005). This is primarily because the early stages of the disease are often asymptomatic. There are, however, risk factors that can help determine a woman's chances of developing the disease.

Family history is the strongest risk factor. If a first- or second-degree relative has ovarian cancer, the risk increases to 3.1 times (5%-7% lifetime risk). If two or three relatives have it, the risk increases to 4.6 times. The BRCA1 gene is also a determining risk factor. Carriers of the gene have up to a 60% chance of developing ovarian cancer by age 70. BRCA2 gene carriers, on the other hand, not only are at risk for ovarian cancer but for other types of cancer as well.

A link between the risk of ovarian cancer and exposure to milk products has also been discovered.

Screening for the CA-125 cancer marker helps determine risk since it signifies ovarian tumor activity. The sensitivity of an abnormal CA-125 is approximately 80%. When the CA-125 level is elevated, a transvaginal ultrasound is usually recommended.

Ultrasound screening is said to detect about 88% of ovarian tumors; however, due to false-positive results the actual accuracy may be lower. According to the US Preventive Services Task Force, the disadvantages of screening still outweigh the benefits.

As mentioned earlier, ultrasound and CA-125 screening may be helpful in some cases. But more often than not, when women finally opt to use these methods, the ovarian cancer has worsened and has already spread.

The best way to detect ovarian cancer in its early stages is to take into account the risk factors as well as some early signs. A study published in the *Journal of the American Medical Association* (2004; 291:2705-2712) revealed several commonly reported symptoms associated with ovarian cancer:

Table 11. Symptoms related with Ovarian Cancer	
Symptom	**Frequency of occurrence in ovarian cancer cases**
Low back pain	45%
Fatigue	34%
Bloating	27%
Constipation	24%
Abdominal pain	22%
Urinary symptoms	16%

Among the 1,709 participants of the 6-month study, 72% had a median of two recurring symptoms. Results from another group of subjects showed similar results. This group consisted of 44 malignant and 84 benign ovarian cancer cases. Those with malignant ovarian cancer experienced symptoms such as bloating, increased abdominal size and urinary urgency 20-30 times per month with higher severity than those with benign conditions.

Additionally, other physical signs can also help determine ovarian cancer. If there are red dots on the tongue and/or cherry angiomas on the abdominal area with one or more of the above symptoms occurring every month or on a regular basis, ovarian cancer screening should be performed promptly.

Case reports:

J.P., DC from MT, has a 34 y/o/f patient who was found to be at risk for estrogen-related conditions (red dots on tongue and abdominal cherry angiomas). She said that she did have an ovarian cyst. But she didn't do anything about it. A year later, she tearfully revealed that her CA.125 is 16 (normal is < 3), indicating the presence of ovarian cancer.

S.L., a 57 y/o/f from IL, had sudden vaginal bleeding, which indicates ovarian cancer risk when it occurs in postmenopausal women. Almost a month later, she was indeed diagnosed with ovarian cancer.

J. Iannetta, DC from ME, has a 57 y/o postmenopausal patient who suddenly had vaginal bleeding and was suspected to have ovarian/uterine cancer. She took Myomin and Angiostop right away. After 14 months, her CA.125 reduced to 4.6 *U*/ml. Furthermore, her estradiol level reduced dramatically from 413 to 43 pg/ml.

R. Shemesh, MD from FL, has a 54 y/o/f who had very low levels of estrogen, progesterone, and testosterone (through a saliva test). At that time, she was given a bio-identical hormone cream by her gynecologist. A year later, she developed ovarian cancer. Her Ca.125 was 499. After undergoing surgery and chemo, she is now on Myomin.

PROSTATE CANCER

Red dots on the tongue and abdominal cherry angiomas in men signify prostate cancer risk. In many cases, these signs are accompanied by one or more of these prostate cancer symptoms presented in the August, 2003, issue of *US Pharmacist*:

- Frequent urination, which continues during the night
- Problems starting or holding back the urine stream
- Incomplete emptying of the bladder
- Pain or burning during urination
- Poor or interrupted flow of urine
- Blood in the urine or semen
- Difficulty obtaining an erection
- Pain during ejaculation
- Pain in the lower back, hip or upper thigh.

Prostate Specific Antigen

The prostate specific antigen (PSA) level has been widely used as a standard clinical marker for prostate cancer. In the December 2003, issue of *Patient Care*, it was proposed that the PSA threshold for prostate cancer should be lowered to 2.5 mg/dL instead of 4.0 mg/dL. This, coupled with a digital rectal exam (DRE), can help promote the early detection of prostate cancer incidence and prevent the need for a biopsy. The *New England Journal of Medicine* (July 2003; 349:335-42) also reports various studies supporting the need to lower the PSA threshold to 2.5 ng/mL for early detection of prostate cancer and biopsy screening. However, there are definite risks as well as missed occurrences associated with biopsy screening. (*NEJM* May 2004; 350(22): 2239-46).

There is a risk of spreading the cancer when a biopsy is performed. Furthermore, biopsies have been found to miss 82% of prostate cancer occurrence in men younger than 60 years old and whose

PSA levels are greater than 2.6. In those over 60 years old who have PSA over 2.6, 65% of cases are not detected through biopsy. This high percentage of missed occurrences can be attributed to the location of the cancer/tumor. A tumor is very difficult to find through a biopsy when it is located in the back of the prostate. In addition to this, a biopsy procedure is performed without anesthesia and can be very painful (*Patient Care*, Dec 2003). To avoid the physical discomfort and missed detection of biopsies, it is necessary not only to clinically monitor PSA levels, but also to watch out for early symptoms of prostate disease as well as physical signs (red dots on tongue, cherry angiomas on abdomen) indicating high estrogen level (Pictures 12g, 12h).

For many years, I have maintained the importance of maintaining optimum PSA levels. Men in their 40s should have a PSA level of less than 0.1, those in their 50s should have a PSA level less than 0.5, and those in their 60s should have a PSA level of less than 1.0. PSA level should not exceed 2.0.

Ronald Wheeler, MD, reinforced my theory at the November 2002 American College for Advancement in Medicine symposium by reporting that men in their 40s who have a PSA > 0.7 will eventually develop prostate cancer. Almost a year after that, he reiterated that prostatitis causes prostate cancer when PSA level exceeds 1.0.

A new study suggests that a rapid rise (or velocity) in PSA level could as easily be a marker for prostatitis as for prostate cancer. In a study of 1,851 men, 468 were diagnosed with prostate cancer and 135 with prostatitis at the time of their first biopsy. Risk for prostate cancer was found in those with a PSA increase of 0.3 to 0.5 ng/ml per year while risk for prostatitis increased for those with a PSA velocity of at least 2.0 ng/ml per year.

In more specific terms, among men with a PSA rise between 0 and 2.0 ng/ml annually before biopsy, 30% had prostate cancer and 5% had prostatitis. In contrast, among men with a PSA velocity of more than 4.0 ng/ml per year, 13% had cancer and 13% had prostatitis.

This study does not imply that PSA velocity should be disregarded as an indicator of prostate cancer. It is still an important tool in prostate cancer risk assessment. However, this can be confusing in some cases. Prostatitis often causes a rapid rise in PSA, prompting a biopsy unnecessarily. According to Dr. Laurence Klotz of the University of Toronto, prostatitis patients treated with antibiotics for a month have a median drop in PSA of 3.0 ng/ml (Ref: ASCO/ASTRO 2006 Prostate Cancer Symposium. Abstract 4).

Whenever there is a rapid rise in PSA level, first rule out prostatitis before making a prostate cancer diagnosis.

Case reports:

V.G., 59 y/o/m from MN, had many red dots on his tongue and abdomen and had a belly fat, indicating he was at risk for a hormone-related problem such as prostate cancer. Although his PSA was 1.85, and still below the official threshold, he was already diagnosed with prostate cancer. This reinforces my recommendation that men around 60 years old should have a PSA level less than 1.0.

A 31-year-old DC at the Parker seminar in Dallas in 2001 had many red dots on his tongue. I advised that he should not wait until he's in his 50s to check his PSA. He admitted he had testicular cancer at age 26 and he's still using DHEA and HGH. He instead used the Chi program. Now he is healthy and doing better.

At the anti-aging meeting in Las Vegas, NV, in December 2000, I saw this one doctor (age 48 at the time) from the US Virgin Islands and told him that he has a high chance of getting prostate cancer (because he had numerous red dots on his tongue). Two weeks later, he found out his PSA is 108.

R. Lynch, MD from FL, had no lunulae on his fingernail and had numerous dots on his tongue, suggesting a possible high PSA or prostate problem. He used Chi products for about a year and his lunulae came back. The red dots on his tongue were also greatly reduced: there were only 2 dots on the left side of the tongue and 7 on the right side.

R. Hendrickson, DC from MN, has a 53 y/o/m patient who was found to have some prostate issues (white spots in the nails and 3 red dots in the abdomen). He then found out his PSA level was 4.

T. Rose, DC from NV, had red dots on his tongue. In 1999, his PSA level was 0.9, which has now increased to 4.2 (free PSA is 15).

R. Lynch, MD from FL, had no lunulae on his fingernails and had numerous red dots on his tongue, suggesting the possibility of a high PSA/prostate problem. He used Chi products for approximately a year, and his lunulae came back. The red dots on his tongue were also greatly reduced: there were only 2 dots on the left side of the tongue while there were 7 on the right side.

D.B., a 65 y/o/m, had red dots on his tongue and abdominal cherry angiomas, indicating a high risk for prostate cancer. He later found that his PSA was 11. He said that he was glad to be alerted to the risk. He is now on the prostate program.

R. B., a 45 y/o/m from WA, reports that in 2007 he had many red dots on his belly, so he was found to be at risk for prostate issues. His father did have prostate cancer. So he went to have his prostate checked. Though his PSA was 0.7, he was still at risk for prostate cancer because of a trend of increasing estradiol and diminishing testosterone. Besides, Ronald Wheeler, MD, a prostate cancer specialist, believes that men in their 40s should have a PSA level of less than 0.7; otherwise, their risk for prostate cancer increases.

D. Metcalf, DC from CA, has a 69 y/o/m patient with prostate cancer who was being treated at the Mayo Clinic. He was given Lupron twice, but his PSA was still 47 in November 2008. Usually Lupron produces very quick results. Around that time, he started taking Angiostop, Myomin, Revivin, Asparagus Extract, and Reishi

Spore Extract. Two months later, his PSA dropped to 1.2. Even his MD was surprised with the quick results.

Simply Natural of Sunrise, FL, has a 68 y/o/m client who has 10 cherry angiomas on the abdomen and two on the forehead. His PSA reduced from 12 to 7 to 4 on the prostate program.

R.S., a 62 y/o/m from MN, had a long, black line on the fingernail, white spots on the fingernails, red dots on the back of the tongue, an ear crease and dark/blue color underneath his tongue. He then revealed that, a year earlier, he had a 1-cm lump in his prostate that has now grown to 1.8 cm. He just had a biopsy for prostate and was still bleeding badly.

SKIN CANCER

The most common of all human cancers occur on the skin. Early detection is very important and any warning signs should be evaluated by a physician. Often, warning signs of skin cancer can be seen in moles. Examine moles with the following signs in mind: **A**symmetry, **B**orders that are irregular, **C**olor variations, and **D**iameter larger than a pencil's eraser.

Basal Cell Carcinoma

This is the most frequent type of skin cancer, which tends to occur in older persons. It is slow growing, rarely metastasizes (spreads), and is usually smooth with a pearly border and may be pigmented with ulceration in the center of the lesion. Treatment is by surgical removal, freezing or local chemotherapy. Use of the MIT and Whole Skin ointment as well as Revivin, Reishi Spore Extract, and AGG is beneficial.

Squamous Cell Carcinoma

This cancer can affect both the skin and mucous membranes. It often occurs in sun-exposed or sunburned areas. The lesions appear as rough scaly nodules that can ulcerate and metastasize. The cancerous keratinocyte cells often extend down through the basement membrane zone into the dermis. Surgical removal is the treatment of choice, with a check and removal of enlarged draining lymph nodes for all the smallest of lesions. However, using the MIT and Whole Skin and taking Angiostop, Revivin, Reishi Spore Extract, and AGG will help.

Malignant Melanoma

This cancer has been increasing in incidence in Caucasians and now account for every significant morbidity and mortality. It has been estimated that in the U.S. an individual's lifetime risk of having malignant melanoma is 1 in 75. Pigment producing cells, melanocytes, are the originating cells of this type of cancer. Risk of this cancer is raised with increased sun exposure, particularly childhood exposure including sunburns. Heredity, congenital or dysplastic nevi, and fair skin are also risk factors. These lesions are known for their invasiveness and metastatic behavior. Prognosis is dependent on the depth of invasion of the tumor. Therefore, early detection and removal are critical. All moles (nevi) should be inspected regularly for irregular borders and surfaces or a change in color.

Since 1997, I have promoted and practiced the idea that a wide, vertical dark band on the nails indicates melanoma risk (Pictures 3c, 3d). In the February, 2003, issue of the *Dermatology Times*, R. Scher, MD, confirmed my theory in his article, "Missed nail diagnosis could actually be squamous cell carcinoma, melanoma."

It is therefore important not to overlook signs manifested on the nails as it can delay treatment and possibly worsen the condition.

Sometimes the tongue may also show a sign of melanoma risk. If there are dark discolorations on the tongue, check first if that is a birthmark. Otherwise, it may be a sign of melanoma.

Approximately 40% of women with black nevi in the vulva area have been found to be at risk for melanoma. Nevi are pigmented spots on the skin such as a mole. Some are smooth while others are rough or have hair. It was discovered that nevi found in the vulva area are more likely to be malignant than nevi found in any other part of the body.

Dermatologists recommend the use of folic acid to prevent melanoma. Among natural sources, Asparagus Extract is a very rich source of organic folic acid.

Case reports:

G. Schucard, DDS, NMD, from CA, has a male patient with a red/dark growing mole on his arm for 2 to 3 months. Then he read *Dr. Chi's Fingernail and Tongue Analysis* book and found out that the dark wide strips on his nails could signal skin cancer. His father had died from melanoma. So on that same day, he cancelled all his patients' appointments in order to see me. He has since been taking the program for melanoma: Angiostop, Revivin, Asparagus Extract, Reishi Spore Extract and AGG.

R. Welch, DC from CA, has a 53 y/o/m male patient with a black band on each of his thumbs as well as on one of his index fingers and a red tongue with white coating. When told that he is at risk for melanoma, he revealed that his father was diagnosed with melanoma in 1990 and died about 1 ½ years later.

S. Lau, ND from FL, has a 64 y/o/f patient who had a 12 mm lump between the breasts in 2007. She also had many cherry angiomas (>50) on her abdomen at that time. She used Angiostop and Myomin for 6 months. A test later found that the lump was melanoma under the skin. She had it surgically removed. A PET scan revealed that she was lucky it hadn't spread.

STOMACH CANCER

Stomach cancer, or gastric cancer, has now been divided into two types: gastric cardia cancer and non-cardia gastric cancer. Gastric cardia cancer affects the top inch of the stomach, the place where it connects with the esophagus. Non-cardia gastric cancer refers to cancer in all other parts of the stomach. For the rest of this discussion, the term gastric or stomach cancer will refer to non-cardia gastric cancer.

If detected in the early stage, 90% of stomach cancer (or gastric cancer) patients can live 5 years longer after treatment. However, early stomach cancer symptoms are often not very clear or distinct. When stomach cancer is usually diagnosed, it is in the late stage and it becomes difficult to treat.

Being aware of the risk factors of gastric cancer is helpful.
- ***Helicobacter pylori.*** Infection with the *H. pylori* bacteria is considered an important risk factor for gastric cancer. According to the U.S. National Cancer Institute, *H. pylori* was classified as a carcinogen in 1994 by the International Agency for Research on Cancer. In 2001, an analysis of 12 studies on *H. pylori* and gastric cancer estimated that the risk for gastric cancer was almost six times higher for *H. pylori* infected people than for those not infected with the bacteria.
- **Chronic gastritis, ulcers, polyps.** Long-term inflammation and ulcer of the stomach as well as polyps can increase the risk for gastric cancer.
- **Diet high in salted, smoked, pickled, dried, fried or poorly preserved foods.** These types of foods are high in nitrates, which increase gastric cancer risk. Aflatoxin, a potent carcinogen found in peanut fungus is associated with stomach and liver cancer risk.

As mentioned, early stage stomach cancer usually does not exhibit specific symptoms. But there are physical signs and symptoms you can look for, such as the following:

- **Deep crack on the tongue**. A crack on the tongue indicates digestive issues (Picture 13f). When the crack is more than 2 mm deep or there are multiple cracks in the tongue and is accompanied by missing lunulae (except on thumbs), the chance of getting stomach cancer is very high.

- **Red tongue.** A red tongue usually signals inflammation or infection, most likely in the digestive system.
- **Abdominal pain.** Upper abdominal pain is usually associated with the stomach. If the pain is accompanied by bloating, reflux and nausea, there may be stomach cancer risk. In some cases, the appetite may drop and weight loss and muscle weakness results. If the severity of the pain suddenly changes (e.g., from mild to severe pain), check for abnormalities in the stomach.
- **Hard lump on abdomen.** If you feel a hard lump about 2 inches to left of the navel or above, this may indicate stomach cancer (Figure 4A). When pressed, this hard spot is painful and is usually about quarter-sized.
- **Auricle lump, wrinkle or thickening.** A lump, thickening or wrinkle on the auricle or outer ear may be a sign of stomach or liver cancer (Pictures 15g, 15h).
- **Dark, oily feces**. If the feces is dark and greasy (looks like tar), then this is definitely a sign of stomach cancer.

It is usual for those with chronic stomach problems to have the same set of symptoms all the time. If the symptoms change, then the presence of stomach cancer should be checked. The pattern of abdominal pain may have changed. For instance, if somebody has mild pain frequently and then suddenly has severe pain and/or burning, then there is a likelihood of a more serious condition. Or if the pain worsens even with meals or food, then there might be a chance of a more serious problem. Additional symptoms are unexplained weight loss, changes in bowel movement, and vomiting with blood.

APPENDIX A

A Quick Guide to Fingernail and Tongue Analysis

I.   **Heart:** Ear crease, lack of lunulae, pinky has lunulae, large lunulae, tip of tongue is red, nail clubbing, vertical ridges on nails, cherry angiomas on the head, central nail canal (fir tree abnormality on nail), xanthomas, red lunulae, shortness of breath, chest heaviness, palpitations.

   Circulation: Lack of lunulae, cold hands and feet, numbness of the limbs. Tongue pale or dark red/purple in color. (If the condition improves, the lunulae should come back). Cherry angiomas on the head indicate stroke or aneurysm risk.

   Heavy metal: Dark protruding veins under the tongue, black or blue-colored fingernails, red/black spots (blood stasis spot) on the side of the tongue, metallic taste, dark blue lines or spots on gums, dark ring around the lunulae.

II.   **Digestion:** Teeth marks, crack(s) on the tongue, nail splitting, horizontal ridges on nail and yellow/brown coating on tongue, bloating (gas) problems and acid belching.

III.   **Lung:** Clubbing nail, white/opaque nail and/or vertical ridges on nail, geographic tongue, white tongue coating, nail looks pale, coughing, shortness of breath.

IV.   **Liver:** Dark blue branching veins under the tongue, large cherry angiomas on abdomen, blue/red spots on the sides of tongue, spider veins on abdomen, tip of nail has dark/red ring, bloating, constipation, fatigue, loss of appetite, bitter taste, dry mouth, dark facial complexion, jaundice. **Gallbladder:** Upper right quadrant pain, nausea.

V.   **Colon/Intestines:** Cyst on frenula, bowel movement problem, tongue cracking on upper middle area, skin tags

VI.   **Kidney:** Solid vertical ridges on nail, teeth marks on tongue, yellow coating on roots of tongue, dark color and bags under eyes and ankle swelling, half-and-half nails. Especially swelling on the hands and the face in the morning, urine foaming, and leg/ankle swelling.

VII.   **Arthritis/Osteoporosis:** Beaded ridges on nail. Finger stiffness (for arthritis).

VIII.   **Hormone Imbalance:** White spots on the nail, red dots on the back and/or side of the tongue and/or cherry angiomas on the abdomen.

IX.   **Aging:** Vertical ridges on fingernails, vision/hearing deterioration, hair loss.

X.   **Cancer/Immunity:** Only thumbs have lunulae (especially if you had lunulae before and they disappeared and you feel cold), clubbing nails, and triangular nails.

XI.   **Thyroid:** Brittle nails, light white swelling tongue sometimes with teeth marks, index finger longer than ring finger using the finger length test (Hashimoto's thyroiditis), fatigue, hair loss, dry skin, weight gain, cold hand/feet and memory loss, bowel irregularity.

XII.   **Tinea/Psoriasis:** Fingernails have indentations (pitting), scaling and/or skin has eruption of reddish silvery-scaled bumps and lesions on elbows, knees, scalp and trunk.

XIII.   **Autoimmune:** Nail pitting, half-and-half nails, geographic tongue, red lunulae.

APPENDIX B

Herbal Formulas

AGG

This is a combination of Astragalus, Green tea and Grape seed extract. AGG is a potent antioxidant designed to strengthen the immune system and reduce free radical-caused tissue damage. Fifty times as powerful as Vitamin C and twenty times as powerful as Vitamin E, AGG protects brain and nerve tissue and has been clinically proven to result in synergistic effects for wide variety of health conditions.

ANGIOSTOP

Angiostop is an RTK (receptor tyrosine kinase) inhibitor, which blocks the associated cancer processes such as angiogenesis, invasion, proliferation, metastasis and inhibition of apoptosis. Angiostop attacks cancer at both the cellular membrane as well as the DNA level (Figure 1).

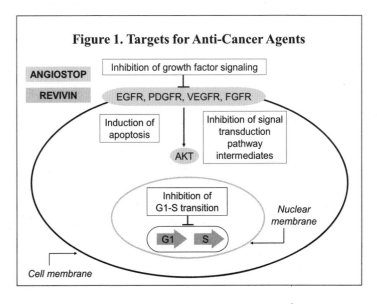

Figure 1. Targets for Anti-Cancer Agents

At the cellular membrane level, it inhibits new blood vessel formation and four different RTKs: vascular endothelial growth factor receptor (VEGFR), platelet-derived growth factor receptor (PDGFR), epidermal growth factor receptor (EGFR), and fibroblast growth factor receptor (FGFR). Simultaneous suppression of these RTKs as well as its associated downstream signaling (e.g. Akt, FAK, Paxillin, Erk) appears to be more effective than suppression of a single RTK. This is because each RTK is associated with one or more cancer process. For example, angiogenesis (or new blood vessel formation) is associated with VEGFR and FGFR. Cell proliferation is associated with VEGFR, PDGFR and FGFR. Apoptosis (or cancer cell death) is associated with EGFR and VEGFR. Metastasis is mainly associated with FGFR and so on.

It is clear that the more RTK targets that are addressed, the higher the chance of completely suppressing associated cancer processes. For example, drugs like Sutent and Nexavar, which inhibit both VEGFR and PDGFR, can address several cancer processes while a drug like Gleevec can only target proliferation and tumor vascular maturation. Or a drug like Tarceva can target apoptosis, mitogenesis and cellular motility only, not all of the processes. None of the drugs target the FGFR. Angiostop, on the other hand, inhibits all 4 RTKs, so it is able to block the more cancer processes.

With more RTK targets, the use of Angiostop is not only confined to one type of cancer but many different kinds, such as those listed in Table 12.

For instance, in cancers of the breast, colon, lung and prostate, multiple RTKs are overexpressed. Inhibiting only one, therefore, will not be effective in completely suppressing the growth. Since Angiostop inhibits all 4 RTKs, inhibition of growth would be much more effective. Furthermore, in Table 12, cancers of the bladder, bone, and esophagus as well as myeloma overexpress FGFR. Compared to the drugs mentioned earlier, only Angiostop has been shown to inhibit FGFR.

Table 12. Angiostop inhibits 4 RTKs and associated cancers

RTK (RTK inhibitor drugs) / Cancer Type	VEGFR (Avastin, Sutent)	PDGFR (Gleevec, Sutent)	EGFR (Tarceva, Erbitux, Herceptin)	FGFR (None)
Bladder				✓
Bone				✓
Brain (Glioma)	✓	✓		
Breast	✓		✓	✓
Colon	✓		✓	✓
Esophageal				✓
Gastric/Stomach	✓	✓	✓	✓
Kidney	✓	✓		
Leukemia		✓		
Liver	✓			✓
Lung	✓	✓	✓	✓
Lymphoma	✓	✓		
Melanoma	✓			
Meningioma		✓		
Myeloma				✓
NSCLC			✓	
Ovarian	✓	✓	✓	✓
Pancreatic	✓	✓	✓	✓
Prostate	✓	✓	✓	✓
Stomach	✓	✓	✓	✓

ASPARAGUS EXTRACT

There are many reasons why Asparagus Extract is very beneficial to our health:
- Most powerful alkaline agent
- Natural diuretic agent, improving kidney function
- Improves intestinal/stomach membranes, thymus and spleen functions
- Highest organic folic acid content for reducing homocysteine levels. An elevated homocysteine level signals a risk for cardiovascular disease. Asparagus Extract has been shown to

increase folic acid level by 39% after 1 month, and, in turn, reduce homocysteine levels by 28% after 4 months

- Increases immunity (IL-2, NK, CD_4/CD_8) and contains asparaginase, an enzyme used to treat some forms of cancer in the blood. The USP Drug information book (1998 edition, p. 3213 and 3215) lists asparaginase as treatment for acute lymphocytic leukemia, chronic lymphocytic leukemia, acute myelomonocytic leukemia, acute myelocytic leukemia (AML), Hodgkin's lymphoma and non-Hodgkin's lymphoma. In order for cells to grow, they need a chemical called asparagine - an amino acid synthesized from aspartic acid. Cancer cells cannot produce their own asparagine, so they rely on the normal cells to live. Asparaginase, however, breaks down asparagine in the body, thereby inhibiting unwanted cell growth
- Reduces the risk of birth defects and miscarriage - Women of childbearing age should take this before becoming pregnant

AUTOCIN

Carefully extracted from unique Chinese herbal compounds, Autocin regulates the immune system to help eliminate symptoms of auto-immune diseases.

Autocin is clinically proven to benefit those with rheumatoid arthritis, psoriasis, eczema, and more.

BAMBOO EXTRACT

Bamboo Extract is made out of the most nutritious part of the bamboo, containing a complex source of amino acids, vitamins and minerals. It is excellent for those who have symptoms associated with upper respiratory problems such as cough with phlegm, fever, runny nose, sore throat, dry mouth, heaviness in the chest and headaches. It works very quickly for acute respiratory problems, even in children and young adults. In fact, it is excellent for ear infections in children.

Bamboo Extract was shown to be effective against these types of bacteria: *Staphylococcus aureus, Pseudomonas aeruginosa, Escherichia coli, Klebsiella pneumoniae, Bacillus dysenterine, Bacillus influenza, Streptococcus pneumoniae*, and *Streptococcus pyogenes Type II* (Group A). Bamboo Extract has antipyretic (fever reducer), expectorant and anti-inflammatory properties as well.

A study was performed on 200 patients, ages 38 to 68 years old, from December 1997 to April 1998 – a period when the flu is usually prevalent. This study suggests that Bamboo Extract is effective even for chronic bronchitis, especially when used with conventional medicine like Cephalexin. Results indicate that Bamboo Extract with Cephalexin is more effective at 26% than Cephalexin alone (8.3%) in subjects 40 to 60 years old. In those who have had the disease for 11-20 years, the combined therapy is 40% effective while Cephalexin by itself is only 5% effective. This means that older people who are at higher risk for respiratory problems will greatly benefit from Bamboo Extract. Moreover, people suffering from chronic lung problems for even longer than 10 years will benefit from it as well.

BATHDETOX

This skin dialysis herbal bath extracts wastes from the body by simultaneously removing toxins through the skin while increasing urine output. This rejuvenating bath engages the olfactory and dermal neural senses and allows the body to secrete various waste products.

Studies show that Bathdetox is effective in improving kidney function. In a study on 358 patients, Bathdetox reduced BUN and creatinine levels in 41% and 26% of the patients, respectively. Proteinuria was improved in 83% of the patients while edema, skin itching and pain was relieved in over 75% of the patients.

Various studies have shown how effective Bathdetox is for kidney function, pain and even skin problems such as eczema, dermatitis, and tinea. It is used either as a whole body bath or a foot bath. Even children as young as 2 years old can safely use Bathdetox for colds, fever and skin problems.

For best results in improving kidney function, use Bathdetox with Asparagus Extract, Kidney Chi and Cordyceps Extract.

CFC

CFC is a natural vegetable polysaccharide from fibrin plants. This dietary supplement exhibits a powerful ability to absorb water. In the intestinal tract, after absorbing fluids, the volume of a CFC capsule expands 50 to 100 times its initial size. In such a manner, it is able to expand the intestinal cavity and moisten stool, making feces fluffy and easy to free.

Once consumed, CFC evolves into sticky fibers after absorbing fluids. It lengthens the period of time food remains in the stomach and, in this way, satiates one's appetite.

CFC is capable of decreasing a user's food intake levels and improving the quality of food control. The sticky fibers can increase the viscosity of the condiments and create a diffusion barrier by recovering the intestinal mucosa and combining the carbohydrate materials. Thus the diffusion and absorption of carbohydrate materials are limited in the intestinal tract, the rate of sugar absorption is decreased, and postprandial sugar is lower. In addition, the absorbed and combined carbohydrate materials can be excreted with stool.

CHI ENERGY

Chi Energy benefits the heart, lungs, adrenal glands, and stomach. It has anti-aging functions as well. It promotes nitric oxide (NO), which makes blood vessels flexible.

In a six-week study on 24 heart failure patients, the addition of Chi Energy to Calcium blockers produced the best. Patients taking both a calcium blocker and Chi Energy were able to endure 56 seconds more running time on the treadmill test than the group taking only the Ca blocker.

Chi Energy is also effective for chronic bronchitis (69.3%) and emphysema (66.7%) patients.

CHI-F

CHI-F is an herbal formula that naturally balances estrogen, progesterone and testosterone levels. In women, it promotes a balanced menstrual cycle by 75% and improves PMS symptoms by over 90%. Chi-F has also been effective in reducing abnormal uterine bleeding by as much as 93%.

Approximately 80% of women around 50 years old (or those who are around the menopausal stage) will also benefit from the hormone-balancing effect of Chi-F. This is evident in one study on 120 menopausal females, ages 40 to 55 years old, who took Chi-F for 3 months and were evaluated for one year (Table 13).

Table 13. Chi-F on Menopausal Syndrome				
Symptom	% Change		Symptom	% Change
Hot Flash	↓ 87.37		Depression	↓ 32.26
Irritability	↓ 43.01		Painful intercourse	↑ 89.18
Insomnia	↓ 23.72		Fatigue	↓ 62.96

Chi-F also nourishes the blood and bone marrow synthesis. One study shows that Chi-F and iron have almost the same effect in increasing red blood cells (RBCs) and hemoglobin. EPO is a glycoprotein hormone responsible for the regulation of RBC production. A reduction in EPO signifies that the body is using it to produce more RBCs. Based on this study, Chi-F allows a more effective utilization of EPO.

DEBILE

Debile is an herbal formula that helps dissolve gallstones, reduce gallbladder inflammation and improve gallbladder disease symptoms.

DIABEND

As the name suggests, Diabend is great for Type II Diabetes. Diabend can promote a system's healthy absorption of fat, protein, amino acids, and zinc.

Scientific studies have shown the efficacy of the Diabend ingredients in terms of lowering blood sugar and restoring pancreatic function. When taken in conjunction with western medicine, it inhibited insulin resistance. It can also allow muscle and fatty tissue to use and turnover glucose at its optimal rate.

Diabend reduces blood glucose, increases glucose tolerance, improves insulin receptor sensitivity, stimulates beta cells of pancreas to produce more insulin, and regulates lipoprotein metabolism.

DIGESTRON

Digestron is an excellent herbal formula for digestive health. It:
- Stimulates the production of your own digestive enzymes.
- Adjusts stomach and intestinal involuntary muscle contractions
- Reduces *H. pylori* bacteria, which is responsible in many cases of ulcers
- Repairs stomach/intestinal membrane
- Balances stomach acidity

Studies have shown that Digestron is has an overall effective rate of 58.9% and an overall improvement rate of 24.97% for various gastrointestinal conditions, such as gastritis, ulcers, irritable bowel syndrome, diverticulitis and colitis.

In comparison to Ranitidine, a histamine H_2-receptor antagonist drug, Digestron has a lower recurrence rate for Duodenal and Gastric Ulcers within 2 years.

GI CHI

GI Chi contains herbs traditionally used for various gastrointestinal conditions. It has mostly been used for chronic colitis, IBS and Crohn's disease. It has also been recommended for GI infections and diarrhea. It has been shown to have anti-microbial effect against bacteria such as *E. coli*, *Streptococcus*, and *Spirillum*. One of its herbs, in particular, has anti-pathogenic activity against bacteria, viruses, fungi (candida), protozoans (trichomonads), helminths, and Chlamydia. For best results, GI Chi should be taken immediately at the first sign of a GI infection.

HAPPY SKIN TONIC

Happy Skin Tonic (HST) is a topical formula for fungal and bacterial infections. It can be used either directly on the affected areas of the skin or as a douche for genital infections. It functions as an antipyretic and anti-itching antidote and an effective sterilizing agent. It has inhibitory effect against bacteria, fungus and trichomonads.

In a study on 766 patients with topical infections, HST was 99.08% effective for bacterial infections, 87.67% effective for fungal infections and 81.29% effective for trichomonal infections.

Studies also show that HST is 92% effective for gonorrhea and condyloma acuminatum and is used in various cases of vaginal inflammation, tinea, eczema, scabies and dermatitis.

HYPERTINE

Hypertine contains herbs, which, individually, has a different effect on circulation and cardiovascular function. Collectively, the herbs work to regulate blood pressure and improve symptoms associated with hypertension.

Hypertine controls the blood pressure through the brain within two hours after consumption. The maximum effect occurs within a day and a half. The level of blood pressure is maintained continuously as long as it is taken regularly.

In one study on 30 hypertensive patients, Hypertine reduced blood pressure to within normal range in 80% of the patients.

JUVENIN

Juvenin is an anti-aging formula which promotes vision, hearing, bone health and hair growth. It also improves symptoms such as ear ringing, dizziness, weak knees and cold sweats.

KIDNEY CHI

Kidney Chi is a great natural formula which can be used as first aid for urinary tract, bladder, kidney and prostate infections.

It improves kidney, bladder, urethra, and urinary tract infections, helps dissolve kidney stones that are less than 7mm over a 3-month period, and changes urine pH to less than 7 which is optimal for preventing kidney stone formation and dissolving them.

LIVER CHI

Liver Chi is an all-natural formula recommended for hepatitis, fatty liver and liver cirrhosis. In the United States, 2% of adults have Hepatitis C, so Liver Chi is a very useful formula.

- Hepatitis C
  In vivo study demonstrates that Liver Chi significantly suppresses Hepatitis C Virus replication and expression in 6 days. This means that the virus stays intact inside the cells and can no longer come out and infect normal liver cells. Then the

virus inside the cells will eventually die. In 7 days, energy will start to increase. In 2 months, the liver enzymes can be checked for improvement. In 4 to 6 months, the virus titer should be significantly reduced.

- Hepatitis A and B
  - 47 Hepatitis A and B patients: average ALT level reduced by 73% in 3 months
  - 10 out of 15 Chronic active Hepatitis B cases reduced their ALT level to within normal range
  - Bloating, constipation and loss of appetite improved
- Fatty Liver
  In 7 fatty liver cases: 100% effective
- Liver Chi increases liver mitosis rate (new cell growth) and reduces liver cell necrosis
- Liver Chi has been effective for abdominal pain (78.21%), vomiting (82.75%), acidic stomach (87.87%), bitter/dry mouth (78.57%) and poor appetite (87.8%).

METAL FLUSH

Metal Flush is an oral herbal formula that chelates metals from the body without stripping away essential minerals. It is even safe for children three years and older to take.

Other chelating agents remove metals through urination, thereby adding burden to the kidneys. Metal Flush, however, removes metals through urination and fecal excretion. Studies have shown that Metal Flush does not damage the liver nor does it inhibit hemoglobin biosynthesis. Those with kidney issues can still use Metal Flush if they take Asparagus Extract and use Bathdetox along with it.

MYOMIN

Myomin is a natural aromatase inhibitor that has been shown to be effective for cysts, fibroids, endometriosis, estrogen-related tumors, and belly fat. By inhibiting aromatase, it reduces estradiol levels as seen through *in vitro*, animal and clinical studies. It also competes with estradiol at target cells' estrogen receptors. Furthermore, Myomin also increases the 2/16 hydroxyestrone ratio, consequently reducing the risk for breast cancer (Figure 2).

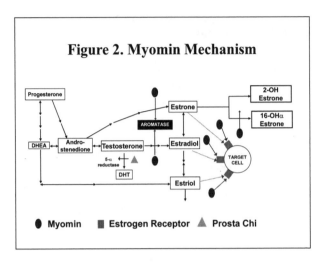

Figure 2. Myomin Mechanism

In 1994, clinical studies showed that Myomin was 57.6% effective on 255 females with ovarian cysts and endometriosis while it was 69.2% effective on 60 female patients with uterine fibroids that exceed 5 cm³ in size. The latter study was conduction in combination with Revivin, another herbal formula. Another alternative would be to combine Myomin with Angiostop, an angiogenesis inhibitor.

One study involved 75 cases of fibrocystic breasts (70 women ages 18 to 52 years old and 5 men ages 62 to 64 years old). Sixty five percent of the women were under 35 years old. Twenty five cases were in the control group while fifty cases were treated with Myomin. Results of the study revealed that, in 14 cases, the fibrocystic breast completely cleared after 1 month of taking Myomin while, in 16 cases, the fibrocystic breast reduced by 50% in size (Table 14). Among the five men in the study, the cysts cleared completely in 3 cases.

Table 14. Myomin on Fibrocystic Breast in 75 Patients		
	Number of cases	
Category	**Myomin group**	**Control Group**
(A) Clear	14	1
(B) Effective	16	5
(C) Improved	15	5
(D) No Change	5	9
(E) Worse	0	5

Table 14 legend: (A) Breast fibrocysts completely gone, symptoms cleared; (B) Breast fibrocysts reduced by more than 50%, symptoms were relieved significantly; (C) Breast fibrocysts reduced by <50%, some symptoms were relieved; (D) No effect; (E) Worse condition - an increase in fibrocyst size by at least 25% or another growth occurred.

Overall, the effective rate of Myomin is more than 60% compared to the control group's 12% rate. In the Myomin group, in 48 out of 50 cases, associated pain cleared or tremendously reduced (p value < 0.05) while in the control group, pain reduced in only 12 out of 25 cases.

In 1998, it was found that one reason for Myomin's beneficial effects on fibroids, cysts and endometriosis was that it reduced estradiol, the bad form of estrogen. In an animal study, Myomin was given to 3 groups of mice for 30, 60 and 180 days, respectively. Myomin was able to progressively reduce estradiol in during this period and it stabilized after 180 days. In a clinical study on 60 postmenopausal women with cysts and fibroids, Myomin was able to reduce estradiol by 47.88% in 10 days.

In 2003, *in vivo* studies showed that, in rat endometrial and ovarian tissues, Myomin reduced aromatase expression tremendously after 28 days of administration by 100% and 85.6%, respectively. In a study on 60 postmenopausal women with fibroids and cysts, Myomin reduced estradiol level by 47.88% after 10 days. In clinical studies on women of various ages with ovarian cysts, endometriosis, and fibrocystic breast, Myomin had over 60% effective rate after 6 months.

R. Santoro, ND from NY, has a 75 y/o/m patient who has tried to reduce his estradiol and increase his testosterone for a long time to no avail. Only Myomin has reduced his estradiol level and increased his testosterone by 100 points after a year.

When on HRT, even bio-identical hormones, add Myomin to avoid hormone-related side effects.

L. Funk, DC from CA, has a 53 y/o/f patient who used bioidentical testosterone cream. After 1 ½ years, she developed breast cancer. Twenty years earlier, she already was aware that she had a reproductive organ problem but she was still prescribed the cream.

MYOSTEO

Myosteo is n herbal formula that benefits the nerve system and microcirculation system. It is very effective in managing pain and improving dizziness.

As a pain controller, Myosteo is particularly effective toward the central nervous system and in regulating the symptoms of fibromyalgia such as muscle pain. In addition to having a relaxing effect on the body, it helps patients with insomnia obtain a restful sleep, Myosteo has been observed to reduce the frequency and the length of convulsion seizures.

Long-term use of NSAIDs like COX-2 inhibitors (Celebrex, etc) and other pain relievers can cause GI bleeding and ulcers. Some can cause side effects like drowsiness and lethargy. Others even worsen headaches. Myosteo is a much better alternative in relieving pain without the risk of bleeding and other side effects.

OXYPOWER

OxyPower is an excellent formula for relieving lung congestion and improving energy. One of its main functions is to increase the oxygen-carrying power of red blood cells. A study shows that OxyPower has even better anti-hypoxia effects than Rhodiola, an herb popular for his anti-hypoxia properties. This makes OxyPower beneficial for those with lung problems and oxygen-deficiency conditions and even those who live in high altitudes.

OxyPower also enhances mitochondrial function by reducing serum lactic acid level for better oxygen delivery to cells and tissues. Unlike coffee and energy drinks which give you energy only temporarily, OxyPower works quickly at the mitochondrial level so it has a more lasting effect in increasing energy. It works even faster than CoQ10.

Smokers, athletes, lung patients and chronic fatigue patients are just some of the people who can benefit from OxyPower. It contains no steroids, narcotics, beta blockers, stimulants or diuretics.

OxyPower has also anti-aging functions. In a 24-hour *in vitro* test using electrophoresis analysis on TK6 human lymphoblast Cells (Comet Test), it was found that OxyPower may protect and repair damage DNA (Figure 3).

Figure 3. OxyPower protects and repairs DNA damage *in vitro*

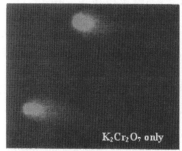

Test shows the $K_2Cr_2O_7$-induced DNA damage of TK6 human lymphoblast cells, evident here as the comet tail.

24 hours after OxyPower was added, DNA damage was repaired, as seen by the absence of the comet tail.

Here are a few of the many case reports showing OxyPower's ability to repair damaged DNA. For fresh keloids, add Whole Skin ointment for better results.

- A 25 y/o/f developed keloids from a C-section (Figure 17a) 3 years ago. She recently took OxyPower (2 soft gels, 3 times daily). After only 3 months, the middle part of the keloid from the C-section has clearly improved (Figure 17b) and the keloid from the C-section has visibly flattened and the color was lightened as well (Figure 17c).
- A 70-year-old patient reports that an old keloid and a small lipoma have both cleared.
- M. Rocco, DC from CO, has a 65 y/o/f patient with mitral valve prolapse. Her doctor already wanted her to have a valve replacement. She has a difficult time walking due to breathing problems. She tried CoQ10 for a while but she didn't feel any difference. When she took OxyPower and Vein Lite, the results were so quick! She says that 1 hour after taking OxyPower, she felt so amazing: no more breathing difficulty and weakness. The following day, she took 2 more OxyPower soft gels and said she felt normal again. Now her doctor says she doesn't need a valve replacement.
- H. Khalsa, DC from CA, has a 67 y/o/f patient who had her upper right lung removed due to a tumor. She's always had breathing difficulties and palpitations. She also had choking-like symptoms, lung discomfort and "pounding" in the chest. After the 1st day of taking OxyPower, she already felt a tremendous difference. After 2 months, she had no difficulty breathing, she can walk longer and even climb a flight of stairs. Her lung discomfort and chest pounding are mostly gone.

PRO-METABOLIC

Pro-Metabolic improves thyroid function in those with hypothyroidism. If you have symptoms such as cold hands and feet, weight gain, fatigue, hair loss, dry skin, then Pro-Metabolic will be beneficial. For those who need to lose weight, Slender All and Myomin are recommended. If you need to lose weight and have low thyroid function, add Pro-Metabolic.

S.L., a 29 y/o/f from NY, weighed 190 lbs when she started Myomin, Slender All, and Pro-Metabolic. After two years, she lost 65 lbs (Figures 19a, 19b).

PROSTA CHI

Prosta Chi is an herbal formula that inhibits the 5-alpha reductase to reduce DHT levels (Figure 2). It works effectively for prostate problems, such as prostatitis and benign prostatic hyperplasia (BPH), and its associated symptoms:
- Reduces frequent urination
- Eases urine urgency
- Relieves abdominal discomfort or pain associated with prostate enlargement
- Improves sexual function
- Improves hair loss in men

PSORICAID

Psoricaid is an herbal formula that inhibits the production of certain inflammatory cytokines. These inflammatory cytokines, such as interleukin 1 (IL-1), interleukin 2 (IL-2), and tumor necrosis factor alpha (TNF-alpha), are overexpressed in such conditions as psoriasis, Rheumatoid Arthritis, Crohn's disease and more. Studies show that Psoricaid more effectively inhibits these cytokines than Celebrex (Figures 4 and 5).

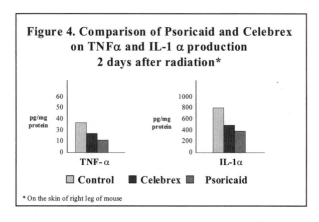

Figure 4. Comparison of Psoricaid and Celebrex on TNFα and IL-1 α production 2 days after radiation*

* On the skin of right leg of mouse

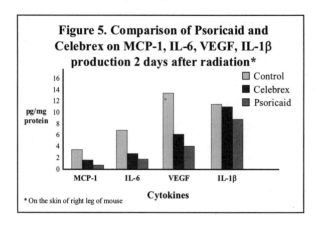

Figure 5. Comparison of Psoricaid and Celebrex on MCP-1, IL-6, VEGF, IL-1β production 2 days after radiation*

*On the skin of right leg of mouse

F. Akbarpour, MD from CA, has a 51 y/o/m patient who has had psoriasis for 45 years. In 2006, he had a severe breakout of psoriasis and couldn't find any relief despite many methods he tried (Figure 20a). After about a month on Psoricaid/Autocin, his psoriasis has improved significantly (Figure 20b). He said that in the 45 years that he's had this disease, this is the first time he's had this much improvement.

RELAXIN

Relaxin is an herbal formula that naturally enhances the GABA receptor activity to engender a relaxing effect. It is effective for sleeping problems, anxiety, aggression and even withdrawal symptoms.

In an animal study, mice in the Relaxin group took the shortest time to fall asleep, even shorter than both the control and GABA groups. Similarly, mice given Relaxin had the longest sleep duration (Figures 8 and 9).

EKG results show that brain waves during sleep after taking Relaxin are very calm. Relaxin induces a deep and restful sleep, leading to more energy when waking up.

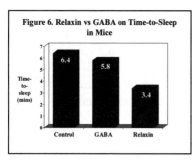

Figure 6. Relaxin vs GABA on Time-to-Sleep in Mice

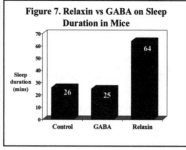

Figure 7. Relaxin vs GABA on Sleep Duration in Mice

To determine the effect of Relaxin on anxiety, the elevated plus-maze was used. This is a cross-shaped maze with 4 equally long arms, two of which have protective walls and two of which are open. Anxious animals avoid the open arms. The animal is placed in the center of the plus-maze suspended well above floor level in a well lit room for a 5-min observation session. Mice given Relaxin were less anxious and entered the open platform more often and spent more time in the open platform than the other 2 groups. In conclusion, GABA did not have any effect at all on anxiety while Relaxin produced a significant calming effect on the mice.

REVIVIN

Revivin is considered a G1-S inhibitor, recommended as an adjunct cancer therapy. It inhibits uncontrolled cell replication by blocking the transition from the G1 phase to the S phase. This ensures that damaged or mutated DNA does not get passed on to daughter cells, in effect, stopping the uncontrolled cell division (cell cycle arrest).

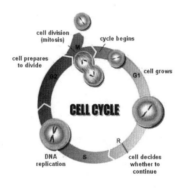

Revivin has been shown to exhibit an effect against several tumor cell lines, including leukemia, melanoma and cancers of the breast, cervix, ovary, liver, kidney, colon, prostate, and bone.

SINUS CHI

Sinus Chi is recommended for sinusitis and nasal allergies. It is best taken before the allergy season starts for optimal effect. It blocks histamine release for the relief of allergy symptoms, regulates immunity to help fight sinus infection, and reduces symptoms associated with respiratory problems.

SLENDER ALL

Slender All is effective for weight management. It removes fat by 51% when taken before meals and helps burn fat faster when taken before exercise.

When you exercise, ATP (energy) is converted to ADP. As ADP accumulates, the fat burning process is inhibited. Slender All removes excess ADP in the metabolic pathway. It also inhibits fat digestion by binding to fat molecules, preventing absorption of fat into the bloodstream. For best results, Slender All is recommended with Pro-Metabolic and Myomin.

S.L., a 29 y/o/f from NY, weighed 190 lbs when she started Myomin, Slender All, and Pro-Metabolic. After two years, she lost 65 lbs (Figures 19a, 19b).

L. Fickes, DC from HI, has a 54 y/o/m patient who lost 18 lbs and 4 inches around his waist after 6 months on Slender All and Myomin.

SYNERGEN

Synergen naturally reduces inflammation in the bronchial tubes for the ease of respiratory symptoms associated with asthma and similar conditions. It also reduces the IgE level and stops histamine release. In a five-year study on 1000 asthma patients, mostly older, chronic and weak patients, 69.8% of the patients recovered.

VEIN LITE

For over 20 years now, Vein Lite has been remarkably effective for circulatory problems. Clinical studies show that it enhances platelet functions, lowers blood pressure, maintains and promotes blood vessel health and reduces cholesterol. It also reduces blood coagulating factors, such as blood viscosity, fibrinogen, red blood cell aggregation and more (Figure 8).

Results of a study on 315 cases of cardiovascular, pulmonary and cerebral conditions showed that Vein Lite alleviates the following symptoms: heaviness of the head, limb numbness, nausea, anxiety, cold chills. Neck stiffness and heart palpitations were symptoms that were alleviated to a secondary degree. Positive results were also seen in the mitigation of symptoms of edema, right upper quadrant pain, portal vein hypertension, jugular vein distension, dark tongue due to blood stasis, cerebral vascular conditions, and senility. Speech capacity and language comprehension abilities were also improved.

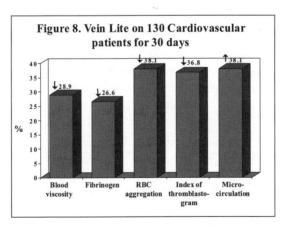

Vein Lite not only reduces the risk for cardiovascular conditions such as CAD and stroke but also increases brain circulation to improve memory and cognitive function after a stroke or in relation to Parkinson's disease. Electroencephalogram (EEG) tests show increased brain wave activity among senile patients after taking

Vein Lite. In 56 patients who suffered a stroke, Vein Lite was able to improve cognitive impairment after 6 months.

Various studies also illustrate that Vein Lite promotes circulation to other organs of the body. In a study on 116 glaucoma patients, Vein Lite reduced ocular blood pressure and improved eye circulation in over 50% of the patients after 6 months. A study on 48 patients with kidney problems showed that Vein Lite was 40% effective in improving blood flow to the kidneys after 2 months. In a study on 37 diabetic neuropathy patients, Vein Lite was 78% effective in improving peripheral circulation after 2 months.

S. Kelly, DC from MN, has a 58 y/o/f patient was found to be at risk for cardiovascular problems. Seven months later, she had heart failure. Afterwards, she couldn't even walk, had shortness of breath, was tired and felt like there was water up to her diaphragm. She started taking Vein Lite and OxyPower. After only a day, she says that the water in her diaphragm reduced by an inch and she can breathe more easily

WHOLE SKIN

Whole Skin is an all-natural, scar-free ointment for burns, wounds, sores, abrasions, dryness, keloids and more. It increases phagocytic activity, helps activate fibroblast, smoothens muscle cells and stimulates angiogenesis which is the reason skin heals quicker. Furthermore, it rejuvenates skin faster at the keratose layer.

According to a May 7, 1990 article in *Newsweek*: "The new remedy not only eases pain of burn injuries, according to proponents, but speeds healing, reduces scarring and drastically cuts the cost of saving lives. There is no need for bandages, no topical antibiotics and no sterile isolation. The conventionally treated skin was rough, scarred and marked by patches of excessive or reduced pigmentation. The herbal treated flesh was supple and unblemished."

Studies show that Whole Skin is much better than silvadene cream for burns and wounds. This is great to have as a first aid ointment.

For faster healing, especially for old scars and keloids, use Whole Skin with OxyPower. Refer to page 218 for some cases on keloids.

M. Rocco, DC from CO, has a 39 y/o/m patient who was caught in a snowstorm for an entire night at -57°F. By the time he was rescued the following day, he had developed frostbite in his feet and hand (Figure 18a). Four days later, his doctors observed that amputation may be needed. At that time he already started on Whole Skin, Vein Lite, OxyPower, Asparagus Extract and Bathdetox. In 2 weeks he has improved significantly that his doctors decided that amputation was not needed at all. After more than 6 months, his foot has recovered well (Figure 18b).

L. Fickes, DC from HI, reports that only Whole Skin has worked on a patient's skin ulcer on the ankle.

WINE EXTRACT

Wine Extract is very effective in reducing overall cholesterol, LDL cholesterol (the "bad" cholesterol), and triglycerides. In a study on 155 hyperlipidemia patients, Wine Extract reduced total cholesterol in 88% of the patients, reduced triglycerides in 80% of the patients, reduced atherosclerosis index in 84% of the patients and increased HDL cholesterol (the "good" cholesterol) in 65% of the patients. For even better results, take it with Vein Lite.

YOUTH CHI

Youth Chi promotes calcium-binding to the bone and increases bone formation without going through the estrogen route. Youth Chi is recommended for osteoporosis patients who have or are at risk for estrogen-related conditions such as cysts, fibroids, breast cancer, etc.

Studies show that Youth Chi improves bone density, increases BGP (the bone formation marker) and reduces both DPD and PYD levels (both bone loss markers).

Youth Chi was found to be very effective for osteoporosis. In one study on 90 women and 6 men with osteoporosis, Youth Chi was effective on 54.17% of the subjects. Improvement was seen in 44.79% while only one person experienced no change at all.

E. Schlabach, DC from OH, has a 79 y/o/f patient with osteopenia with an elevated DPD level. Research studies show that a high level of DPD is associated with both rapid bone loss and fracture risk. The patient took Youth Chi at 2 capsules, 3 times daily. In July 2008, after 4 months, DPD reduced by 43 without any other medication. When Youth Chi was increased to 3 capsules, 3 times daily, it resulted in a 45% reduction in DPD levels within 2 months.

	MAR 2008	JULY 2008	SEP 2008	REFERENCE VALUES
DPD level	20	11	6	Healthy: 3.0-7.2 Std units Osteoporotic: >7.2 Std units

APPENDIX C

Fingernail and Body Diagrams

Fig 1A - Vertical ridges

Fig 1B - Dark ring on tip

Fig 1C - Extremely narrow nails

Fig 1D - Triangular nails

Fig 1E - Indented nails

Fig 1F - Clubbing

Fig 2A – Short and wide nail

Fig 2B – Spoon-like

Fig 2C – Bumpy raised dots

Fig 2D – Horizontal ridges

Fig 2E – Horizontal ridges/dips

Fig 2F – Dark line, small splotch

Fig 3A – Blackish or yellowish tone

Fig 3B – Red or circular spots

Fig 3C – Nail pulls away from skin that is bluish in color

Fig 3C – Brittle nails

Fig 3E – Shoot out like growth from the lunula

Fig 3F – Ridges, easily tears or splits

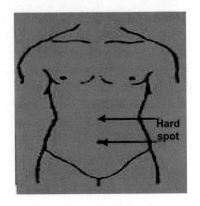

Figure 4A
Hard lump or spot 2 inches to the left of the navel or above it, painful when pressed: Stomach or liver problem.

APPENDIX D

Pictures of Fingernail, Tongue and Body Markers

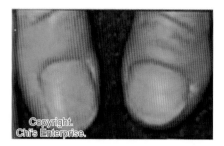

Picture 1a
Short, wide nail:
Cardiovascular

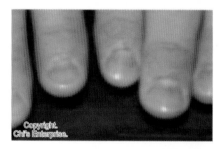

Picture 1b
Triangular or Shell-shaped
nails: Bone marrow or blood
disease (leukemia,
lymphoma, anemia, etc.)

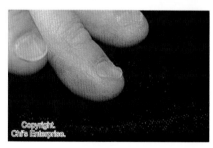

Picture 1c
Spoon-shaped nails: Anemia

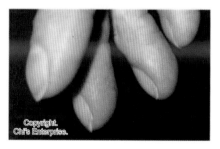

Picture 1d
Nail clubbing: Primarily lung
issues, may also be a heart
problem, cancer, liver
cirrhosis, or Crohn's disease

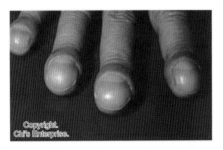

Picture 1e
Drumstick fingers (Nail clubbing): Major heart problem. May also be lung problem or cancer

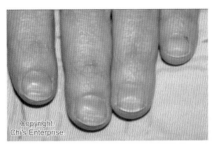

Picture 1f
Beau's lines: An interruption in nail growth caused by trauma, diet, heart disease or chemotherapy

Picture 1g
Dark yellow nails towards the tip, normal nails toward the base. Nail growth was interrupted by chemotherapy.

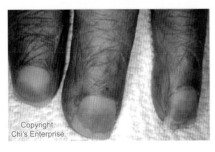

Picture 1h
Half-and-Half nails (dark on upper half, white on bottom half): Mostly kidney problems (autoimmune-related), sometimes liver problems

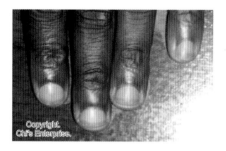

Picture 2a
Terry's nails: Kidney, Heart failure, Diabetes or Autoimmune disease. If the nails are opaque, as in this picture, then it is definitely a kidney problem

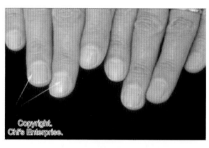

Picture 2b
Mee's lines (white lines that parallel the lunulae on all nails, moves with nail growth): Heavy metal, Hodgkin's disease, chemotherapy, carbon monoxide poisoning

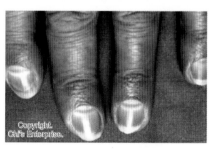

Picture 2c
Muehrcke's lines (white lines that parallel the lunulae, does not move with nail growth): Kidney disease, particularly hypoalbuminia

Picture 2d
① Solid vertical ridges: Ridges signify aging, adrenals, kidney, digestive, respiratory, or peripheral blood disease, vitamin or mineral deficiency;
② Yellow nails signify digestive/liver problem

Picture 2e
Red lunulae: Heart,
Autoimmune condition
(Rheumatoid arthritis or
lupus)

Picture 2f
Normal appearance of nails:
Four lunulae, except on
pinkies and no ridges

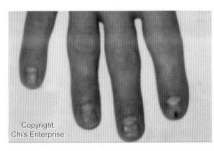

Picture 2g
Lunula on pinky: Heart
condition; Horizontal ridges:
Cardiovascular problem or
malnutrition; Black spots: If
not trauma, may be internal
bleeding or digestive
problem

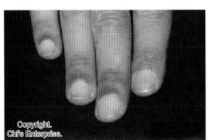

Picture 2h
No lunulae: Circulatory
deficiency, high risk of cancer

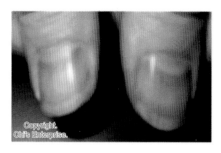

Picture 3a
Azure lunulae: Most likely heavy metal toxicity, may also be Wilson's disease, Raynaud's disease, lupus, or Rheumatoid arthritis. This patient has silver toxicity.

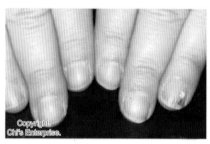

Picture 3b
Solid vertical ridges: Aging, Adrenals, Kidney, Peripheral blood vessel disease, Respiratory, vitamin or mineral deficiency.

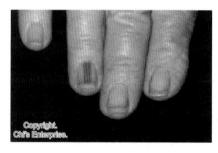

Picture 3c
Dark or brown vertical band: Melanin deposition on the skin, high chance of melanoma.

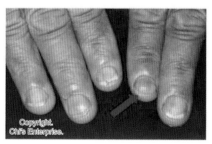

Picture 3d
Dark strip on nail: Melanoma, if a birthmark and continues to grow, may also be melanoma

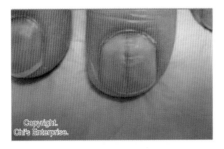

Picture 3e
Central Nail Canal or Ridge:
If not trauma, may be
malnutrition

Picture 3f
Central Nail Canal (Fir tree
abnormality): Peripheral
artery disease, heart
problem

Picture 3g
Beads on a string:
Osteoporosis, Arthritis

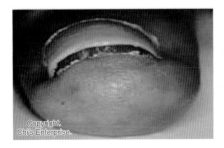

Picture 3h
Onycholysis: Fungal
infection, Poor capillary
function, chemical reaction,
malnutrition, psoriasis,
protein deficiency, anemia.
This is a drug reaction.

Picture 4a
①White spots: Hormonal imbalance; ②White strips: Proteinuria, Kidney problem

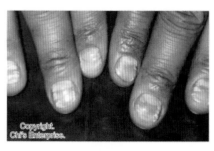

Picture 4b
White lines on nails: Proteinuria

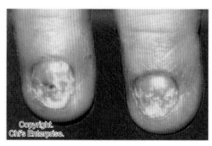

Picture 4c
Pitting with massive scaling and crusting: If not a fungal infection, then psoriasis or eczema.
This is a psoriasis patient.

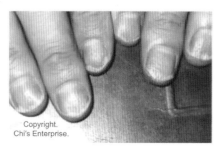

Picture 4d
Pitting: Fungal infection, psoriasis, or eczema

Picture 4e
White spots: Hormonal imbalance, Zinc deficiency. May be normal for children, but not for adults.

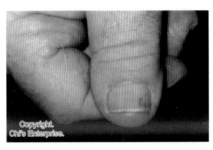

Picture 4f
Black spot/line on nail: Internal bleeding

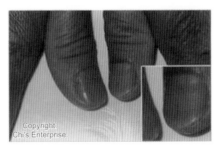

Picture 4g
Black line on nail: Internal bleeding

Picture 4h
Dark rings around lunulae: Heavy metal or carbon monoxide poisoning

Picture 5a
Terry's nails (Dark or red band on tip of nails, the rest of the nail is pink): Liver problem

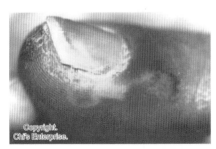

Picture 5b
Yellow skin on hands: Jaundice, liver

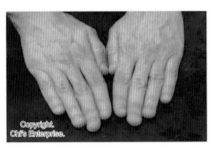

Picture 5c
Periungal erythema (thickening and discoloration): Diabetes, transplant recipients, or AIDS. If scaling around the nail: fungal infection

Picture 5d
Index finger is longer than the ring finger: Hashimoto's thyroiditis if hypothyroid symptoms are present

Picture 6a

Ear crease: heart condition

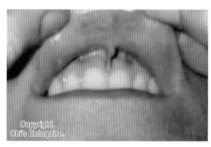

Picture 6b

Frenula cyst (top): Small intestines or upper colon

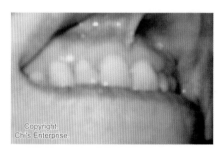

Picture 6c

Frenula cyst (close to gum): Colon or rectum

Picture 6d

Multiple cysts on frenula: High risk of multiple colon polyps

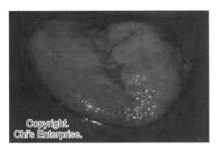

Picture 7a
Deviated tongue: Whiplash,
heavy metals, or stroke

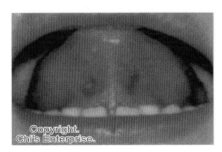

Picture 7b
Branching, bulging varicose
veins, red spots: Liver
problem, poor circulation,
heavy metal accumulation.

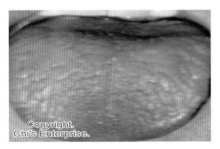

Picture 7c
Four or more dark veins
under the tongue: Liver
cirrhosis or liver cancer

Picture 7d
No vitality (dry, dull,
cracking tongue): No saliva,
no energy, chronic disease,
poor digestion, poor
absorption

Picture 7e
Teeth marks: Pancreas
(hypoglycemia), kidneys

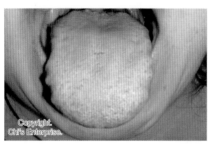

Picture 7f
Teeth marks on a large and
swollen tongue: Water
retention/ Hypoglycemia

Picture 7g
Normal appearance of
tongue surface (38 y/o/f):
no teeth marks, light red
with a thin white coating

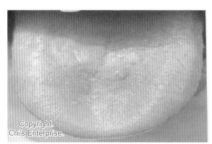

Picture 7h
Pale tongue: Anemia, Lungs,
Large intestines

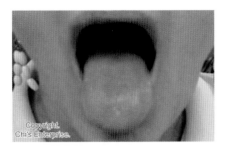

Picture 8a
Pale and small tongue: Anemia, may also be a sign of cancer risk

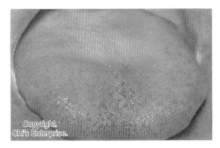

Picture 8b
Red tongue with crack on the center towards the tip, covered by coating: Fever, heart, small intestines/ digestive problem

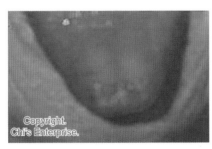

Picture 8c
Dark red tongue: If not fever, may be heart or liver problem

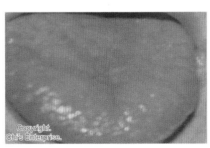

Picture 8d
Purple tongue: Blood stasis, heart, or lung. If dry, kidney or lung problem

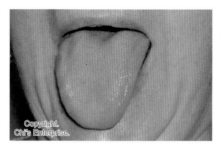

Picture 8e
Blue tongue: Pancreas, serious condition

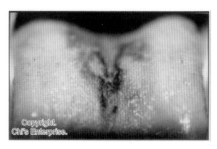

Picture 8f
Black coating that cannot be scraped off: May be severe digestive, lung or kidney problThis is the tongue of a patient with a kidney tumor.

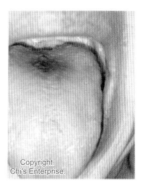

Picture 8g
Yellow/Brown coating in the back or root of the tongue: Signals early kidney or digestion problem

Picture 8h
Black, dry, spiky coating in center of the tongue: Liver, digestive issues

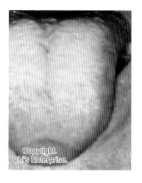

Picture 9a
Yellowish coating on center:
Fever, local inflammation
(maybe in the stomach);
White coating: lung

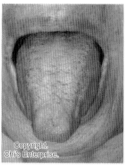

Picture 9b
Dry, yellowish coating:
Digestive problem. This is
the tongue of a patient with
a digestive problem (yeast
overgrowth) caused by long-
term antibiotic use.

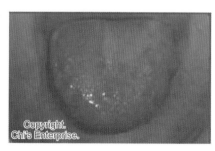

Picture 9c
Coating on left side only:
Inner organs problem, more
serious than coating on the
right side only.

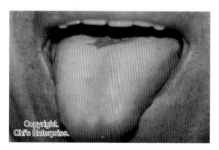

Picture 9d
No coating on root:
Serious condition (can be
likened to grass with no
roots)

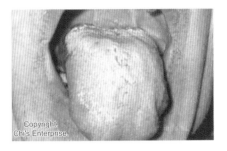

Picture 9e
White coating: Respiratory;
White, greasy chunks:
Pneumonia, low immunity

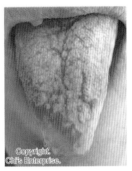

Picture 9f
Snow-like coating: Very
serious conditions, may also
be an autoimmune disease

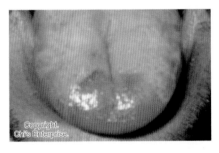

Picture 9g
Geographic Tongue: ① Lung,
allergies, asthma, sinus
problem; ② IBS, colitis,
Crohn's disease (presence of
crack on tongue). Can also be
both a lung and a digestive
problem.

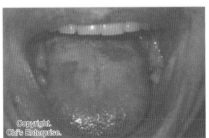

Picture 9h
Geographic Tongue: Lung,
sinus, allergy, asthma

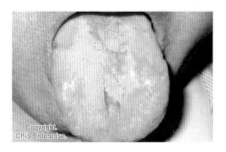

Picture 10a
Geographic tongue with off white/yellowish coating, cracking and very patchy: poor digestion, colitis.
This is a colitis patient.

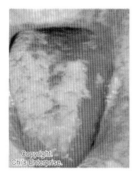

Picture 10b
Coating is peeling off irregularly: Patient's condition is very serious.

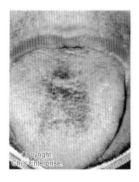

Picture 10c
Yellow coating on root and dry, spiky, burnt coating on center: very poor digestion

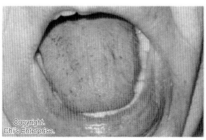

Picture 10d
Burnt yellow spikes on tongue: Pancreatitis

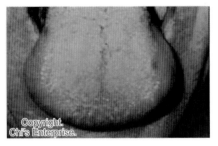

Picture 10e
Hammer-shaped tongue:
Hormone depletion, patient
is oversexed, can also be
kidney problems

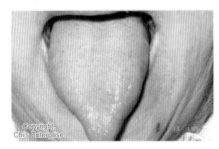

Picture 10f
Tip of tongue is elongated:
Heart disease

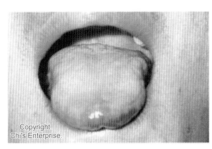

Picture 10g
Thick and wide tongue:
Liver/Digestive problem.

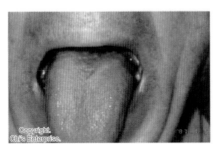

Picture 10h
Grey coating on root:
Kidneys

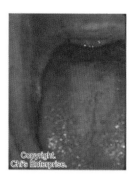

Picture 11a
Coating splits on center of the tongue, no coating on surrounding area of tongue: Serious condition. This particular case is of a patient with a digestive problem.

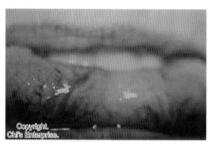

Picture 11b
Dark blue, bulging, and branching veins under the tongue: Liver problem

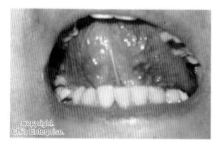

Picture 11c
Dark, branching veins under the tongue: Liver or circulation problem

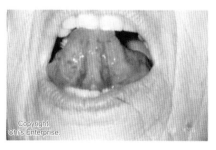

Picture 11d
Very dark or black protruding veins under the tongue: Lung problem. This is an emphysema patient.

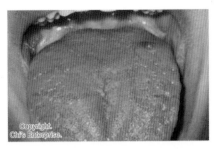

Picture 11e
Roadmap-like tongue: In young people: hormonal imbalance or blood disease. In older people: hypochlorydia, can also be digestive problem.

Picture 11f
Fissured tongue: Poor digestion (especially lambda-shaped cracking), stomach, pancreas

Picture 11g
Red tongue, dry, cracking: Gallbladder

Picture 11h
Protruding spots on the side of the tongue: Poor liver function, could also be menstrual problems

Picture 12a
Red spikes on tip of tongue: Heart problem, nervousness, insomnia, thyroid

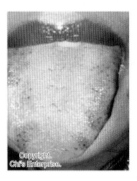

Picture 12b
Dark marks on tongue, especially on the tip: Coronary heart disease

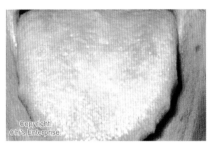

Picture 12c
Case of pulmonary/heart problem due to tuberculosis, smoking. Patient also has poor digestion, spleen and kidney problem (Continued on Picture 12e).

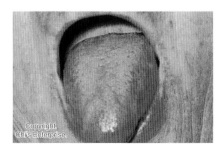

Picture 12d
Over a month later of the pulmonary heart problem case (Picture 12d): After taking Chi supplements, improvement is apparent

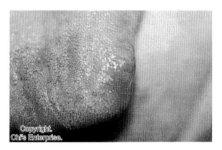

Picture 12e
White coating, Bulging
sides: Lung problem,
asthma

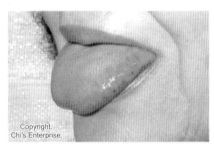

Picture 12f
Bruised spots or marks on
the side of tongue: Liver and
poor circulation

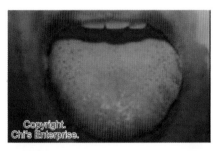

Picture 12g
Red dots on tongue:
Hormonal problem (mostly
estrogen is too high).
This is a breast cancer
patient.

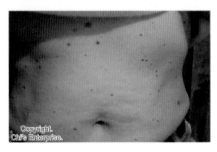

Picture 12h
Cherry Angiomas on the
abdomen in a man: Liver,
prostate problem

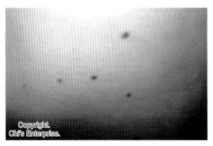

Picture 13a
Cherry Angiomas on the abdomen in a woman: Liver, breast, ovarian problem

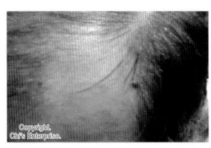

Picture 13b
Cherry Angiomas on the forehead, hairline area or head: Stroke, aneurysm risk

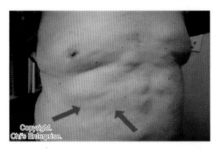

Picture 13c
Cherry Angiomas, Spider veins: Liver problem; Lipomas on abdomen: fat deposit (cellulite)

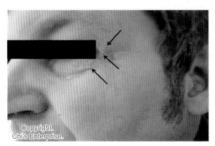

Picture 13d
Xanthomas (bumps around the eye): cholesterol is high

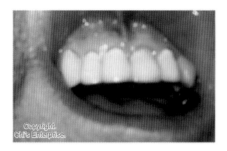

Picture 13e
Heavy metal deposit in gums. Deposits in this area are usually of mercury.

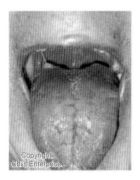

Picture 13f
Deep cracks: Stomach or GI tract problem.
This is a stomach cancer patient.

Picture 13g
①Teeth marks: hypoglycemia;
②Brown/yellow coating on center, cracking on upper center of tongue: Stomach/ GI tract problem.
This is the tongue of an esophageal cancer patient

Picture 13h
Foamy urine: Proteinuria

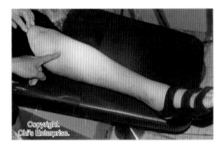

Picture 14a
Leg edema: Kidney or heart problem.

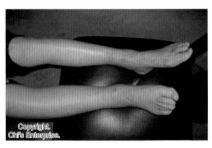

Picture 14b
Leg edema (right leg visibly swollen and larger than left leg): Kidney.
If edema occurs in the morning: kidney problem.
If edema occurs in the afternoon: heart problem.

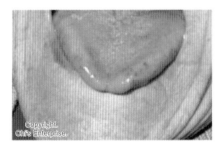

Picture 14c
Sides of the tongue are inflamed, red dots on the side of tongue: Lung

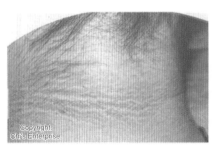

Picture 14d
Skin texture resembles an orange peel (or wrinkly) and is dark: Diabetes. If in children: Juvenile diabetes

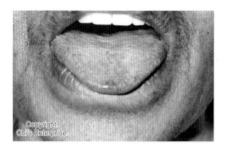

Picture 14e
Red dots on tip: Coronary
Heart Disease; White
coating: lung

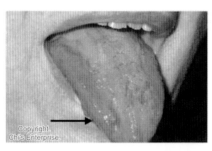

Picture 14f
Tongue ulcer

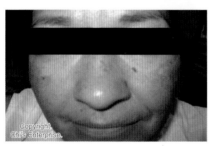

Picture 14g
Dark patches on the cheeks
(may be on one or both
cheeks) starting in the 30s:
Sign of female hormone
problem (elevated estrogen
and exposed under the sun)

Picture 14h
Soft baby hair on cheek
(new growth): Lung or
colorectal cancer risk

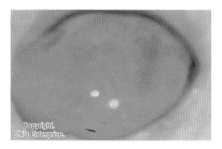

Picture 15a
Mirror-like tongue: Serious condition.
This patient has low serum albumin.

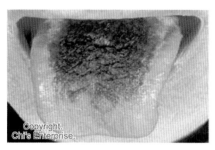

Picture 15b
Black coating on tongue: Respiratory, digestive or kidney system. This is a patient with respiratory problems.

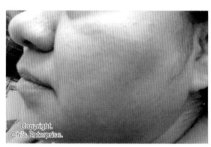

Picture 15c
Rough skin, overweight, hirsute: Polycystic ovarian syndrome, insulin resistance

Picture 15d
Hirsute/Hairy (females): Polycystic ovarian syndrome (PCOS)

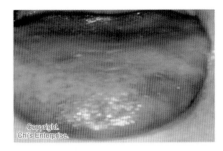

Picture 15e
Roadmap-like tongue in a young person: Hormonal imbalance

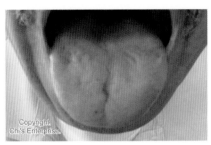

Picture 15f
Yellow coating, deep crack, shiny edges, pale tongue: Digestive issues, Anemic

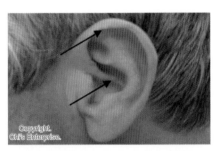

Picture 15g
Progressive growth of lump, thickness or wrinkle in the auricle: Stomach or liver cancer risk.

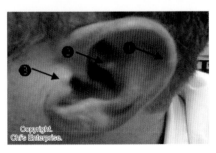

Picture 15h
Lumps on the helix (1), anti-helix (2) and tragus (3): Stomach, liver or esophageal problem.

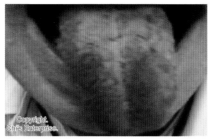

Picture 16a
Tongue is very red with deep cracks and a thick coating: Patient has very severe GERD.

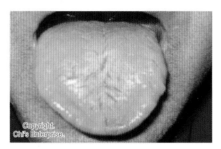

Picture 16b
Red tongue, geographic tongue (white coating on center only), deep cracks: Colitis, infection/inflammation

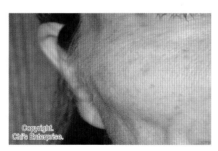

Picture 16c
Soft baby hair on cheek (newly grown): Lung or colorectal cancer risk. This is a colorectal cancer patient.

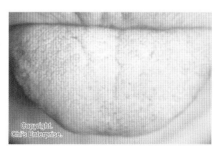

Picture 16d
Tiny or fine white spots spread throughout the tongue: hypertension risk is high

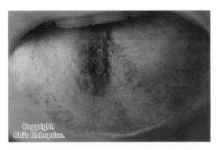

Picture 16e
Greasy tongue, crack in the center covered by yellow/brown coating: Serious digestive problem. This is a stomach cancer patient.

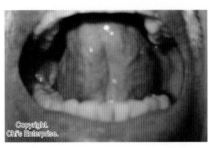

Picture 16f
Dark branching veins (more than four) under the tongue of a patient with fatty liver/Hepatitis C that developed into liver cirrhosis.

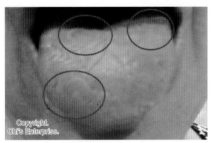

Picture 16g
Circular patches on the tongue, white in the rims: Colon problem. This patient has had colitis for years which developed into colon cancer.

Picture 16h
Skin tags: colon problem

CASES OF IMPROVEMENT

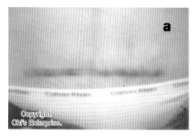
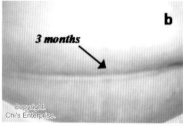

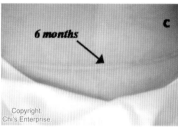

Figure 17
(a) Keloids on a 25 y/o/f from a C-section. **(b)** After 3 months on OxyPower, keloid from the C-section has visibly improved. **(c)** After 6 months on OxyPower, keloids from the C-section has flattened

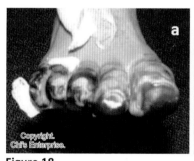
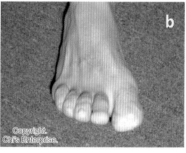

Figure 18
(a) A 39 y/o/m suffered from frostbite. **(b)** After more than 6 months on OxyPower, Whole Skin, Vein Lite and Asparagus Extract, his foot has recovered well.

Figure 19
(a) A 29 y/o/f patient weighed 190 lbs when she started on Slender All, Pro-Metabolic and Myomin. **(b)** After two years, she has lost 65 lbs.

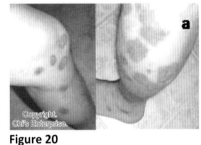
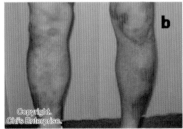

Figure 20
(a) Severe psoriasis flare-up on a 51 y/o/m who has been suffering from psoriasis for 45 years. **(b)** After more than a month on Psoricaid/Autocin, his psoriasis improved much.

INDEX

D

Debile, 210
Diabend, 210
Diabetes, 70, 93
Diagnostic wheel, 129-133
Digestive conditions, 68-69, 70, 145-147, 201
  Bowel movement, 97-99
  Constipation, 97-98, 148
  Crohn's disease, 145
  Diverticulitis, 150
  Gas, 100-101
  Gastritis, 71, 198
  GERD, 181
  Irritable Bowel Syndrome, 145
  Stool, 99-100, 176, 199
  Ulcer, 70, 198
  Ulcerative colitis, 145, 167, 176
Digestron, 210-211
Diverticulitis, 150
Dizziness, 115
DPD, 159, 225

E

Ear markers, 80-82, 169
  Auricle lump, 183, 199
  Ear ringing, 169
  Earlobe crease, 23, 37, 80-81, 136-137, 201
Edema, 101, 156, 202
eGFR, 155
Emphysema, 70-71
Estrogen, 148, 154, 160, 214
Eyes, 30, 84-86

F

Facial color, 83
Female disorders, 126-127
Fever, 116
Finger length test, 32, 93, 202
Fingernails
  Beading, 21, 30, 158, 159
  Black lines, 20, 25, 28, 145
  Brittle nails, 32, 202
  Central canal or ridge, 21, 139
  Clubbing, 6-8, 27, 29, 138, 166, 184, 201, 202
  Color of nails, 9-13
    Black nails, 13
    Blue nails, 13

Half-and-half nails, 10, 156, 202
  Purple nails, 12, 29
  Red nails, 11
  White nails, 9
  Yellow nails, 11
Gray dots, 25
Horizontal indentations, 8, 22
Horizontal ridges, 22-23, 27, 202
Horizontal white lines, 23, 29, 156
Index fingernail, 1
Length of nails, 5
Middle fingernail, 1
Narrow nails, 5
Opaque, 29, 184, 201
Pinky fingernail, 1-2
Pitting, 23, 32, 167, 202
Red lines, 25
Red spots, 25
Ridges, 19-22
  Vertical ridges, 19, 29, 138, 156, 167, 201
Ring fingernail, 1
Shell-shaped nails, 6, 31, 186
Short and wide nails, 5, 27
Spoon-shaped nails, 6, 30
Thinning, 159
Triangular nails, 6, 31, 186
White spots, 24, 29, 160, 202
Fir tree abnormality, 21, 27
Foamy urine, 105, 156
Frenula cyst, 28, 79-80, 147, 149-150, 175, 201
Frequent urination, 105
Fungal infection, 24, 25, 30, 202

G

Gallbladder conditions, 154-155, 175, 183, 201
Gas, 100-101
Gastritis, 71, 198
Geographic tongue, 54, 145, 167, 168, 201, 202
GERD, 180
GI Chi, 211
Greasy tongue, 53
Gums, 90, 144

H

H. pylori, 198
Hair, 82
Hammer-shaped tongue, 57